Antonio Buero-Vallejo

FOUR TRAGEDIES OF CONSCIENCE

Antonio Buero-Vallejo

FOUR TRAGEDIES OF CONSCIENCE
(1949–1999)

STORY OF A STAIRWAY
(*Historia de una escalera*)

BEFORE DAWN
(*Madrugada*)

THE BASEMENT WINDOW
(*El tragaluz*)

MISSION TO THE DESERTED VILLAGE
(*Misión al pueblo desierto*)

TRANSLATIONS AND EDITION BY
Patricia W. O'Connor

University Press of Colorado

Published by the University Press of Colorado
5589 Arapahoe Avenue, Suite 206C
Boulder, Colorado 80303

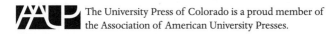 The University Press of Colorado is a proud member of
the Association of American University Presses.

The University Press of Colorado is a cooperative publishing enterprise supported, in part, by Adams State College, Colorado State University, Fort Lewis College, Mesa State College, Metropolitan State College of Denver, University of Colorado, University of Northern Colorado, and Western State College of Colorado.

∞ The paper used in this publication meets the minimum requirements of the American National Standard for Information Sciences—Permanence of Paper for Printed Library Materials. ANSI Z39.48-1992

Library of Congress Cataloging-in-Publication Data

Buero Vallejo, Antonio, 1916–2000
  [Plays. English Selections]
  Antonio Buero-Vallejo : four tragedies of conscience (1949–1999) / Antonio Buero-Vallejo.
    p. cm.
  Includes bibliographical references.
  ISBN 978-0-87081-902-5 (hardcover : alk. paper) — ISBN 978-0-87081-903-2 (pbk. : alk. paper)
  I. Title.
  PC6603.U4 2008
  862'.64—dc22

                                                                                2007047544

Design by Daniel Pratt

17   16   15   14   13   12   11   10   09   08   10   9   8   7   6   5   4   3   2   1

Contents

Preface

Antonio Buero-Vallejo (1916–2000), widely known at home and abroad simply as "Buero," is Spain's most important dramatist of the second half of the twentieth century. The four plays in this volume, representative of the author's concerns and style, have timeless, universal appeal and illustrate why he was called "the conscience of Spain."

Buero's emblematic first play, *Story of a Stairway* (1949), chronicling thirty years in the lives of several Madrid families, catapulted the young author and former political prisoner into unlikely prominence and marked a milestone in Spanish theater. *Before Dawn* (1953), reminiscent of Greek tragedy and Ibsen's *Ghosts*, is a riveting whodunit and the poignant odyssey of one woman's search for truth. *The Basement Window* (1967) is an Orwellian science-fiction experiment that explores the moral climate of the late twentieth century as examined by ethically enlightened researchers of a distant century. *Mission to the Deserted Village* (1999), the author's final play, is particularly relevant for our times in its scrutiny of the ethics in war. A reiteration of several favorite themes and a stressing of conscience, this play brings the author's theater and this collection full circle.

I wish to express my gratitude to Carlos Buero, Victoria Rodríguez, Darrin Pratt, and Laura Hynes for their invaluable contributions in the preparation of the manuscript. Without their support, this book would be considerably diminished if not impossible.

PATRICIA **W.** O'CONNOR

Antonio Buero-Vallejo
FOUR TRAGEDIES OF CONSCIENCE

Introduction

ANTONIO BUERO-VALLEJO: HIS LIFE AND TIMES

Antonio Buero-Vallejo, Spain's most important dramatist since Federico García Lorca (1898–1936), was born in the Castilian city of Guadalajara in 1916 and even as a small child showed remarkable talent for drawing, acting, and creating plays for his cardboard theater.* Buero also loved music and well into adulthood spent many happy hours at his aunt's player piano. Because his primary dedication was to art, after graduation from high school in 1934, he went to Madrid to study painting at the San Fernando Art Academy. His father, an army officer, was transferred soon thereafter to Spain's capital, and the reunited family established residence in a modest apartment building not unlike the one depicted in *Story of a Stairway*. But Buero's tranquil young life was soon interrupted and forever altered by political circumstances, and his future would involve—rather than the visual images he planned—verbal and philosophical reflections on the devastating

---

* Because the author used both last names professionally (the first paternal, the second maternal), he requested that, in order to avoid confusion, these names be hyphenated for translations and productions abroad. He is widely known simply as "Buero," and this shortened form often is used in the introduction.

1

Self portrait, 1947

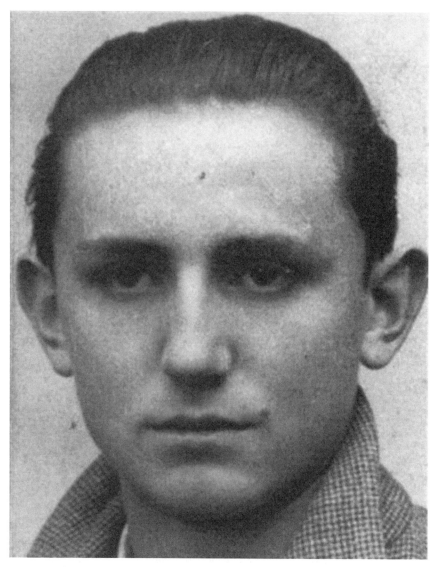

Buero at eighteen, 1934

events he witnessed. His vision of responsible conduct is impossible to separate from the new theatrical mode he would one day set in motion.

In 1931, a national referendum peacefully replaced the traditional Catholic monarchy with a republic, but the ensuing liberal reforms—like civil marriage, the legalization of divorce, the penalization of the landed aristocracy, and the specter of agrarian reform—enraged conservatives, and the extremes of wealth and poverty fueled social unrest. Mounting polarizations of the left and the right led to acts of violence (including assassinations by death squads) and were a grim prelude to civil war.

In the May 1936 elections, the liberal Manual Azaña ousted conservative president Niceto Alcalá Zamora, but Azaña's cutting of funds to the military and reducing the number of officers angered the army's upper echelon. At that point, a group of generals began plotting to overthrow the government and in July 1936 launched a military offensive from North Africa that marked the official beginning of the civil war (1936–1939). In Madrid nervous policemen detained Buero's army-officer father, a sincere defender of the Republic, and in an action that had become all too common, shot him. Deeply affected by this tragic event, Buero, not yet twenty, joined the Republican sector (about half of the total) of the army and served for a time in the Division to Preserve Artistic Treasures. The young painter's experiences there would find expression in his final play, *Mission to the Deserted Village.*

Spain's three years of civil war constituted a savage struggle, physical and ideological, between Republican loyalists (principally intellectuals, the educated middle class, Basque and Catalan separatists, trade unions, socialists, anarchists, and communists) and the Nationalist rebels (a large sector of the army, the Catholic Church, the wealthy, monarchists, Carlists, the National Front, the Falange, and other right-wing political parties).[1] Europe's fascist powers, Germany and Italy, provided the insurgents military support (like the devastating bombings by Hitler's Condor Legion), while Russia intervened on behalf of the Republic. Although the world's democracies officially sat on the sidelines, many of the world's citizens, including George Orwell, Ernest Hemingway, and other writers who would one day be famous, joined the International Brigades to defend Spain's fragile democracy. Eventually, however, the Germans' military power proved too much for the loyalists, and in April 1939 the Republic conceded defeat. General Francisco Franco (1892–1975), the victorious general, headed the military dictatorship established in October 1939 and remained in power until his death in 1975.

At war's end, Buero was in Valencia, the last Republican stronghold. As part of a large contingent of soldiers and other displaced loyalists fleeing for their lives, he was either unable or unwilling to fight his way aboard one of the few trains that might have saved him from prison, at least initially. The train incident, so pivotal in *The Basement Window,* is intimately related to the author's own experi-

As a prisoner in Ocaña, 1945

ence, for it was in that Valencia train station that Nationalists captured him and took him to the local bullring where he and hundreds of others would remain for days before being assigned to prisons.

Perhaps because Buero had not been a combatant in the war, he was soon paroled, but his failure to report to authorities as mandated and his participation

5

In Julio Diamante's film, "El arte de vivir" (The Art of Living), 1966

in clandestine political activity led to a second arrest. Sentenced to death this time, he was placed with numerous other prisoners to await execution. But Buero's name was not called during the long period of multiple executions each dawn, and within a year his sentence was commuted to life imprisonment.

In 1946, after surviving seven years in various prisons, Buero was again paroled. This time he reported to authorities as required and avoided overt political activity. Because he was then thirty years old and found painting discouraging after the long hiatus, he turned to another early passion: theater. He performed in several films, but writing was his forte and an area in which his considerable visual, verbal, and acting talents served him well. Buero's experiences in the war and in prison also prepared him uniquely to champion a new dramatic genre that would eventually be called "social realism," "critical realism," "theater of commitment," and "opposition theater."

By nature serious, intellectual, and introspective, Buero consistently reflected his personality in his works. Understandably cautious given his political antecedents, he frequently impressed interviewers and photographers as cold and aloof, qualities that contributed to his public image as the somber, unsmiling author. He captivated friends, however, with his openness, stimulating conversation, and subtle sense of humor. In the presence of children, whose candor he loved, Buero became another child happily sitting on the floor, working puzzles with

Buero, 1952

them, playing make-believe games, or fashioning paper birds. This gentle man also showed surprising talent, energy, and joy for dancing.

Unlike many other Republicans who had a choice, Buero opted to remain in Spain during the difficult Franco years to show solidarity with his Spanish brothers. Even at the end of the 1950s, when he was firmly established as a major playwright, Buero continued to share the Spartan existence of his widowed mother in the apartment of his young adulthood. During those years, he wrote at his own measured pace and shunned materialism. He rejected with particular verve the "necessity" in Spain's new consumer society, the automobile.

In 1956 Buero met his future wife, actress Victoria Rodríguez, in the course of rehearsals for his *Today's a Holiday* (*Hoy es fiesta*), in which she played a major role and won the coveted award for best actress of the year. They were married in 1959, and it was to the longtime family home that Buero brought his young bride. It was there, as well, that their two sons, Carlos (1960–) and Enrique (1961–86), were born, where the family would remain, and where Buero's widow lives even now. Victoria Rodríguez has continued to be professionally active over the years and has performed in many of her husband's plays. In the works included here, she played Elvira in the 1968 revival of *Story of a Stairway*, Asuncion in the most recent (2003) production, and the mother in the 1997 revival of *The Basement Window*.

7

Wedding picture, with actress Victoria Rodríguez, 1959 (Courtesy, Estudios Iñumeta)

On April 23, 2000, a few months after the opening of *Mission to the Deserted Village*, Buero was able, despite failing health, to accompany his wife and applaud her performance at the National Theater, the scene of her early triumph in *Today's a Holiday*. But on April 28, a mere five days later, a cerebral hemorrhage took the life of Antonio Buero-Vallejo, and it was Victoria Rodríguez's turn to accompany

With son, Carlos, 1962 (Courtesy, Basabe)

her husband to the National Theater and observe as thousands of mourners paid final respects to the dramatist who had challenged them for fifty years to heed their consciences.

Buero's Tragedies of Conscience

The dictionary defines "conscience" as the set of ethical principles that controls or inhibits the actions and thoughts of an individual. Long known as "the conscience of Spain," Buero created highly successful dramas that artfully recommend compassion and empathy. Rather than attempting to purge the audience's emotions as did the classical tragedians, Buero sought to awaken and provoke as he planted seeds for thought.

Comparable to works by such contemporary American tragedians as Arthur Miller, Eugene O'Neill, and Tennessee Williams, Buero's plays often feature the common man or woman caught in moral or existential dilemmas. These works suggest that catastrophe results from character flaws such as selfishness, passivity, denial, haste, and procrastination, all of which produce a failure to examine

A few months before his death, 1999 (Courtesy, Patricia W. O'Connor)

inadequacies and make corrections. The lament that people do not learn from their mistakes until it is too late permeates Buero's theater and echoes the wisdom of the world's great historians and thinkers: Thucydides (fifth century BC), the "father of history," identified knowledge of the past as the best guide to action; British poet and philosopher Samuel Taylor Coleridge (1772–1834) observed ruefully that experience, like a lantern on the ship's stern, illuminates only the waves behind; Spanish-born Harvard philosopher George Santayana (1863–1952) asserted simply that those who ignore history are doomed to repeat its mistakes.[2]

The themes of ethics, history, war, art, freedom, time, and the search for truth permeate Buero's plays and find expression in a variety of ways. Although the author drew much inspiration from his own life and often featured Spain's history, his plays transcend the personal, local, or political to portray timelessly relevant issues of universal importance. His characters are often hampered by the limitations of their own humanity and, like the creatures of Plato's cavern (*The Republic*, Book 7), yearn to know the unknowable. As did another Spanish philosopher and dramatist, Miguel de Unamuno (1864–1936), Buero believes that man's responsibility is to search for life's meaning despite overwhelming odds against ever achieving that goal. Although progress toward ultimate truth is slow in human terms, Buero's tragedies are never without hope, for each lonely cry in the wilderness includes the possibility of a response.

In order to underscore human imperfections as well as a broad groping toward ultimate truth, Buero often portrays the existential search allegorically through blind characters. In works that include a political layer, a characteristic structure involves conflict between the passive dreamer and the thoughtful activist; or, conversely, a man of action whose haste and aggressiveness preclude reflection confronts the patient, thoughtful intellectual. To increase dramatic tension, these men often compete for the love of the same woman. Buero's heroes are the "givers" who place ideals and others above self. Negatively portrayed are the "takers," especially those motivated by power, money, or prestige.

Although all the art forms find expression in theater, Buero, with a painter's eye and musician's ear, makes special use of image, sound, light, and shadow, all of which may convey meaning. Foregrounded, for example, is the visual when Buero portrays painters who confront obstacles analogous to those faced by Spain's creative community during the Franco years. Using projected images, Diego Velázquez and his art are central to *Las Meninas* (1960, the title of a Velázquez painting), and Francisco Goya is the main character in *The Sleep of Reason* (1970, *El sueño de la razón*, the title of a Goya painting). In *Mission to the Deserted Village*

(1999), audiences see vague representations of a possible El Greco painting for which a painter risks his life.

Not surprisingly, the social, philosophical, and political implications of Buero's theater provoked brushes with the ultra-conservative censorship of the Franco dictatorship. Refusing to sacrifice deeply held principles or write in simplistic fashion, Buero used his ingenuity to express himself authentically within the letter if not the spirit of the law, and his oblique references often slipped through censors' fingers like quicksilver.

CENSORSHIP DURING THE FRANCO DICTATORSHIP

For much of the thirty-six-year period that followed the civil war, Spain was Europe's last fascist-style regime, and from 1939 until the death of General Franco in 1975, that dictatorship practiced a system of prior censorship. This "prior" control meant that all printed, visual, or aural matter (newspapers, magazines, books, pamphlets, theater, nightclub acts, films, television, radio, recordings, drawings, and cartoons) intended for the public must first have government approval.

In the early years of the dictatorship, officials handed play scripts to priests or other individuals of unquestioned loyalty who evaluated them in predictable fashion: they summarily prohibited all works considered out of step with conservative official positions on religion, politics, and morality. This cavalier approach to theatrical censorship was in force until Franco's least reactionary minister of information, Manuel Fraga Iribarne, ordered not only the establishment of specific censorship rules but the formation of a formal committee to evaluate plays and films based on those rules.

The norms for theater, printed by the ministry of information in a non-circulating ten-page pamphlet dated February 9, 1963, consisted of thirty-seven articles that essentially formalized existing attitudes and policies: they demanded exclusively positive presentations of the dictatorship's values and representatives, including orthodox presentation of Catholic dogma and all the regime's laws and practices. Specifically protected from any criticism as well was the man at the top of Spain's absolutely vertical government, General Franco. But in addition to requiring this doctrinaire vision, other rules expressly prohibited any presentation or allusion to suicide, mercy killing, vengeance, dueling, divorce, sexual relations outside of marriage, prostitution, contraception, or abortion unless there was expressed disapproval or punishment of the individuals involved. Other specific prohibitions in the aforementioned pamphlet included "colloquial expressions"

12

(swear words, youthful jargon, slang); images that provoked "low passion" or offended conjugal love; images of brutality toward persons or animals; scenes that denied one's obligation to defend the homeland; the "undignified" presentation of political ideologies; the "falsification" in the reporting of facts, personalities, or historical events; works that fostered hatred between peoples; "pornographic" or "blasphemous" scenes; and works offensive to "the most elementary standards of good taste."[3] None of the foregoing terms, debatable in an open society, was defined but rather was left to the discretion of ultra-rightist censors empowered to prohibit or authorize and, in case of authorization, to detail obligatory cuts or modifications. Serving on all censorship committees was a priest who held veto power.

Also controlled by the theater committee were the venues in which authorized plays might be performed. Spectators in Madrid and Barcelona, for example, might view material considered mildly subversive, because the more sophisticated urban populations were likely already "corrupted." Further, some plays were authorized for the larger theaters, whereas the more suspect works were limited to small alternative stages and might be authorized for single performances only.

In this period, the majority of Spain's intellectual writers were silent; largely Republican, they had either died in the war, been executed, were in prison, or had chosen exile. Because the Franco government forbade expressed opposition to declared values, those who lost the war obviously lacked a voice in the early years of the dictatorship. *Story of a Stairway* showed that theater might be a way to express disagreement.

Buero's New Dramatic Language in Context

When Buero began writing in 1946, three types of plays geared toward conservative bourgeois audiences predominated on Spanish stages: (1) propaganda dramas that extolled the Nationalist values of God and country by portraying the civil war as a heroic "crusade" against atheistic forces; (2) "well-made" romantic comedies and dramas; and (3) escapist and absurdist comedies. Serious, committed, and determined to return a social component to theater, Buero created a new dramatic language through a subtle interweaving of politics and philosophy. Beginning with *Story of a Stairway*, Buero approached social and existential issues through allusion, omission, analogy, metaphor, simile, and visual signs. Some plays evoke the dictatorship's social or political abuses by portraying characters in jail-like enclosures from which they struggle to free themselves. These and other techniques, such as historical parables and Brechtian distancing in time or space, enabled Buero to question or even subvert the dominant theatrical discourse.

As Buero observed just before the 1949 opening of *Story of a Stairway*, his purpose was to write a play that would be appreciated and enjoyed by a broad spectrum of the theater-going public.[4] When this first work was performed the following year (1950) in Barcelona, the author courageously stated his position more openly: "In confronting the serious crises of the world today, I see two possibilities: to take refuge in the trivial diversions so widely available or face bravely and sincerely our problems."[5] Buero's ambitious aesthetic not only produced the desired results but dignified an art form and inspired a new generation. Because of the enormous success of *Story of a Stairway*, writers who had previously believed any critical reflection on Spain would be futile now followed Buero's lead. These playwrights, with Buero, drew positive international attention to Spain's theater during the Franco era. The most famous members of the new group, known as the Realistic Generation, were Alfonso Sastre, Lauro Olmo, Carlos Muñiz, José Martín Recuerda, and José María Rodríguez Méndez. Because Buero continued to be the most visible dramatist on the scene, he was the target of attacks by not only the conservatives in power but even by some authors of like mind who felt that he was not openly critical enough or that he received special favors in the censorship process.

The most highly publicized dispute took place between Buero and Sastre in 1958. Their tart assertions and rebuttals published in the theater journal *Primer Acto* came to be known as "possibilism" (Buero's position of working within the "possibilities" of the system) and "impossibilism" (Sastre's tactic of testing and rebelling against established norms). Catherine O'Leary summarizes the polemic this way: "Both dramatists agreed that Spanish theatre was dominated by commercial interests that cared little about artistic or social merit and that concentrated instead on satisfying the entertainment needs of bourgeois audiences; both insisted on their own desire to change the situation. The entire debacle seems to have arisen from Sastre's belief that Buero was failing to address strongly enough certain social and political issues in his works."[6]

Both dramatists were simply expressing their own personalities in their respective styles. Sastre—aggressive, provocative and daring—preferred the frontal attack and valued the social message above the aesthetic. Buero, the calm intellectual concerned with artistic expression, preferred the allegorical, distanced, dialectical approach and was willing to negotiate when censors ordered cuts. Time proved Buero's position much more effective, for his plays were performed in mainstream theater, whereas Sastre's voice was often silenced or relegated to minority venues. Buero, however, enjoyed the advantage of winning the Lope de Vega Prize at a key moment and of having his first play a major success. He was also a driving force in theater when Sastre, ten years his junior, appeared on the scene. As Buero explained years later: "If less established authors had written their plays exactly as I wrote mine, they would have had more problems, because censorship could have silenced them more easily. Perhaps the secret of the whole affair lies in that particular point rather than in the assertion by some that my plays made more accommodations than others."[7] In a related commentary about his professional beginnings, Buero later provided additional details that illustrate his little-known sense of humor:

> I came upon the theater scene and have persisted in writing tragedies and confronting people with uncomfortable or problematic aspects of human life. These expressions, especially when I first began writing, were frowned upon, because the official party line stubbornly affirmed that Spain was the best of all possible worlds; that everything here was wonderful and that nothing happened in Spain that could possibly be a cause for tears, disagreement or even discussion. Therefore, when somebody comes along and suggests there are things to discuss or even cry about, people say: "that guy must have terrible indigestion; and he certainly has no sense of humor."[8]

Spanish Theater in the Post-Franco Years

Franco's death in November 1975 made possible a return to democracy. In the immediate power vacuum, censorship, still nominally operative, relaxed, for most Spaniards wanted to appear modern, socially as well as politically. The two most obvious novelties in theater during the so-called transition period (1975–1978) prior to the formalization of democracy were the "recuperations," plays by authors whose works had been forbidden during the Franco years, and an explosion of onstage nudity (*destape* or *despelote*). These two impulses were not isolated phenomena but rather part of a three-pronged rebellion involving politics, religion, and sex. Men cast in women's roles as well as sexual symbolism in stage settings were particularly prevalent in this period.

In the area of erotic images, after thirty-six years of sexual repression, Spanish audiences demanded—and got—visual gratification. This relatively tardy sexual revolution in Spanish life and art often found expression in creative new versions of the "recuperated" plays. Several works by Lorca, murdered by a Nationalist death squad and the Republic's most famous martyr, were staged. In 1976, actor

Ismael Merlo played the title role in *The House of Bernarda Alba* (*La casa de Bernarda Alba*) and, in various scenes, sat enclosed in an almond-shaped form symbolic of female genitalia in front of windows that bore similar but closed configurations to emphasize control and restriction. Also in this period, *The Monster* (*El adefesio*), by the communist exile Rafael Alberti (1902–1999), was performed. In this production, a bearded, defeminized María Casares as Gorgo brandished a phallic cane, and the popular actress, Victoria Vera, titillated in a G-string as the victimized Altea in a scene of sadistic violence against a backdrop of simulated female genitalia.

One of the most irreverent (blasphemous, some would say) of Franco's prohibited authors was Fernando Arrabal (1932–), who, in his self-imposed exile in France, had missed no opportunity to sneer at Franco publicly from Paris where his plays were greatly appreciated and subsequently performed all over the world. In a collage of Arrabal's short works presented in Madrid in 1977 under the title of *The Automobile Graveyard* (*El cementerio de los automóviles*), Victoria Vera again appeared in the G-string (despite pleas from the director for total nudity) as she provided room service and sex to guests of a broken-down hotel and emptied chamber pots filled in the course of the action in noisy simulations of nature's way. Other plays by world-famous authors in this period, combining semi-nudity, scatology, sex, violence, and politics in attention-grabbing productions, brought international attention to Spain's contemporary theater, which some had formerly dismissed as an artistic wasteland.

Of the contemporary "recuperations" by dramatists living and working in Spain, the most important and successful was Buero's play prohibited by censorship in 1964: *Two Sides to Dr. Valmy's Story* (*La doble historia del doctor Valmy*). Probably the longest-running of Buero's plays, this one premiered 1976 and deals with police brutality in the treatment of striking miners.

In his own subtle way, Buero had already trod the forbidden terrains of nudity, politics, and religion. *Las Meninas* (1960) portrayed the enlightened seventeenth-century painter, Velázquez, confronted by the Inquisition, which prohibited representation by Spanish painters of the unclad human body but voiced no objection to the many foreign masterpieces featuring the nude body occupying places of honor in the royal palace. Utilizing an imaginary painting of a nude Venus by Velázquez that the artist necessarily kept hidden, Buero succinctly alluded to the hypocritical dictatorship's limiting effects on the country's artistic community.

In 1971, Buero pushed a little more in the areas of politics and nudity with *Arrival of the Gods* (*Llegada de los dioses*). Reflecting on the physical and psychological devastations of war, Buero alternated scenes of body parts strewn grotesquely on a desolate battlefield with those of healthy, scantily clad young people on a beach. In another section of the same play, the blind protagonist visualized a nude portrait of his fiancée. Sharing this character's inner vision, spectators glimpsed briefly a shadowy image in which the actress appeared to be nude but actually wore a body stocking.

The political transition ushered in other advances as well. Despite struggles for power by hard-line Francoists, in 1976 Spain held its first elections for parliament since 1936. The centrists won a majority of seats, and the following year the National Movement, a conglomeration of the old right-wing groups and the only political party permitted under Franco, saw the handwriting on the wall: after serving as the dictator's rubber stamp for thirty-seven years, the National Movement literally voted itself out of existence, thus laying to rest what had been a long and painful period for many.

The transition was complete in 1978 when a national referendum ratified a new Spanish constitution drafted by the duly elected parliament. This document included, among others, the following reforms: Juan Carlos, heir to the throne, would be the symbol of national unity; presidents of government would be elected; civilians (not generals) would have ultimate authority over the military; the Catholic Church was no longer the official religion; and censorship was abolished.

By the 1980s, Spanish writers and audiences had satisfied initial cravings for the formerly forbidden erotic fruit and entered into a more mature phase of life and art. Published translations and performances in various parts of the world of plays by Buero, Arrabal, Ana Diosdado, José Luis Alonso de Santos, Jordi Galcerán, Paloma Pedrero, and others have brought positive attention to contemporary Spanish theater.

COMMENTARY ON
STORY OF A STAIRWAY (HISTORIA DE UNA ESCALERA)

After a lapse of fifteen years, in 1949 Madrid's city council reinstated its prestigious Lope de Vega Prize for the best new play submitted to competition. Encouraged by friends, Buero entered the contest with two plays written in the three years since his release from prison: *Story of a Stairway* and *In the Burning Darkness*. Of the hundreds of works submitted, *Story of a Stairway* won the coveted prize and, as a condition of the award, was to be performed in Madrid's magnificent municipal theater, the Español. When the author's political circumstances came to light, there was strong opposition in official quarters to honoring the work of a former political prisoner. Nevertheless, the play was performed as scheduled and made theater history.

Despite its serious implications and tragic tone, *Story of a Stairway* (1949) was an enormous success and marked a milestone in Spanish theater. As critic Ricardo Doménech observed: *"Story of a Stairway* put the brakes on theatrical jokes. *Story* said 'Let's get serious' as opposed to comic theater's 'Let's tell lies.' "[9] The immediate, dramatic, and enduring impact of *Story of a Stairway* on Spanish theater is impossible to overstate. When the play was revived in 1968, another major critic, José Monleón, wrote: "This play represents not only a considerable effort within Spanish theater, but a point of departure for an attitude characteristic of a whole new generation. We might say that all who have taken Spanish theater seriously during the last twenty years are indebted to that *Story of a Stairway*, for it all began there."[10]

The three acts of this play take place in 1919, 1929, and 1949, respectively. Why these particular years, one may ask, and why does the dramatist skip 1939? The answer for some Spaniards was simple: any politically incorrect vision of Spain in the year the war ended would have been futile. Nevertheless, the omission of 1939 coyly invites curiosity about what happened to the characters in the war and what observations they might have made.

A saga of economic and social stagnation, *Story of a Stairway* chronicles the misfortunes of several Madrid families living in a modest apartment building. The first act (1919) introduces all the characters but focuses principally on the young adults. Fernando, a handsome but less-than-reliable clerk, loves Carmina, as does Urbano, the responsible factory worker. The dialogues between the passive dreamer, Fernando, and the union activist, Urbano, lay out the ideological dynamic of the play as they discuss their hopes for the future and their ideas about how best to "move up" in life. Fernando plans to rise on individual effort but procrastinates; Urbano believes in solidarity (a Republican theme) and touts collective action as the means of making life better for everyone.

The stairway, a central visual symbol, is the heart of the apartment building. The vertical structure of the set alludes to the vertical hierarchy of the dictatorship, and those who live in the building represent in microcosm Spain's forgotten lower-middle classes. The narrow confines of the set reinforce the idea of enclosure, suggesting limitations on the characters not only because they are poor and members of a controlled society but as beings caught in the snare of their human imperfections. The stairway's appearance reflects as well the passage of time and illustrates the stinginess of the well-heeled landlord, who neither installs an elevator nor maintains the interior adequately. Similarly symbolic is that the characters do not ascend the stairway to upper floors, a sign that does not bode well for those who dream of "going up."

This play bears a certain resemblance to the conventional Spanish *sainete*, a popular and traditionally comic form that features contrasting stock characters whose interactions in familiar situations spark laughter. In *Story of a Stairway*, such contrasting stereotypes include the handsome playboy versus the rough-hewn proletarian; wholesome girl-next-door versus the spoiled manipulator; outspoken older woman versus timid, retiring one; and the weak but well-meaning sister victimized by love versus the dutiful sister who sacrifices self for family. Making appearances as well are the neighborhood pimp and a variety of supporting types familiar to Spanish audiences. Any similarity between this play and the *sainete* ends with the establishment of type, however, for the characters in the Buero play are multilayered and tragic rather than simplistic and comic.

The final scene of the first act has special significance and involves a submerged reference to La Fontaine's fable of the dreaming milkmaid: carrying on her head a pitcher of milk she will sell at the market, the young girl fantasizes about the pretty dress she will buy with money realized from the sale and the handsome husband she will attract. Carried away by her dreams, the maiden jumps for joy, the pitcher falls, and the milk, along with her dreams, are lost. In the Spanish scene, Fernando stops Carmina as she returns from the market with her pitcher of milk and persuades her to sit on the steps with him. He then speaks of his love for her and of what he can do if she marries him. He will, he tells her, become a sought-after engineer as well as a successful poet. At that point, he assures her, they will live far from the ugliness that currently surrounds them and will be so happy. As Fernando leans over to kiss the captivated Carmina, he carelessly knocks over the pitcher. The spilled milk spreads out over the floor and foreshadows doom for the young couple's dreams.

In the second act (1929), the results of Fernando's passivity as well as the failure of Urbano's hopes are portrayed. The final scene of the third act, taking place after another twenty years have passed, brings the play full circle as Young Fernando and Young Carmina sit on the steps where their parents sat so long ago to articulate poignantly similar dreams. Buero's dramatic genius shines as he juxtaposes the aging Fernando and Carmina on opposite sides of the landing above the young couple to observe this scene, so movingly reminiscent of the one they played there long ago. As their children look into one another's eyes adoringly and so full of hope, the parents gaze at each other across the empty stairwell, their eyes betraying infinite sadness. Are they thinking of what might have been had they made different choices? Spectators respond emotionally at first but then ask questions: Can Young Fernando and Young Carmina break the cycle? Why do people self-destruct? Do they fail because they don't observe closely enough and heed the lessons of the past, or is it because they learn these lessons too late? Is youthful optimism an incurable blindness? Are time and experience the only teachers of such truths as wishing does not make it so? Although with respect to the current generation the play's conclusion remains open, in its circular structure the sad implication is that history will repeat itself.

COMMENTARY ON *BEFORE DAWN (MADRUGADA)*

A contrast to *Story of a Stairway*, *Before Dawn* (1953) is a thriller with social and political statements as well as a virtuoso tour de force on the classical unities if time, place, and action. The time factor constitutes a particular challenge and requires not only extreme precision on the part of the author but careful calibration by director and actors. The large grandfather clock standing on stage front and center as the curtain goes up marks the hour: 4:15. The clock's sizeable hands, fully visible to the audience at all times, move relentlessly in real time as the play progresses. The dramatic action, realized in a single space and on a single theme, requires perfect synchronization, for this play in two acts must end as the clock strikes six.

Although the passage of time and the search for truth are entwined in all of Buero's plays, these themes stand out sharply in *Before Dawn*. In exploring the intricacies of human nature, this play features a determined detective as protagonist. In unraveling the mystery, not only are the questions specific but answers are provided gradually and, in the end, with clarity. Most audiences find that kind of mounting tension exhilarating, and the sought-after solution provides satisfaction and closure. But because Buero would not be satisfied with writing a simple drama of intrigue, he adds other layers to *Before Dawn* as he depicts the passions, noble and ignoble, that drive us all.

Before Dawn is one of the few Buero plays to feature a female protagonist. In previous plays, the author portrayed women as sweethearts, sisters, wives, and mothers, and the most admirable were devoted to their families, supportive of their men, and quietly unassuming. Amalia represents a departure, for she is not only assertive but shows sharp intelligence and steely will in her search for truth. Stressing her motivation rather than her personal qualities, Buero commented on opening night: "The completely feminine woman lives for and through love. Amalia is completely feminine."[11]

As *Before Dawn* opens, Mauricio, a highly successful painter, has just died of a heart attack. Unbeknownst to anyone, Mauricio had quietly married Amalia, his longtime model and lover, and had made her principal heir to his considerable estate. In the final months of his life, however, the relationship with Amalia had become strained, and on his deathbed he murmurs words to the effect that although it was too late to clear up certain misunderstandings, he might win her back from the grave. Because Amalia loves Mauricio deeply and needs to know what he meant, hers will be a quest for a personal truth: the hoped-for confirmation that Mauricio loved and trusted her, for therein lie Amalia's identity and self-worth. Why, she wonders, were certain family members omitted from the will, and did someone tell Mauricio lies about her at a family gathering? Is his marriage to her proof of his love and desire to protect her, or is the money left her payment for services rendered?

In order to obtain the answers she seeks, Amalia devises a bold plan shared only with Sabina, the maid. The latter will be her ally in this very tricky undertaking, for as Mauricio lies dead in the next room, Amalia must keep the secret of his death and, before dawn, acquire the information vital to her future well-being. Adding to the pressure, Mauricio's nurse, awaiting daylight to leave the house, may thwart her attempts with inconvenient remarks, as may the arrival of friends and admirers who have heard the news of the painter's death on the radio. In the approaching contest, Amalia faces a test of endurance and a race against the clock. In anticipation of the forthcoming challenges, she works to suppress the considerable grief she feels and dons an elegant "costume" for the role she is about to play.

Amalia calls together her husband's relatives, most of whom covet the painter's wealth, and tells them that Mauricio lies in a coma and will not survive the night. Suspecting that one or more of the relatives tried to turn Mauricio against her, Amalia threatens to awaken him if no one confesses. She explains that the nurse can accomplish this action via injection only once. At that point, she tells them, she will ask Mauricio to sign a will she has prepared leaving everything to her. Because the relatives are unaware of the marriage and believe that if Mauricio dies without a will, they will inherit his entire estate, they are motivated to stall Amalia in hopes that Mauricio will die before she awakens him. Amalia, on the other hand, must pressure the relatives for immediate information, even though the responses given may fail to console her. The strain her face reflects is not counterproductive, for the relatives interpret her emotion as normal under the extreme circumstances they assume them to be.

The ethical component, always evident in Buero's plays, finds negative expression in the relatives whose materialism contrasts to the spiritual values of selfless love demonstrated by Amalia and Monica. Further, love is allowed partial triumph, and even one of the antagonistic relatives may have learned an important lesson, for he observes ruefully: "I hope this night teaches us something." In the play's final moments, Amalia draws back the drapes of the large picture window and the clarity of dawn floods the room. Symbolizing philosophical and personal enlightenment, this "dawning" is the ethical hope implicit in all of Buero's plays.

COMMENTARY ON *THE BASEMENT WINDOW (EL TRAGALUZ)*

The Basement Window opened in 1967 and was the first new Buero play performed since his highly successful historical parable of 1962, *The Concert at St. Ovid (El concierto de San Ovidio)*.[12] The explanation for the long absence is that in 1963 Buero had not only signed a document with other intellectuals criticizing the government's torture of striking miners (an exceedingly bold gesture for a former political prisoner), but his new play, *The Double Case History of Dr. Valmy (La doble historia del doctor Valmy)*, alluded precisely to that abusive situation and was immediately banned. During these five "silent" years, Buero had also written *Myth (Mito)*, an opera libretto planned as a joint venture with the well-known composer, Cristóbal Halffter. Featuring elements of science fiction as well as antigovernment sentiment, *Myth* concerns a quixotic actor who believes in flying saucers. Unfortunately, Halffter did not produce the musical score, and the work remains unperformed.[13] After Buero's long absence from the theater scene, *The Basement Window*, repeating many of the ideas and concerns of *Myth*, became not only the play to see but one that generated heated discussion during its long run. On opening night, a Franco sympathizer was so enraged by what he saw that he leapt onto the stage and launched into a verbal attack on the author.

In *The Basement Window*, researchers of a distant future study certain events and attitudes of the twentieth century as an exercise in ethics. When a reporter asked Buero if these characters were part of the twenty-first century, he replied: "I'm not that optimistic. The lies and catastrophes [portrayed there] may well be part of that era, but the temporal setting is imprecise. The future in which I set the experiment is quite distant and could be the twenty-fifth or thirtieth century."[14]

A challenge to Spain's slumbering conscience, *The Basement Window* assumes, as its subtitle announces, the form of an experiment and, as one of the characters states, unless the spectator participates as both accused and judge, the experiment has failed. Much more than an exercise in aesthetics, the play pleads for examination of our responsibilities to one another and draws a fine line between guilt and innocence, moral aggression and moral authority.

He and She, the researchers of another century, project holograms representing thoughts as well as actions of a remote past captured by the all-seeing eyes of their sophisticated computers. The temporal distancing and the positioning of the researchers as narrators invite spectators to identify with the ethically enlightened figures of the future and thus view their own times from a seductively objective angle. This detached contemplation of contemporary phenomena invites judgment, and the blurring of the boundaries between action and thought attempts portrayal of the total human experience. Although the prostitute surely represents Encarna's fears about the future, less clear is whether certain scenes in the basement apartment actually took place or were intense thoughts. The sound of the train, an element added by the researchers, has special importance in underscoring emotional intensity.

The researchers have elected to study a specific Spanish family because there they find primitive variants of a simple yet all-important "question" basic to their advanced moral code: Who is that person? Unlike historians who focus on historical events and important people, these researchers devote their professional lives to the study of obscure individuals as a reminder that each tree, each blade of grass, and each person has importance. It is significant that their research is devoted to improving the lot of human beings through ethical—as opposed to material—progress.

The Basement Window articulates its principal ideological thrust through Cain-Abel confrontations between Mario and Vicente. Important as well is a character cloaked in shadows and who never speaks; he is Eugenio Beltran, a novelist famous for his "Secret Story," a title that evokes Buero's own emblematic *Story of a Stairway*. Beltran suffers professional prejudices similar to the dramatist's own and, like Buero and the researchers, seeks material for his literary works in the lives of obscure individuals as he observes patiently and imagines empathetically the possible stories they might tell him.

In Spain's postwar period, idealism had become something of an anachronism. In addition to bowing before dictators, royalty, and symbols of a powerful Catholic Church, Spain's neo-capitalistic society illustrated its spiritual bankruptcy through worship of such consumer products as cars, refrigerators, and television sets. Comparable to the brief exchange about a new Fiat that takes place between the Well-Dressed Older Man and the Well-Dressed Younger Man in *Story of a Stairway* are the Mother's remarks in *The Basement Window* about Vicente's new car and his purchases for the family, including a television set. The small square "window" of the latter device not only promotes the consumer mentality through blaring commercials but provides fantasy through shallow situation comedies. Through the basement window of the family's humble dwelling, on the other hand, one may see real people with real problems. Significant in this regard is the Father's action regarding the television set.

"Out of the mouth of babes," a leitmotif of this play, pleads for the innocence of children who express interest in strangers without regard for their money or power. As young boys, Vicente and Mario played a special game analogous to the work of the researchers and "experiment" of the subtitle: they peered out at the world through the barred windows of their basement dwelling as they asked each other a question about passersby that demanded imagination and empathy: Who is that person? Children on the street peep into the window and ask similar questions, as does the "infantile" Father regarding the paper figures he compulsively cuts from magazines and postcards to "save" them as he was unable to save his baby daughter. Because the Father's rejection of contemporary reality reflects a moral lucidity as well as an ironic maturity, his role must be ambiguous. But it is not solely to placate censorship that Buero presents this character as he does. The play is much enriched by this metaphor of the loneliness of the ethical man caught in a selfish and cruel world. The Father bears a cross similar to that borne by Don Quixote, as does his son, Mario.[15] Like Cervantes's knight errant, Mario wants to right wrongs and protect the innocent, and like Don Quixote, he idealizes his own Dulcinea and is distraught when he learns that she is, as her name—Encarna—implies, a flesh-and-blood woman and hence imperfect.

Meaningful as well are the Mother's antiwar expressions ("Only awful people start wars!") and her seemingly trivial preoccupation with food. Her obsession with feeding the family is related to the death of her baby daughter and suggests that hunger and war leave permanent scars. In fact, all the characters, victims in some way of the war, continue to suffer the war's consequences. Poignant as well as risky for the author are Vicente's recollections of the war's horrors briefly detailed in Part Two. Family members are particularly marked by a specific memory they repress until feelings explode. In this sense, *The Basement Window* is a narrow shaft of light beamed on Spain's subconscious and aimed specifically at the national conscience. Supporting the play's ideological focus, the bright lights associated with the researchers suggest moral enlightenment, whereas the sparse illumination of the basement dwelling and the bars on the window denote repression and frustration.

In a technique reminiscent of *Today's a Holiday* (1956), a play in which the roof of an apartment building supports the characters' reaching for the sky and a better life, the dark and partially sunken basement apartment with a barred window is an apt metaphor for both the human condition and the situation of the vanquished in Spain's postwar society. Like the family exiled in its dungeon-like cellar, the losers are symbolic prisoners relegated to the lowest economic levels as well as to the depths of the collective subconscious of the country's victorious segment. The basement window and the train are particularly important signifiers and have multiple meanings. Since the window is situated on the invisible fourth wall, spectators assume the position of the people who pass by the window and whose shadows are projected grotesquely on the apartment's rear wall as behind bars.

The train stands not only for the physical means of locomotion utilized by Vicente in 1939 but as a metaphor for his "ride to success." Once Vicente tasted the exhilaration of mechanized forward motion ("upward mobility"), he never again chose to "walk" (live modestly), despite the consequences to others. The rest of his family, invisible to or ignored by the ruling class, had quite simply "missed the train." The goal of the victors and of those who traveled with them was ideological dominance and material success. Despite the victors' much touted religiosity, many in positions of power hypocritically exploited those beneath them, as Vicente does with Encarna. The planned silencing of Beltran by the new under-writers of the publishing house also exemplifies the hidden censorship exercised over and above that of government practices. Although perhaps Vicente's more dramatic victims are his father and baby sister, he demonstrates willingness to shove Beltran and even his unborn child beneath the wheels of that self-serving train to which he has clung since fighting his way aboard a real train in a struggle for survival after the war. The train, then, represents postwar materialism and illustrates Vicente's life-altering choices: he fought his way aboard that train and rides with the victors by stifling his conscience. Encarna is a mere "hanger-on," and Mario refuses to consider the train at all. But Buero does not suggest that "taking the train" to material success is always evil; he simply draws attention to the manner of "boarding" and "riding" that train.

In addition to its social implications, *The Basement Window* is a study of the human condition in its portrayal of solitary man's search for meaning and justice in an absurd world. The play suggests that man does not truly live until he has acknowledged responsibility for his destiny and emerges from passivity to conscious choice. In answer to Encarna's rationalization of her decisions, "We have to live," Mario responds ruefully: "That's our cross to bear: we have to live." Mario thus suggests, as does the action of Sartre's *Huis clos* (*No Exit*), that man is condemned to live.

The Basement Window shares a general kinship with other Buero plays that cry out from the void to affirm that man is not completely alone. Both the Father and Mario call out to those they find immobilized in pictures, just as they symbolically reach out to passersby through their basement window. Like the people in the images the Father collects, both the Father and Mario remain trapped, immobilized in their own uncommon idealism and sensitivity. This play suggests that if people paused in their hurried pursuit of material gain, turned off the numbing fantasies of television, and looked out of the various "windows" of the heart to see real people empathetically, the world would be a better place.

Mario hints at the meaning of the humanistic "great question" when he empathizes with a passerby (Beltran, not incidentally) and remarks: "His look really got to me. It's as though I were a part of him." Rejecting the contention that man is totally and eternally alone, both Mario and Beltran sense a mystical solidarity with everyone who has ever lived. The researchers offer solace by suggesting that humanity's cries will one day be heard.

The powerful and disturbing climax of this complex and provocative drama assigns guilt, pleads for conscience, and casts us all as judges as well as the judged. In the words of the researchers: "If, at some moment, you have not felt like beings of the twentieth century observed by a kind of future conscience; if at some time you have not felt like beings of a future made present who pass judgment with rigor tempered by mercy on people of a distant past perhaps just like you, this experiment has failed."

Despite the selfishness and frustration portrayed, *The Basement Window* offers hope. Buero writes with guarded optimism in this quasi utopia of a time in which war and its corollaries—arrogance, cruelty, greed, and exploitation—have disappeared and people have learned the lessons of history. From the perspective of a distant future, the woman researcher provides a tentative response to some of the questions posed: "We know now that we are solidly linked not only to those now living, but also to everyone who has ever lived. We stand innocent with the innocent and guilty with the guilty. . . . That person is you, and you and you; I am you, and you are me. We have all lived—and will live—all lives."

Spectators may initially have felt a smug detachment because of the tantalizingly guiltless perspective proffered but ultimately will find little comfort in that implacable eye that inexorably records not only all actions and words but all thoughts as well. The author hopes they leave the theater with the burden of their own times and shortcomings to ponder, for such is the goal of *The Basement Window*.

COMMENTARY ON *MISSION TO THE DESERTED VILLAGE (MISIÓN AL PUEBLO DESIERTO)*

Exactly fifty years after the performance of *Story of a Stairway* (1949) at Madrid's municipal theater, Buero's final play, *Mission to the Deserted Village*, came to life on the same stage. In an interview two days prior to the opening, Buero, eighty-three years old, told reporters that although *Mission to the Deserted Village* was not meant as the conclusion to his career, it could be seen as a summary of sorts in that it returned to the key issues of his previous plays.[16] Not only do ethics, history, memory, time, the search for truth, art, and music stand out in his final work, but Buero directly addresses for the first time the civil war. As the author himself had observed on several occasions, memories of that war were his constant companions. When asked why he had chosen to write about something that had ended sixty years before, he replied simply, "Because that war is not over yet."[17]

In *Story of a Stairway*, the author pointedly avoided setting his final act in 1939, the year of the war's official conclusion, but alluded to the tragedy of a divided people through feuding neighbors. More daring yet, *The Basement Window* showed a Republican family destroyed by the war and featured a confrontation with political overtones between brothers. *Mission to the Deserted Village* focuses on a Republican operation of the civil war that prompts reflection on the ethics of all wars.

This final play also reemphasizes Buero's lifelong love of art. Velázquez, Goya, and their paintings held center stage in *Las Meninas* and *The Sleep of Reason*, and in *Before Dawn* his devotion was expressed in the idealized characterization of the deceased painter, Mauricio. Inspired by personal experiences early in the war when, as dedicated painter and soldier, the author served in the Commission to Protect Artistic Treasures, *Mission to the Deserted Village* portrays three art specialists, all partial authorial surrogates, who risk their lives to rescue a possible El Greco painting. Utilizing a distancing technique reminiscent of *The Basement Window*, the author blurs temporal boundaries by alternating scenes involving present-day narration of the mission at a discussion club and portrayal of those events. The audience blends into the play as club members directly charged with judging the contemporary relevance of the ideas and actions presented.

The symbolic name of the village, Brushfire, is rooted in the Old Testament story of Exodus in which the Angel of the Lord, speaking from a burning bush, instructs Moses to lead his people out of bondage and into a land of milk and honey. Sharing Moses's mission will be his brother, Aaron. Catholic tradition has long associated this Old Testament story with the Angel Gabriel's Annunciation to the Virgin. This relationship has inspired such artistic treasures as the "Buisson ardent" ("Burning Bush") by the French master, Nicolas Foment, a painting that features Virgin and child nestled in the miraculous bush.

Recovery of an unauthenticated El Greco Annunciation constitutes the play's surface mission, but those familiar with Buero's covert challenges will consider other matters as well. What, for example, are the possible relationships between the mission and the motto inscribed over the palace portals: "The burning bush leads me to victory"? Damian, the man of action, suggests that the fire symbolizes the passions of love that assure continuation of the human species. But could this flame be the passion for art that fuels the characters' willingness to die for an irreplaceable painting? And might the absence of fire in the village brush (indication that the Republicans left the village intact) represent Aaron's dream of a democracy capable of eradicating war's violence and destruction? Do the bush's smoldering remains allude to the civil war that, according to Buero, continues? Does the blaze suggest illumination through reasoned reflection on the past? Is victory the recuperation of the long-stifled Republican memory of the war and recovery of a national conscience? Could the redemption of Spain's very soul be at stake? Do the embers represent the humane values of the Republic that lie dormant but might one day burn brightly and be respected? Is victory eradication of war itself? Such victories may be Aaron's wish, subsequently echoed by the club's president in an undefined hope that "all is not lost." Although readers and spectators will reach their own conclusions in these matters, Buero's position is likely contained in the stands taken by Aaron, Lola, and the club's president. Important, too, are the questions themselves, for they challenge reflection and awaken consciences.

Likewise meaningful are some characters' symbolic Spanish names that may fail to resonate with English-speaking audiences. The author gave the play's mature authorial voice to Plácido (literally, "Placid"), a name evocative of the personal calm and balance Buero admired. There is no equivalent name in English, and Plácido might sound comical, all wrong in the context of tragedy. Because in the Biblical parable of the burning bush, Moses's older brother and ally, Aaron, serves as messenger and peacemaker—precisely Plácido's roles in the play—I chose to call this character Aaron in the translation. He contrasts to Damian, the brilliant paleographer and brash young guerilla fighter who earned his nickname, "the Jackal," through animal quickness and cunning. A second alter ego, Damian evokes two facets of Buero's past: the art scholar and the impetuous young soldier.

A third authorial surrogate is the art historian, Lola, who shares Aaron's self-less devotion to Republican principles and to artistic treasures. It is important to note that "Lola" is an abbreviation of "Dolores" (María de los Dolores, Our Lady of Sorrows) and means, literally, "sorrows." Her name alludes to Lola's inexperience in love as well as to her past sorrow as it foreshadows future pain. The tragedy lived out by Aaron, Damian, and Lola reinforces a core idea of the play, possibly related to the village motto as well, that heeding the voice of conscience and the lessons of history leads to victory.

Because conflicting ideologies divided Spain into two large camps during the civil war, there existed a range of differences within each, and *Mission to the Deserted Village* highlights some of these among Republicans.[18] The Captain and the Commanding Officer, for example, sneer at President Azaña as an "intellec-tual" and object to his jeopardizing war plans and soldiers' lives for a painting. Azaña's portrayal is historically accurate, as his recorded statement demonstrates: "It is more important to save an artistic treasure than to save the Republic: if the latter is lost, it can be restored; if destroyed, however, it can never be replaced."[19] A related discussion about the value of art and the mode of transporting and "saving" the painting takes place among the three central characters. Damian wants to prevent the treasure from falling into enemy hands at all cost and favors removing the canvas even though it will likely be damaged beyond repair. Aaron and Lola, on the other hand, are determined to preserve the painting, even if that means leaving it to the Nationalists.

On the broader issue of war, Aaron rejects violence—specifically, the tor-ture of prisoners, the destruction of property, and executions by roving death squads—as he gives voice to the stated but not always practiced humanitarian ideals of the Republic. The contemporary relevance of *Mission to the Deserted Village* is unmistakable. The world's political and religious hardliners and fundamental-ists are, like Damian, much less concerned about the treatment of adversaries and favor any method to eradicate those considered "evil." The more thoughtful moderates, like Aaron and Lola, believe that the truly noble cause is dedication to peace and to the humanitarian treatment of all people. Their solution to war is civil discussion and decisions made democratically.

The personal challenge of all Buero's plays, dramatically reinforced in *Mission to the Deserted Village*, is to listen to the voice of conscience, for conscience will always advise empathy, and empathy leads to compassion and peace. Small individual triumphs over self-serving choices, Buero whispers between the lines, make a difference, for they represent progress toward moral enlightenment and a better world for all.

NOTES

1. Adolf Hitler founded Germany's nationalistic and anti-communist Nazi Party in 1920, and in 1923, Benito Mussolini, asserting that democracy was corrupt and inefficient, established Italy's similarly nationalistic Fascist Party. Spain followed their leads in creating such far-right parties as the National Front and the Falange, and "fascist" became a generic term for ultra-conservative autocratic systems (or individuals) of non-Marxist leanings. Even after the Second World War, totalitarian regimes like those of Hitler, Mussolini, and Franco have existed in South America, Central America, and Western Asia.

2. Additional details, quotations, and documentation of the famous concepts expressed by these thinkers are readily available via google.com.

3. A file containing censorship documents is available in the Archives and Rare Books section of the University of Cincinnati library and contains, among other items, the following relevant documents: (1) the theatrical censorship bulletin listing prohibitions; (2) eight published articles on censorship by Patricia W. O'Connor; and (3) press reports, magazine articles, and correspondence on the government-to-government protest regarding O'Connor's expulsion from Spain in 1972 because of her censorship studies. She not only had official permission from Spain's highest authority under Franco (Manuel Fraga Iribarne, Minister of Information) to pursue her research but was illegally denied access to the U.S. Embassy in the expulsion event.

4. Antonio Buero Vallejo, *Antonio Buero Vallejo: Obra Completa*, 2 vols., ed. Luis Iglesias Feijoo and Mariano de Paco (Madrid: Espasa Calpe, 1994), 2: 319.

5. Ibid., 320.

6. Catherine O'Leary, *The Theatre of Antonio Buero Vallejo: Ideology, Politics and Censorship* (Woodbridge, Suffolk, UK: Tamesis, 2005), 125.

7. Patricia W. O'Connor and Anthony M. Pasquariello, "Conversaciones con la Generación Realista," *Estreno* 2:2 (1976): 10.

8. Quoted in Mariano de Paco, ed., *Buero Vallejo: Cuarenta años de teatro* (Murcia: CajaMurcia, 1988), 129–130.

9. Ricardo Domenéch, "Introducción," in *Antonio Buero Vallejo: El concierto de San Ovidio, El tragaluz* (Madrid: Castalia, 1971), 15.

10. José Monleón, "Reposición: *Historia de una escalera*," *Primer Acto* 96 (May 1968): 66.

11. Buero Vallejo, *Obra Completa*, 2:397.

12. Buero's only other contributions to Spanish theater in that five-year period were in 1963 with performance of his long-forbidden *Adventure in Gray* (*Aventura en lo gris*) and his adaptation of Bertolt Brecht's antiwar play, *Mother Courage*.

13. The Spanish version of *Myth* (*Mito*) is published in the theater journal *Primer Acto* 100–101 (November–December 1968) as well as in a separate volume by Escelicer (Madrid, 1968).

14. Ida Molina, "Note on the Dialectics of the Search for Truth in *El otro* and *El tragaluz*," *Romance Notes* 14:1 (1972): 4.

15. For additional information on this theme, see Carmen Caro Dugo, *The Importance of the Don Quixote Myth in the Works of Antonio Buero Vallejo* (Lewiston, NY: Mellen University Press, 1995).

16. Virtudes Serrano and Mariano de Paco, "Las últimas obras de Buero Vallejo: Principio y fin de una búsqueda," *Estreno* 27:1 (2001): 48.

17. *El País*, October 1, 1999: 19.

18. It is important to recall that Spain's Republicans of the 1930s were the progressive educated middle class who fought to keep their government democratic and separate from the Church, whereas the conservative Nationalist coalition of monarchists, aristocrats, and staunch Catholics vowed a return to the traditional Catholic monarchy. The latter scorned Republicans as atheistic communists, whereas Republicans disdained Nationalists as dictatorial fascists.

19. Cited in Gregorio Torres Nebrera's critical edition of Rafael Alberti's *Noche de Guerra en el museo del Prado* ["A Night of War in the Prado Museum"] (Sevilla: Alfar, 1991), 86.

The Plays

STORY OF A STAIRWAY

(*Historia de una escalera*)

Drama in Three Acts

By Antonio Buero-Vallejo

Translated by Patricia W. O'Connor

This play opened in Madrid's Español Theater on October 14, 1949.

For the son dishonoreth the father, the daughter riseth up against
her mother, the daughter-in-law against her mother-in-law; a man's
enemies are the men of his own house.

MICAH 7:6

Characters

BILL COLLECTOR

GENEROSA, mother of Carmina and Pepe

PACA, mother of Urbano, Trini, Rosa

ELVIRA, daughter of Manuel

ASUNCION, mother of Fernando

MANUEL, father of Elvira

TRINI, daughter of Paca

CARMINA, daughter of Generosa

FERNANDO, son of Asuncion

URBANO, son of Paca

ROSA, daughter of Paca

PEPE, son of Generosa

JUAN, husband of Paca

WELL-DRESSED OLDER MAN

WELL-DRESSED YOUNGER MAN

YOUNG CARMINA, daughter of Carmina and Urbano

YOUNG FERNANDO, son of Fernando and Elvira

MANOLIN, son of Fernando and Elvira

Stage directions (right, left, etc.)
are from the audience's perspective.

ACT ONE

The action takes place in the hallways of a modest urban apartment building. The set features upper and lower landings connected by a flight of stairs. Downstage left, steps not visible lead to floors below. Extending horizontally across the stage to define the lower landing's limits is a cheap iron handrail. Stage right, an ascending flight of approximately ten steps is bordered on the left by the railing that curves left at the top of the stairs and extends across the stage to define the upper landing. At the bottom of these stairs, a wall with a dingy window turns at right angles to form an empty space that the younger characters call their "clubhouse," an area used first for play and later as a meeting site. Encased in wire, a dusty bulb dangles over the empty stairwell. On the upper landing there are four doors: two face the audience, and two on the side walls face each other. These doors indicate four apartments identified, right to left, by the numbers I, II, III, and IV. In Acts One and Two, spectators witness a time gone by. The costumes are only vaguely retrospective.

As the curtain goes up, the **BILL COLLECTOR** *trudges wearily across the stage with his worn leather satchel and climbs the stairs. He pauses briefly to catch his breath before knocking on all four doors. He then returns to door I, where* **GENEROSA,** *a woman about fifty-five and of obviously meager means, awaits him in the doorway.*

BILL COLLECTOR: The light bill: two sixty. (*He hands her the bill as door III opens and* **PACA,** *an overweight, outspoken woman also in her fifties, emerges. The* **BILL COLLECTOR** *extends her bill as he speaks.*) The light bill: four ten.

GENEROSA: My goodness! It goes up every month! I don't know how we'll get by. (*She goes inside.*)

PACA: You can say that again! (*To the* **BILL COLLECTOR.**) Is upping the bill all you people know how to do? The electric company is a pack of thieves! You bloodsuckers should be ashamed of gouging us like this. (**BILL COLLECTOR** *shrugs his shoulders.*) And you shrug it off! I guess you think it's funny!

BILL COLLECTOR: No, ma'am; I'm not laughing. (*To* **ELVIRA,** *who opens door II.*) Good morning. The light bill: six seventy-five. (**ELVIRA,** *a pretty and well-dressed young woman, takes the bill and goes back inside.*)

PACA: But I'll bet you're laughing to yourself. You people down there are all alike. According to my son, Urbano, we could fix a lot of things if we tossed a bunch of you leeches down the stairwell!

BILL COLLECTOR: Watch your tongue, madam. You're getting offensive.

PACA: Thieves! That's what you are!

BILL COLLECTOR: Are you going to pay the bill or not? I don't have all day.

PACA: All right, all right. You take advantage of us little people . . . (*She continues muttering as she goes inside.* **GENEROSA** *emerges, pays the* **BILL COLLECTOR,** *and closes the door. He bangs on door IV again. This time,* **ASUNCION,** *a thin little woman dressed all in black, opens the door immediately.*)

BILL COLLECTOR: The light bill. Six twenty.

ASUNCION: (*Looking at the bill.*) Yes, of course . . . Good morning. Just a minute, please. I'll be right back. (*She goes back into the apartment as* **PACA,** *grumbling, returns to count out the money.*)

PACA: Here! (*She thrusts the money into his hand.*)

BILL COLLECTOR: (*After counting out the money.*) All right.

PACA: No, it's not all right! It's a disgrace! Let's see if there's a little justice around here when you start down those stairs! (*She slams the door as* **ELVIRA** emerges.)

ELVIRA: Here you are. (*Counting out the money.*) Forty, fifty, sixty, sixty-five . . .

BILL COLLECTOR: Fine. Thank you, ma'am. (*He touches his hat in a gesture of respect and moves back to door IV.*)

ELVIRA: (*Looking back.*) Aren't you coming, papa? (*She stands in the doorway as* **ASUNCION** *returns, furtively rehearsing several different smiles.*)

ASUNCION: Oh, I'm so sorry! You're going to have to excuse me this month! You caught me just after I did the shopping, and my son isn't here right now . . .

MANUEL, **ELVIRA**'s *father, emerges dressed to go out. The clothing of both indicates higher economic status than that of the other neighbors.*

MANUEL: (*To* **ASUNCION.**) Good morning. (*To his daughter.*) Let's go.

ASUNCION: Oh, good morning! Good morning, Elvira! I didn't see you standing there!

ELVIRA: Good morning, Miss Asuncion.

BILL COLLECTOR: Look, ma'am; I don't have all day.

ASUNCION: Oh, yes, yes. . . . As I was saying: it just so happens that I can't pay right now. . . . Maybe you could come back a little later?

BILL COLLECTOR: Look, ma'am; this isn't the first time, and . . .

ASUNCION: What do you mean?

BILL COLLECTOR: I mean, every month, it's the same old story. Every month! And you're not the only one! And no, I can't come back later. And no, I can't pay it out of my own pocket either. So if you don't pay up, I'll have to terminate your service.

ASUNCION: But it's just a coincidence that you came now, really! My son isn't here, and . . .

BILL COLLECTOR: Excuses, excuses! You just like to leave the lights on like some grand lady and not go on the budget plan. I'll have to cut off your electricity.

ELVIRA *whispers something to her father.*

ASUNCION: (*On the verge of losing her composure.*) Oh, please! I'm begging you! Don't do that! I promise . . .

BILL COLLECTOR: Why don't you borrow the money from a neighbor? . . .

MANUEL: (*Following his daughter's suggestion.*) Excuse me for interrupting here . . . (*Taking the bill.*)

ASUNCION: Oh, no! I can't let you do that!

MANUEL: Think nothing of it, really. You can pay me anytime.

ASUNCION: This very afternoon, I promise.

MANUEL: No hurry at all. (*To* **BILL COLLECTOR**.) Here you are.

BILL COLLECTOR: All right. (*He tips his hat as he exits.*) Have a good day.

MANUEL: The same to you.

ASUNCION: (*To the* **BILL COLLECTOR**.) Yes, and you have a good day, too. Thank you so much. By this afternoon . . .

MANUEL: (*Handing her the receipt.*) Don't bother. It's no problem. By the way, what's Fernando doing these days? (**ELVIRA** *joins them and takes her father's arm to hear the response.*)

ASUNCION: He's working at the office supply store, but he doesn't like it. The salary is ridiculous! And it's not just because he's my son that I'm saying this, but he's so talented! He deserves so much more. He has big plans, like being a draftsman, an engineer, and I don't know what all. He reads and thinks a lot; always lying on the bed, making plans. And he writes, too. Sometimes it's poetry; such pretty poetry! I'll tell him to write a poem about Elvira.

ELVIRA: (*Embarrassed.*) Oh, you don't have to do that . . .

ASUNCION: You deserve it, my dear. (*To* MANUEL.) I'm not saying this because she's standing here, but look how pretty Elvira has gotten. She's just like a rose. The man who wins her heart . . .

MANUEL: All right, all right. Please don't go on; you'll turn her head. As I was saying (*Removing his hat and extending his hand.*) . . . , my regards to Fernando.

ELVIRA: (*Preparing to leave.*) Good-bye.

ASUNCION: Good-bye, and thank you so much. . . . Good-bye. (*She closes the door.*)

As MANUEL *and* ELVIRA *start down the stairs, the latter suddenly stops and impulsively hugs her father.*

MANUEL: Hey! Watch out! You're going to make me fall down the steps!

ELVIRA: Oh, my little poppy, I love you so much! You're so good!

MANUEL: Enough of your flattery, you little devil. What I am is weak. I give in to you.

ELVIRA: Don't call doing a good deed a weakness. Those poor people never have any money. I feel so sorry for Miss Asuncion!

MANUEL: (*With his hand under her chin.*) The one you're concerned about is that good-for-nothing Fernando.

ELVIRA: Papa, don't say that about Fernando! If you could just hear him talk!

MANUEL: He's a good-for-nothing, I say. Sure, he knows how to talk! But that's all he knows how to do! And he doesn't have a dime to his name. Listen to me, my darling daughter: you deserve better.

ELVIRA: (*On the landing at the top of the stairs, she stamps her foot childishly.*) Don't talk about him that way. He's going to do big things; you'll see. What difference does it make that he has no money? What does my little poppy need a rich son-in-law for?

MANUEL: Oh, honey!

ELVIRA: Listen. I'm going to ask a big favor.

MANUEL: How little respect you show me, my dear.

ELVIRA: But I love you, and that's better than respect. Will you do what I ask?

MANUEL: That depends . . .

ELVIRA: Oh, I know you will.

MANUEL: So what is it?

ELVIRA: It's really very simple, papa. You don't need a rich son-in-law; what you need is an industrious one who will help out with the business. You could take Fernando away from that store and give him a job with a good salary. (*Pause.*) What do you say?

MANUEL: But Elvira, what if Fernando doesn't want it? Besides . . .

ELVIRA: Oh, no! (*Covering her ears.*) I can't hear you!

MANUEL: But, honey; I'm your father!

ELVIRA: I'm deaf! Can't hear a thing!

MANUEL: (*Taking her hands away from her ears.*) That Fernando has turned your head, just like he does with all the girls. Yes, I know he's the best-looking fellow in the whole building, but I don't trust him. Suppose he ignores you. . . .

ELVIRA: You do your part, and I'll do mine. . . .

MANUEL: Elvira . . .

ELVIRA *laughs as she takes her father's arm and affectionately guides him toward the stairs. Pause.* TRINI, *a pleasant-looking young woman, emerges from door III carrying a pitcher as she listens to* PACA.

PACA: (*From inside.*) Be sure you get red wine; you know your father doesn't like the white.

TRINI: Yes, mother. (*She closes the door and goes toward the stairway as* GENEROSA, *also carrying a pitcher, emerges from door I.*)

GENEROSA: Hello there, Trini.

TRINI: Morning, Miss Generosa. Going down for wine? (*They go down the stairs together.*)

GENEROSA: Yes, and milk, too.

TRINI: Where's Carmina?

GENEROSA: Oh, she's busy straightening up the house.

TRINI: Have you noticed how the light bill has gone up lately?

GENEROSA: Oh, yes! And if it were just the lights . . . , but it's also the milk . . . and the potatoes!

TRINI: (*Confidentially.*) Did you hear that Miss Asuncion couldn't pay her light bill this morning?

GENEROSA: Really?

TRINI: My mother told me. She was standing right there and heard everything. Mr. Manuel paid it for her. His darling daughter is crazy about Fernando, you know.

GENEROSA: Well, he's lazy, but he *is* an attractive devil.

TRINI: And Elvira's a conniver.

GENEROSA: A spoiled brat . . .

TRINI: A real schemer, I say.

> *They continue the chatter as they go down the stairs. Pause.* CARMINA *emerges from door I. She is a pretty girl with a simple, modest manner. She wears an apron and carries a milk pitcher.*

CARMINA: (*Leaning over the railing and calling down the empty stairwell.*) Mother! You forgot the milk pitcher! Mother! (*Making a face, she quickly takes off the apron, tosses it inside the apartment and closes the door. As she hurries down the stairs, door IV opens quietly, and* FERNANDO *observes her as he silently closes the door behind him. In her rush,* CARMINA *does not notice him and disappears. He leans on the railing and watches the young girl go down the stairs.* FERNANDO *is, indeed, quite handsome. He wears a casual shirt and the black pants that signal mourning. Door IV opens and* ASUNCION *observes her son.*)

ASUNCION: What are you doing out there?

FERNANDO: (*Irritated.*) I think what I'm doing is pretty obvious.

ASUNCION: (*Repentant.*) Are you angry with me?

FERNANDO: No.

ASUNCION: Did something happen at the store?

FERNANDO: No.

ASUNCION: Why didn't you go to work today?

FERNANDO: I didn't feel like it. (*Pause.*)

ASUNCION: Did I tell you Elvira's father paid our light bill?

FERNANDO: (*Turning toward his mother.*) Yes! You told me! (*Walking toward her.*) Leave me alone!

ASUNCION: But, son . . .

FERNANDO: Why are you always doing that? Do you enjoy reminding me that we're poor?

ASUNCION: Fernando . . .

FERNANDO: Go back inside! (*Pushing her gently but firmly inside and slamming the door. With a sigh of irritation, he leans on the railing again. Pause.* URBANO, *wearing dark blue overalls, reaches the landing. He is a well-built young man with the rugged but expressive features of the classic laborer.* FERNANDO *watches him approach in silence.* URBANO *pauses on his way up when he spies* FERNANDO.)

URBANO: Hey! What are you doing there?

FERNANDO: Nothing much.

URBANO: Looks like you're angry.

FERNANDO: It's nothing.

URBANO: Come on down to the clubhouse. (*Indicating the small space by the window.*) I'll treat you to a cigarette. (*Pause.*) Come on, buddy! (*Fernando begins to go down the steps, but he's in no hurry.*) Something's bothering you. (*Taking out his tobacco pouch.*) Aren't you going to tell me?

FERNANDO: (*Joining* URBANO.) Oh, the same old stuff. . . . (*He leans against the wall in the little clubhouse space as both begin to roll cigarettes.*) I'm just fed up with things!

URBANO: You're right; that's nothing new. I thought something else was wrong.

FERNANDO: Go ahead and laugh, but I'm telling you, I don't know how I put up with everything. (*Short pause.*) Anyway, what's the use of talking about it? What's new at the factory?

URBANO: Lots of things! Ever since the last steelworkers' strike, people have been joining the union like mad. Let's see when you office workers wise up and do the same.

FERNANDO: I'm not interested in that stuff.

URBANO: Because you're out of it. What good is all that reading going to do you?

FERNANDO: You want to tell me what you people get out of all your efforts?

URBANO: Fernando, you're pathetic. And the worst part is that you don't know it. Poor devils like us will never get anywhere or make things better if we don't help each other. And that's what the union's about. All for one, and one for all! Solidarity! That's our motto! And it can be yours, too, when you realize that you're just a clerk in a store; an ordinary chump like so many others, struggling to get by. But you think you're above it all, like you're special. You act like royalty or something!

FERNANDO: No, I don't. I just want things to get better, you know? I want something more; a better life. I want to leave this sordid existence behind.

URBANO: And to hell with everybody else, right?

FERNANDO: What have I got to do with other people? Nobody really helps anybody else. You guys join the union because you don't have what it takes to get ahead on your own. That's not my way. I know I can do it, and I'll do it on my own.

URBANO: Mind if I laugh?

FERNANDO: Do whatever you want.

URBANO: Listen, you dummy. For you to get ahead, just you, you'd have to work at least ten hours every day, and you could never just take off, like you did today . . .

FERNANDO: What makes you think I didn't go in?

URBANO: It's written all over your face, you idiot! And I'll tell you something else: if you want to be successful, there are things you love doing that you won't be able to do, like lying around writing poetry with your head in the clouds. You'll be so busy looking for odd jobs to make ends meet that you'll go to bed about three in the morning, happy, I suppose, that you can even scrimp on sleep, because, for sure, you'll have to save like a miser. And you'll have to eat less, buy fewer clothes, and cut down on cigarettes. And when you've done all that and run out of business schemes, you'll wind up taking some lowly job with a miserable salary just to keep body and soul together. You're not tough enough to make the kind of money you're dreaming about.

FERNANDO: We'll see. Starting tomorrow . . .

URBANO: (*Laughing.*) You're always "starting tomorrow." Why didn't you start yesterday, or a month ago? (*Brief pause.*) Because you can't; you're a dreamer. And on top of that, you're lazy. (**FERNANDO**, *livid, glares at him but controls his anger as he makes a move to leave.*) Hey, wait! Don't get mad. I'm telling you this for your own good. (*Pause.*)

FERNANDO: (*Calmer now, but with an air of superiority.*) Let me tell you something: time will tell who's right. We'll come back to this conversation someday. . . . Let's say . . . in ten years. Then we'll see whether you get farther with your union, or I do better on my own.

URBANO: I already know I won't be a whole lot better off. But you won't either. If things are better for me, it'll be because they're better for everybody. In ten years, we'll probably still be going up and down this same stairway smoking in this little clubhouse of ours.

FERNANDO: Oh, no; not me. (*Pause.*) Although maybe ten years isn't long enough . . .

URBANO: (*Laughing.*) Hey! You don't sound too sure about those pipe dreams.

FERNANDO: That's not it. It's the passage of time that scares me. It's awful to see how the days turn into years, and nothing changes. It seems only yesterday we were kids sneaking down here to smoke our first cigarettes. . . . That was ten years ago! We've grown up without realizing it, going up and down these stairs, surrounded by parents who didn't understand us and neighbors who gossiped about us, just like we talk bad about them now. . . . And everybody's just looking for ways to survive; pay the rent, the light bill, buy groceries, and all the while putting up with the humiliations that go along with having no money. Tomorrow, or ten years from now . . . , and those years can pass like a day, just like the past ten have. . . . It'll be awful if nothing changes. Here we are, going up and down these stairs; stairs that lead nowhere. We cheat on our bills, we hate our jobs, we get behind. . . . (*Pause.*) I need to make a clean break with all this.

URBANO: Yeah? How are you going to do that?

FERNANDO: I don't know. Somehow.

URBANO: And you'll do it all alone?

FERNANDO: Alone. (*Pause.*)

URBANO: Completely alone?

FERNANDO: Sure.

URBANO: Well, let me tell you something. Whether you think so or not, we always need other people. You can't fight life's battle alone without getting worn out.

FERNANDO: Are you going to lecture me about the union again?

URBANO: No. I'm just saying that when people fight hard for something, in order to keep their spirits up they need . . . (*He stops.*)

FERNANDO: Need what?

URBANO: A partner . . . in life. A wife, for example . . .

FERNANDO: No problem. You know that. . . .

URBANO: I know you're handsome and that women fall at your feet. But being so good-looking has its drawbacks. What you need to do is quit playing around and fall in love. (*Pause.*) We haven't talked about things like this for a long time. . . . Before, if we liked this girl or that girl, we'd tell each other right away. (*Pause.*) Anything serious with you these days?

FERNANDO: (*Holding back.*) Well, maybe . . .

URBANO: You don't mean my sister, do you?

FERNANDO: Your sister?

URBANO: Trini.

FERNANDO: Oh, no; no.

URBANO: And I don't think Rosa is your cup of tea.

FERNANDO: Definitely not. (*Pause.*)

URBANO: I don't think you've got your sights set on Generosa's daughter, either . . . (*He looks at* **FERNANDO** *a little anxiously out of the corner of his eye.*) Or is she the one? Is it Carmina? (*Pause.*)

FERNANDO: Nope.

URBANO: (*Laughing as he slaps him on the back.*) All right, buddy! I won't dig any more! You'll tell me when you're ready. Want another cigarette?

FERNANDO: No. (*Brief pause.*) Somebody's coming up the stairs. (*They lean over the railing and look down the stairwell.*)

URBANO: It's my sister.

ROSA, young, pretty, and provocative, appears. As she passes the men, she greets them a little contemptuously. Without stopping, she continues up the next flight of stairs.

ROSA: Hi, guys.

FERNANDO: Hi, Rosie.

URBANO: You've been out on the streets up to no good, I suppose.

ROSA: What I do is none of your business.

URBANO: One of these days, I'm going to knock somebody's teeth out!

ROSA: What a brave man! You better watch out for your own teeth.

She continues up the steps. URBANO is disconcerted by her boldness. FERNANDO laughs and pulls him aside. Before ROSA knocks on door III, door I opens and PEPE emerges. CARMINA's brother is about thirty years old and has the look of the classic hustler. ROSA turns, and they look at each other approvingly. He is about to say something when she gestures for him to be quiet and indicates that there is someone below in the clubhouse area not visible to him. PEPE mimes an invitation to go dancing with him later, and she does not hide her enthusiasm in responding affirmatively. PACA opens the door to interrupt their silent communication.

PACA: What a pretty little scene! (*Furious, she whirls her daughter around.*) Get inside! I'll show you a good time right here!

FERNANDO and URBANO lean over the railing to watch.

ROSA: Don't push! You can't treat me like this!

PACA: I can't?

ROSA: No! I'm an adult!

PACA: And who do you think supports you? You ungrateful little floozy!

ROSA: Hey! Hold the insults!

PACA: (*Shoving her inside.*) Get in there! (*To PEPE, who has descended a couple of steps.*) And you, you dirty pimp! If I catch you around my daughter again, I swear, as sure as my name is Paca, my frying pan is going to leave a mark on your skull!

PEPE: Oh, you scare me to death!

PACA: Outta here! Get outta here! (*She slams the door as* **PEPE,** *unperturbed, continues down the stairs. He is about to pass* **FERNANDO** *and* **URBANO** *without stopping, but* **URBANO** *grabs him by the sleeve.*)

URBANO: What's the hurry?

PEPE: (*Turning toward him angrily.*) Great! Two against one, huh?

FERNANDO: (*Hastily.*) No, no, Pepe. (*Smiling slightly.*) I'm not a part of this. It's none of my business.

URBANO: No; it's my business.

PEPE: Get your hands off me. What do you want anyway?

URBANO: (*Seething.*) I just want to tell you something: if my silly sister doesn't know what kind of guy you are, I do. If she can't see that you've been living off of Luisa and Pili, after getting them to turn tricks out there on the streets, I know it. And if I catch you with Rosa again, I swear: you're going right over that railing. (*He releases him violently.*) Now get out of here. (*He turns his back on* **PEPE.**)

PEPE: You can't do anything I don't let you do. Oh, these little boys! Huh! When they grow to a certain height, they think they're men! If it weren't for . . .

URBANO *pays no attention to him, but* FERNANDO *intervenes, trying to calm things.*

FERNANDO: Forget it, Pepe. Don't let it bother you. You'd better go.

PEPE: Yeah; you're right. (*He begins to leave, but stops and turns around.*) That little snot-nose thinks he can scare me. Me! (*He goes down the steps, grumbling to himself.*) One of these days, I'm going to get into it with him. I'll show that little punk what being a man is all about. . . .

FERNANDO: I don't know why you enjoy shouting and threatening people like that.

URBANO: (*Matter-of-factly.*) Everybody's different. Why are you nice to a low-down rat like that?

FERNANDO: It's better than making empty threats.

URBANO: What do you mean: "empty threats"?

FERNANDO: That you'll never do those things! Throw somebody down the stairwell? You? Hell, no! You don't even scare anybody! (*Pause.*)

URBANO: I don't know how we do it, but you and I always end up arguing! I'm going home to eat. See ya around.

FERNANDO: (*Satisfied with his small revenge.*) See ya, union guy.

URBANO *goes up the stairs and knocks on door III.* PACA *opens it.*

PACA: Hello, son. Are you hungry?

URBANO: Hungry as a bear!

URBANO *goes inside and closes the door.* FERNANDO *leans on the railing and stares into the empty space below. With a gesture of irritation, he returns to the little clubhouse and looks out of the window, feigning distraction. Presently* MANUEL *and* ELVIRA *come up the steps. When* ELVIRA *spots Fernando, she presses her father's arm. They stop for a moment before continuing on.*

MANUEL: (*Looking slyly at* ELVIRA, *who seems very anxious.*) Hello, Fernando, my boy.

FERNANDO: (*Turning around disinterestedly and without looking at* ELVIRA.) Good morning.

MANUEL: Home from work so early?

FERNANDO: (*Hesitantly.*) Yes. . . .

MANUEL: Well, fine. (*He is about to continue on, but* ELVIRA *holds him back, stubbornly indicating that he should speak to* FERNANDO *now. The father gives in, against his will.*) One of these days, I need to talk to you about something.

FERNANDO: Whenever you say.

MANUEL: There's no hurry. I'll let you know. Until then, my regards to your mother.

FERNANDO: Thank you; and the best to you, too.

As they go up the stairs, ELVIRA *turns frequently to look at* FERNANDO, *who has his back to her.* MANUEL *unlocks door II and they go in.* FERNANDO *grimaces and leans on the railing again. Pause.* GENEROSA *comes up the stairs, and* FERNANDO *greets her, smiling broadly.*

FERNANDO: Good morning.

GENEROSA: Hello, Fernando. Would you like something to eat?

FERNANDO: No; thanks anyway. How is Mr. Gregorio?

GENEROSA: He's been down in the dumps ever since they forced him to retire. He'd reached the age limit, you know. . . . It's like he says: "What good does it do to drive a streetcar for fifty years, if then they toss you out?" If they retired people with a decent pension, that'd be different . . . , but what they give you these days is next to nothing; you sure can't live on it. And Pepe is no help. Nobody's been able to straighten him out! (*Pause.*) What a life! I don't know how we're going to get by.

FERNANDO: You're right. It's a good thing Carmina . . .

GENEROSA: Carmina is our only consolation. She's a good girl, a hardworker, and knows how to keep a nice house. . . . Now, if our Pepe were like her . . .

FERNANDO: I'm not too sure, but I think Carmina was looking for you before.

GENEROSA: Yes, I'd forgotten the milk pitcher. I saw her already. She'll be up in a minute. See you later.

FERNANDO: See you.

GENEROSA *goes up the steps, opens her door, and enters. Pause.* ELVIRA *comes out very quietly and leaves her door ajar. She leans on the railing as she looks down at* FERNANDO, *who pretends not to notice. She calls out to him.*

ELVIRA: Fernando . . .

FERNANDO: Yes . . .

ELVIRA: Can you go with me to buy a book later on today? I have to get a gift, and I thought you might help me pick something out.

FERNANDO: I don't think I have time. (*Pause.*)

ELVIRA: Please try. I need your advice. And I need the book by tomorrow.

FERNANDO: I'm not making any promises. (*She pouts.*) In fact, don't count on me. (*He continues to gaze down the empty stairwell.*)

ELVIRA: (*Unhappy, but forcing a smile.*) You really don't like doing things for other people, do you? (*Pause.*) Can't you at least look at me? I don't believe it's all that hard. . . . (*Pause.*) Is it?

FERNANDO: (*Looking up.*) What?

ELVIRA: Weren't you even listening? Or maybe you just don't want to hear what I have to say.

FERNANDO: Oh, leave me alone.

ELVIRA: (*Resentful.*) How easily you humiliate others! It's easy . . . but it's cruel to talk to anybody like that! You take advantage of how much people like you, because you know they won't hurt you back . . . but they could, if they wanted to. . . .

FERNANDO: (*Turning to her, furious.*) Explain what you mean by that!

ELVIRA: It's easy to be arrogant and look down on people who are fond of you; ready to help out . . . and are helping already. . . . It's so easy to overlook that help.

FERNANDO: (*Furious.*) How dare you throw up your money to me? You're just so ordinary and boring! I can't stand the sight of you! Go away!

ELVIRA: (*Repentant.*) Oh, Fernando, I'm sorry! Please forgive me! It's just that . . .

FERNANDO: Go away! You make me sick! I can't stand your favors and your stupidity. Go away! (*She moves back, obviously upset. She goes into her apartment tearful and hardly able to control herself. Also agitated, Fernando pulls out a cigarette, lights it, and tosses the match away as he exclaims.*) What a crock!

FERNANDO *returns to the clubhouse. Pause.* **PACA** *comes out of her door and knocks on door I.* **GENEROSA** *opens it.*

PACA: Could I borrow some salt?

GENEROSA: Table or cooking?

PACA: The coarse kind, for my stew. (**GENEROSA** *goes back inside, and* **PACA** *raises her voice.*) Just a little. (**GENEROSA** *returns with a folded paper containing the salt.*) Hey, thanks!

GENEROSA: You're welcome.

PACA: How much was your light bill this month?

GENEROSA: Two sixty. And that's ridiculous! I hardly ever turn the lights on, but I never get away with owing less than two pesetas.

PACA: Don't complain! I had to pay four ten.

GENEROSA: But you have one more room than we do, and there are more of you living there.

PACA: So what? I never turn the lights on in our bedroom. Juan and I get undressed in the dark. At our age, there's nothing to see anyway. . . .

Story of a Stairway (Germany, 1965), Act I, Paca (Leonie Dielmann) and Generosa (Impa Strick)

GENEROSA: Oh, my!

PACA: Am I embarrassing you?

GENEROSA: Well, no, but the things that come out of your mouth!

PACA: What's a mouth for anyway? I say it's there to use!

GENEROSA: But in good ways.

PACA: I didn't say anything bad.

GENEROSA: Even so . . .

PACA: Look, you're a timid soul; that's for sure! You don't even dare gossip!

GENEROSA: Lord, forgive me! I gossip way too much.

PACA: Gossip's a fun thing! (*Confidentially.*) By the way, did you know that Manuel paid Asuncion's light bill?

With an expression that shows increasing disgust, FERNANDO *overhears it all.*

GENEROSA: Trini told me.

PACA: Darn that Trini! She could let *me* tell you! (*Changing her tone.*) But in my opinion, Elvira got her father to do it.

GENEROSA: Well, it's not the first time they've done things like that for her.

PACA: But who really set the whole thing up was Asuncion.

GENEROSA: How do you figure that?

PACA: Well, sure! (*Mimicking* ASUNCION's *voice and manner.*) "Oh, I'm so sorry; I can't pay the bill just now. Oh, good morning, Mr. Manuel. Oh, my goodness, Mr. Bill Collector, I can't pay right this minute! Oh, hello there, Elvira! How pretty you look!" You think her hand wasn't out?

GENEROSA: You always think the worst of people.

PACA: Me? Think the worst? I'm not knocking what she did. What else can a woman in her situation do? Her widow's pension is only sixty-five pesetas a month, and her son doesn't do a lick of work.

GENEROSA: Fernando has a job.

PACA: And what do you think he makes? It's a pittance! After paying bills for rent, heat, and food, they have nothing left! And of course they don't pay him for those times he doesn't show up. One of these days, the store is just going to fire him.

GENEROSA: Poor boy. Why would they do a thing like that?

PACA: Because he rarely goes to work. He's not reliable. I have a feeling he's after Elvira . . . and her father's money.

GENEROSA: Isn't it the other way round?

PACA: Heavens no! That guy knows what he's doing, and he knows how to get just what he wants. He's so good-looking, you know; because he *is* good-looking! No denying that.

GENEROSA: (*Looking over the railing and then coming back.*) I wonder what's keeping Carmina . . . Listen, Paca. You really think Manuel has money?

PACA: Well, you know he was just an office clerk in the old days. But with that agency he's put together, he's making a bundle with all his contacts and his slick little deals . . .

GENEROSA: What kind of agency is it anyway?

PACA: Just something to get money out of people. He sells certificates and permissions; government-bureaucracy stuff. Well, I got to go; it's getting late. (*She starts to leave but pauses.*) How's your husband getting along?

GENEROSA: Not too well, as you can imagine. When he reached the age limit, they retired him. . . . It's like he always says: you give them fifty years of your life driving a streetcar, and at the end they just toss you out like garbage . . . because the pension is ridiculous; a pittance. But you know all that, Paca. What a life! My goodness, I just don't know how we're going to get by. And my Pepe is no help . . .

PACA: Pepe's bad news. Excuse me for saying so, but you already know that. I've said it before and I'll say it again: I don't want him hanging around my Rosa.

GENEROSA: (*Humiliated.*) I know you're right. My poor child!

PACA: Poor child? When you come right down to it, he's sort of like my Rosie. I guess they're two of a kind. I've got to admit it. And the poor parents . . . us! What did we ever do to deserve this? Do you know?

GENEROSA: All I know is that children make us suffer, and plenty.

PACA: Yeah, that's for sure! Suffering is all we get out of it. What a life! See you later, Generosa. And thanks for the salt.

GENEROSA: See you later.

Both women go into their respective apartments and close the doors. FERNANDO, *depressed, leans on the railing. Pause. Suddenly he straightens up and listens, facing the audience.* CARMINA *comes up the steps with the milk pitcher. They look at each other; then, with eyes downcast,* CARMINA *tries to pass.* FERNANDO *reaches out to stop her.*

FERNANDO: Carmina.

CARMINA: Leave me alone, please. . . .

FERNANDO: No, Carmina. You're always avoiding me. This time you've got to hear me out.

CARMINA: Please, Fernando. . . . Let me go!

FERNANDO: When we were kids, we were close. . . . Why are you so cold now? (*Pause.*) Don't you remember the old days? I was your beau, and you were my little sweetheart. . . . Yes, that's what we were. . . . And when we got tired of playing, we'd sit here (*Pointing to the step.*) on this very step, and play at being grown-up sweethearts.

CARMINA: Hush.

FERNANDO: We were close then, and . . . you loved me.

CARMINA: I was a child. I don't even remember that.

FERNANDO: You were such a pretty little girl playing grown-up. You were beautiful then, just like you're beautiful now. You can't have forgotten all that. I certainly haven't! Carmina, wonderful memories of those times are what keeps me going in the midst of this sordid reality. And I wanted to tell you . . . that always . . . that for me, you're still what you were back then.

CARMINA: Don't make fun of me!

FERNANDO: I'm serious, I swear!

CARMINA: What about all those girls you've gone out with . . . and kissed? . . .

FERNANDO: Well, sure. I understand why you might have doubts. But a man . . . It's hard to explain. You were the one I couldn't talk to; the one I couldn't kiss . . . Because I loved you. I loved you then, and I love you now!

CARMINA: I don't believe you. (*She starts to walk away.*)

FERNANDO: No; don't go, please. I need you to listen . . . and to believe me. Come over here. (*He leads her to the first step.*) I want you to trust me now, like you used to.

Tugging slightly, he gets her to sit down beside him, her back against the wall. He takes her milk pitcher and places it beside him before taking her hand.

CARMINA: They're going to see us!

FERNANDO: So what? Carmina, please believe me. I can't live without you. I'm desperate. Everything around us is so ordinary; so monotonous. I need you to love me and stand by me. If you don't, I'll never be able to do anything.

CARMINA: Why don't you talk to Elvira? (*Pause; then he looks at her, excited and happy.*)

FERNANDO: You love me! I knew it! You had to love me! (*He raises her head, and she smiles, in spite of herself.*) My Carmina, my Carmina! (*He is about to kiss her, but she stops him.*)

CARMINA: What about Elvira?

FERNANDO: I hate her! She tries to tempt me in with her money. I can't stand her!

CARMINA: (*Smiling slyly.*) I can't either! (*They giggle like happy children.*)

FERNANDO: I have a question for you, too. What about Urbano?

CARMINA: What a good guy! I'm crazy about him! (**FERNANDO** *frowns.*) Silly!

FERNANDO: (*Putting an arm around her waist.*) Carmina, starting tomorrow, I'm going to work so hard for you. I want to get away from all this poverty and ugliness and take you with me. I'm tired of gossipy, bickering neighbors. . . . I don't want to worry about money or those embarrassing favors that come like slaps in the face. I'm tired of parents wearing us down with their clumsiness, their smothering love, their stupid . . .

CARMINA: (*Holding back.*) Fernando!

FERNANDO: Yes. I want to get out of here. Help me! Listen; I'm going to study so hard, you know? Really hard. First, I'll become a draftsman. That's easy! I can do that in a year. By then I'll earn good money and will study to become a building tech. That'll take about three years. In four, I'll be a foreman, and all the architects will be after me! I'll earn lots of money. By then, you'll be my wife, and we'll live somewhere else, in a nice place in a quiet neighborhood. But I'll keep on studying, and, who knows? Maybe I'll even become an engineer. And since I can do other things, too, I'll write a book of poetry that will be a huge success . . .

CARMINA: (*Listening, entranced.*) We'll be so happy!

FERNANDO: Carmina!

As he leans over to kiss her, he knocks over the pitcher of milk. Shocked by the clatter, both jump up and watch as the white liquid spreads out over the floor.

CURTAIN

ACT TWO

Ten years have gone by. The stairway continues shabby, the window dingy, and the apartments still have no doorbells.

As Act Two opens, GENEROSA, CARMINA, PACA, TRINI, *and* JUAN *are onstage.* JUAN, *a tall, bony, aging gentleman with a long, thin moustache, looks like a modern-day Don Quixote. All the characters show the passage of time:* PACA *and* GENEROSA *are now quite gray;* TRINI *is mature-looking but still lively;* CARMINA's *beauty, though still apparent, is fading. The attire of all is more contemporary but continues to suggest poverty. Doors I and III are wide open; doors II and IV are closed.*

The characters lean on the railing of the upper landing and stare into the space below. PACA *and* GENEROSA *cry, and* TRINI *has an arm around her mother's shoulders. Soon* GENEROSA *starts down the stairs, her gaze still fixed on some object below, as* CARMINA *follows her.*

CARMINA: Come on, mother . . . (GENEROSA *pulls away, but her tearful eyes continue fixed on something farther down.*) Come on . . . (*She looks into the stairwell, too. They both sob and hug each other gently, eyes still fixed on the object of their gazes.*)

GENEROSA: They're just getting to the front door. (*Pause.*) You can hardly see him anymore . . .

JUAN: (*On the upper landing, to his wife.*) They were really struggling with the casket. I guess he weighed a lot. (PACA *gestures for him to keep his voice down.*)

GENEROSA: (*With an arm around her daughter.*) We're all alone now, dear; completely alone. (*Suddenly, she frees herself and hurries up the steps.* CARMINA *follows her.*) Let me watch from your window! Let me look out from there!

PACA: Of course, dear.

GENEROSA *rushes through door II, followed by* CARMINA *and* PACA.

TRINI: (*To her father, who continues leaning on the railing lost in thought.*) Aren't you coming, papa?

JUAN: No, honey. What for? I've seen enough caskets and hearses to last me a lifetime. (*Pause.*) Remember Miss Asuncion's funeral? That one was really first-class, velvet-lined casket and all.

TRINI: I heard Mr. Manuel paid for that one.

JUAN: Very possible. His own funeral was more modest.

TRINI: That's because the kids paid.

JUAN: You're right about that. . . . (*Pause.*) And now Gregorio is gone. I don't know how he survived these last ten years. They broke his spirit when they made him retire. (*Pause.*) We all have to go sometime!

TRINI: Papa, don't talk like that!

JUAN: It's true, honey! And my time's coming.

TRINI: Don't think about those things. You're just fine. . . .

JUAN: Don't be too sure about that. On the inside . . . , there's a lot of pain. (*He seems drawn to door I and points to it timidly as he looks at* TRINI.) Right there; that's what's killing me.

TRINI: (*Approaching him.*) No, papa. Rosie's good. . . .

JUAN: (*Moving away from her with a sad smile.*) They haven't said a word.

TRINI: No, they haven't.

Pausing in front of door I, the father touches the doorframe as he peers into the empty interior.

JUAN: No more playing cards, old friend!

TRINI: (*Tugging at him sadly.*) Let's go home, papa.

JUAN: Now his family is all alone with no means of support. (*Looking toward door I.*) And there's that good-for-nothing son . . .

TRINI: Papa, please stop it.

JUAN: We all have our problems . . .

She shakes her head disapprovingly. GENEROSA *comes out of door III flanked by* PACA *and* CARMINA.

PACA: Hey! That's enough tears! What we have to do now is live; move on.

GENEROSA: I don't think I have the strength. . . .

PACA: You'll just have to find it; it's the only way.

GENEROSA: My Gregorio was such a good man!

PACA: We've all got to go someday; that's a law of life.

GENEROSA: My Gregorio . . .

PACA: Come on; we need to do something. Let's sweep up out here. My Trini will go to the market and fix dinner. Did you hear that, Trini?

TRINI: Yes, mother.

GENEROSA: I'll die soon, too.

CARMINA: Mother!

PACA: Who's thinking about dying?

GENEROSA: I'd just like to see my daughter married to a good man before I go.

PACA: Better yet, see it a long time before you go.

GENEROSA: What good would that do?

PACA: You could enjoy the grandchildren, my dear! Wouldn't you like that?

GENEROSA: (*Pause.*) All I can think about right now is my Gregorio.

PACA: All right; that's enough. Let's go in. Would you like to come with us, Juan?

JUAN: I'll join you a little later. Listen to what she says, Generosa. You have to keep your spirits up! (*He hugs her gently.*)

GENEROSA: Thank you . . .

> JUAN *and* TRINI *enter their apartment and close the door.* GENEROSA, PACA, *and* CARMINA *walk toward door I.*

GENEROSA: (*Before going in.*) Lord, what's to become of us? And what about my daughter? Oh, Paca, what is going to become of Carmina?

CARMINA: Don't take it so hard, mama.

PACA: Of course she won't. We'll all get along somehow. Think about your friends.

GENEROSA: You're all are so good to me.

PACA: Hey, we're not all that good! Sometimes I feel like treating you like a little kid and giving you a couple of swats!

> *They go inside, leaving the stairway vacant. Pause. Door II opens slowly and* FERNANDO *appears. The years have given him a more ordinary look. He surveys the landing and emerges, speaking in the direction of his apartment.*

FERNANDO: You can come out now. The coast is clear.

ELVIRA *emerges with an infant in her arms.* FERNANDO *and* ELVIRA *are modestly dressed. She is still pretty, but her face betrays none of her former vivaciousness.*

ELVIRA: So what'll we do? This is embarrassing. Should we say something or not?

FERNANDO: Let's not do anything right now. We'll decide when we get downstairs.

ELVIRA: "We," you say! I'm the one who'll end up deciding, as usual. If we left things up to you, we'd never do anything! (FERNANDO *says nothing but looks glum. They start down the stairs.*) And speaking of decisions! When are you going to make up your mind to earn more money? We can't go on living like this. Can't you see that? (*Pause.*) Of course, you were counting on your father-in-law to support you! Well, your father-in-law is in his grave! And if your wife isn't in hers, I don't know why!

FERNANDO: Elvira!

ELVIRA: Yes! Now you get mad because someone's telling you the truth. Getting mad is all you know how to do. You were going to be a draftsman, an engineer; maybe even a senator! Ha! That was the line you used on all the girls! Silly me, falling for it, just like the others did. If I had known how things were going to turn out . . . If I had known that you were just a spoiled brat; because all your stupid mother knew how to do was give in to you.

FERNANDO: (*Stopping.*) Elvira, I won't let you talk about my mother like that, you hear me?

ELVIRA: (*Angrily.*) You were the one who taught me to talk like that! You never said anything nice about her!

FERNANDO: (*Speaking between clenched teeth.*) You've always been stubborn, demanding, and inconsiderate.

ELVIRA: Demanding? There was only one thing I ever really wanted! Just one! And . . .

FERNANDO *tugs on her sleeve to warn her that* PEPE *is coming up the stairs.* PEPE's *appearance tells us that he has successfully fought to preserve his image.*

PEPE: (*As he passes.*) Good morning.

FERNANDO: Good morning.

ELVIRA: Good morning.

FERNANDO *and* ELVIRA *continue down as* PEPE, *amused, watches them from the stairway. Then he continues up the stairs, talking to himself.*

PEPE: She still looks pretty good, that one.

He goes toward door I, his old home. After a moment's hesitation there, he turns decisively toward door IV and knocks. ROSA *opens the door. She has lost weight and is pale.*

ROSA: (*Bitterly.*) What do you want?

PEPE: I'm home for dinner, princess.

ROSA: For dinner, huh? You spend your time out there with other women, getting drunk, then at dinnertime you waltz home to see what Rosa has managed to put on the table.

PEPE: Don't get mad, kitten.

ROSA: You lazy! . . . What about money? Money to buy food with! You think I can just cook something out of thin air?

PEPE: Look, baby. You're boring me. I told you already: you need to bring in some of that folding stuff, too.

ROSA: And you dare to . . . ?

PEPE: Wake up and hear the birdies chirp, lovey. If you're going to nag me, I'll leave. You know that. (*She begins to cry and closes the door while* PEPE *watches her in amused perplexity.* TRINI *emerges from door III with a basket.* PEPE *turns around.*)

PEPE: Hi, Trini.

TRINI: (*Without stopping.*) Hello.

PEPE: You get prettier by the day. . . . You improve with age, just like fine wine.

TRINI: (*Turning around suddenly.*) If you think I'm gullible like Rosa, you're sadly mistaken.

PEPE: Hey, don't get like that, doll.

TRINI: Aren't you ashamed? Out there on the streets up to no good while your father dies! Don't you realize that your mother and sister are in there right now (*Pointing to door I.*) crying their eyes out because he's being buried today? And what do you suppose they'll do now? Take in sewing? (*He shrugs his shoulders.*) And you don't care. Oh, you make me sick!

PEPE: Always thinking about money. All you women know how to do is ask for money!

TRINI: And all you know how to do is sponge off of women. You're the lowest of the low! A despicable pimp!

PEPE: (*Smiling.*) Hey, don't get all worked up, baby! Whoa! And all over a little compliment!

URBANO, *coming up the stairs, in casual clothes, pauses to hear the last words and then rushes up the steps as he speaks.*

URBANO: I'd like to knock that compliment down your throat, and other things, too, this very minute! (*He grabs* PEPE *by the lapels and spins him around.*) I don't ever want to see you bother Trini again, you hear me?

PEPE: Hey, what's the big deal?

URBANO: You bastard! What are you trying to do? Turn her into a prostitute, too? You good-for-nothing slug! (*He forces* PEPE's *upper body over the stairwell railing.*) You couldn't even be bothered to attend your own father's funeral. One of these days, you're going over this railing, you know?

ROSA *rushes out of door IV to intervene. She tries to separate the men and beats on* URBANO *to release* PEPE.

ROSA: Stop it! You don't have to hit him!

TRINI: (*Wearily.*) Urbano's right. I don't want him bothering me.

ROSA: Oh, shut up you helpless ninny!

TRINI: (*Hurt.*) Rosa!

ROSA: Leave him alone, I said!

URBANO: (*Without releasing* PEPE.) And you still defend him? Are you crazy?

PEPE: Hey! Don't insult her!

URBANO: (*Ignoring him.*) And to think you ruined your life for a bum like that; for a gutless leech.

PEPE: Those words . . .

URBANO: You shut up!

ROSA: What business is it of yours, I'd like to know! Do I meddle in your life? Do I say anything if you get involved with some girl? I'm better off with Pepe. He at least puts up with me when nobody else wants me . . .

URBANO: Rosa!

Door III opens and JUAN, *infuriated, comes out.*

JUAN: Be quiet! Stop it, all of you! You're going to be the death of me yet! Yes, I'm going to die! I'll die just like Gregorio!

TRINI: (*Rushing toward him.*) Papa! Don't . . . !

JUAN: (*Pushing her away.*) Leave me alone! (*To* PEPE.) Why couldn't you take her some place else? But no! You had to stay right here and ruin our lives, too!

TRINI: Please don't talk like that, papa!

JUAN: You're right; it's better for me to keep quiet. (*To* URBANO.) And take your hands off that piece of trash!

URBANO: (*Forcefully shoving* PEPE *toward* ROSA.) There! You can have him!

PACA: (*Coming out and closing the door behind her.*) What's all this commotion about? Don't you realize that there's been a death here? You're acting like animals!

URBANO: Mother's right. We haven't shown much respect for these poor people's grief.

PACA: Of course I'm right! (*To* TRINI.) And what are you waiting for? Get to the market! (TRINI *bows her head and starts down the stairs. Then* PACA *turns to her husband.*) And why is this trashy pair any business of yours? (*Stung by her mother's insult,* ROSA *enters door IV and slams the door.*) Come on! Inside! (*She takes* JUAN *by the arm and leads him to the door. From there, she speaks to* URBANO.) Is it . . . over?

URBANO: Yes, mother.

PACA: Why don't you go tell them?

URBANO: Yes! I'll do that right now.

PEPE *starts down the stairs, straightening his clothes as he goes.* PACA *and* JUAN *go into their apartment and close the door.*

PEPE: (*From the landing and watching* URBANO *out of the corner of his eye.*) And to call me gutless! If I don't hit back, it's because you make me sick! Me, gutless! Imagine! These neighbors are like some filthy plague! No class; they don't know how to deal with people or . . .

PEPE *continues down the stairs, muttering to himself. Pause.* URBANO *walks toward door I, but before he arrives,* CARMINA *comes out with a basket and closes the door behind her. She and* URBANO *face each other. Silence.*

CARMINA: Is it . . . over?

URBANO: Yes.

CARMINA: (*Brushing away a tear.*) Thank you, Urbano. You've been so kind to us.

URBANO: (*Stammering.*) It's not important. You know that I . . . that we . . . want to do anything we can . . .

CARMINA: Thank you. I know that. (*She pauses and goes down the steps beside him.*)

URBANO: Are you going to the market?

CARMINA: Yes.

URBANO: You don't have to do that. Trini can go for you later. I don't want any of you burdened by anything.

CARMINA: I thought she was going, but I figured she'd forgotten. (*Pause.*)

URBANO: (*Stopping.*) Carmina . . .

CARMINA: Yes?

URBANO: Can I ask . . . what are your plans now?

CARMINA: I don't know. . . . I guess we'll take in sewing.

URBANO: Can you get by on that?

CARMINA: I don't know.

URBANO: Your father's pension wasn't much, but without it . . .

CARMINA: Please . . . Let's not talk about it.

URBANO: I'm sorry. I shouldn't have said anything.

CARMINA: That's not it. (*She tries to continue on her way.*)

URBANO: (*Stepping in front of her.*) Carmina, I . . .

CARMINA: (*Cutting him off quickly.*) You're so good, Urbano; so good. You've done everything you can for us. I'm very grateful.

URBANO: It's nothing, really. I'd like to do a lot more.

CARMINA: You've done enough. Thanks, anyway. (*She tries to leave.*)

URBANO: Wait a minute, please! (*He leads her over to the clubhouse.*) Carmina, I . . . I love you. (*She smiles sadly.*) I've loved you for years; you know that. Forgive me for saying these things today; that's clumsy of me. I just don't want to see you suffer another day. I don't want things to be hard for you or your mother. It would make me so happy if . . . you told me that maybe someday . . . (*Pause. She looks down.*) I know you don't love me. That doesn't surprise me. I'm not much. I'm nothing, compared to you. But I would try so hard to make you happy. (*Pause.*) You're not saying anything. . . .

CARMINA: I didn't plan to . . . marry.

URBANO: (*Looking down.*) Maybe you're still in love with somebody else. . . .

CARMINA: (*Agitated.*) No! No!

URBANO: Then . . . maybe you're not attracted to me . . .

CARMINA: No, that's not it!

URBANO: I know I'm just a common laborer. I'm not cultured, and I'll never be important. So I guess it's better this way. Then I won't be disappointed like other people.

CARMINA: Urbano, please . . .

URBANO: But better a common laborer than an idle dreamer. . . . If you accept me, I know I can do things; make things better. Yes, I will! Because with you at my side, I'd have so much energy and desire to work! I'd work because of you! I'd learn more about mechanics and earn more money. (*She nods sadly, remembering a similar scene from the past.*) Your mother could live with us, and we'd make her final years happy. And you'd make me happy, too. (*Pause.*) Please accept me, please.

CARMINA: You're so good!

URBANO: Carmina; I'm begging you. Please accept me. Say you'll be my wife.

CARMINA: (*Crying and taking refuge in his arms.*) Thank you! Thank you!

URBANO: (*Beside himself with joy.*) Then it's "yes"? (*She nods.*) I'm the one who should say thank you! I really don't deserve you!

They stand holding one another for a moment. When they separate, their hands remain joined as she smiles through her tears. PACA *comes out of her door and automatically casts an inquisitive glance over the railing and seems to notice some-*

thing in the clubhouse area. In order to see better, she approaches door IV, leans over the railing, and recognizes CARMINA *and* URBANO *on the floor below.*

PACA: What are you two doing down there?

URBANO: (*Leaning out with* CARMINA *toward* PACA.) I was explaining something to Carmina. . . . I was telling her about the burial.

PACA: Some conversation! (*To* CARMINA.) Where are you going with that basket?

CARMINA: To the market.

PACA: Didn't Trini go for you?

CARMINA: No . . .

PACA: With all the commotion up here, she probably forgot. You stay home. I'll go. (*To* URBANO, *as she starts down the stairs.*) You stay with Carmina and her mother; go on. (*She stops; then speaks loudly.*) Aren't you coming up? (*They hasten to do so.* PACA *goes down the stairs and, meeting them halfway, speaks to* CARMINA *as she takes the basket.*) Let me have your basket. (*She continues down the stairs, but stops to look back at the couple. Flustered, they likewise stop to look at* PACA *when they get to their apartment. After* CARMINA *unlocks the door, they enter and close the door.* PACA *gestures knowingly.*) Aha! (*Close to the lower landing, she calls over the banister to* TRINI, *who is coming up the stairs.*) Why didn't you take Generosa's basket with you?

TRINI: I forgot. That's why I came back. (*She appears with her own basket empty.*)

PACA: Let me have yours. I'll go. Keep your father company. You're good at cheering him up.

TRINI: What's wrong with him?

PACA: (*Sighing.*) Same old thing: Rosa. (*She sighs again.*) Let me have the money. (TRINI *hands her some coins and prepares to go in as* PACA *speaks in a low, confidential tone.*) Hey, guess what . . . (*Pause.*)

TRINI: (*Stopping.*) Yes?

PACA: Oh, never mind. See you later.

PACA *continues down the stairs as* TRINI *comes up. Before* TRINI *arrives at the upper landing,* JUAN *comes out of his apartment and sees her as he closes the door.*

TRINI: Where are you going?

JUAN: To keep those poor women company. (*Short pause.*) Weren't you on your way to the market?

TRINI: (*Catching up with her father.*) Mama decided to go instead.

JUAN: Oh. (*He goes toward the door as she is about to enter. He stops and turns around.*) Did you notice how Rosa defended that good-for-nothing louse?

TRINI: Yes, papa, I did. (*Pause.*)

JUAN: It's disgraceful. . . . I'm ashamed she's my daughter. . . .

TRINI: Rosie's really not a bad person, papa.

JUAN: Huh! What do you know? (*Angrily.*) I don't ever want to hear her name in this house again! And I don't want you going to see her or even talking to her! As far as I'm concerned, Rosa has ceased to exist. . . . It's over! (*Pause.*) But she's not getting along very well, is she? (*Pause.*) Although I don't really care . . .

TRINI: (*Going over to her father.*) Papa . . .

JUAN: What?

TRINI: Rosie told me yesterday . . . that what hurt her most was your rejection.

JUAN: She's a hypocrite!

TRINI: She was crying when she said it, papa.

JUAN: Women cry at anything. (*Pause.*) But how is she getting along?

TRINI: It's pretty awful. That bum doesn't have a real job, and it makes her sick to . . . bring in money . . . other ways . . .

JUAN: (*Pained.*) I don't believe it. She's no good; she's become a common whore! That's what she is! A whore!

TRINI: Don't say that, papa! Maybe she's flighty, but she's not that! She started living with Pepe because she loved him. . . . And she still loves him. He's always telling her that she should bring in some money, and then he threatens to leave her. And . . . he beats her, too.

JUAN: That cowardly pimp!

TRINI: Rosa doesn't want him to leave her, and she doesn't want to take to the streets either. She's in a lot of pain.

JUAN: She's not the only one!

TRINI: So, with the little bit of money Pepe gives her from time to time, she feeds him and goes without. She hardly ever eats at night. Haven't you noticed how thin she's gotten? (*Pause.*)

JUAN: No.

TRINI: It's very obvious! And it hurts when he tells her she's ugly . . . and he rarely comes home. (*Pause.*) Poor Rosie may end up on the streets so he won't leave her.

JUAN: Poor Rosie? Don't pity her! She brought it on herself. (*Pause. He starts to leave but pauses.*) And you're affected, too, because of her, right?

TRINI: I feel so sorry for her, papa. (*Pause.*)

JUAN: Look; I don't want you hurting because of her. She's not important to me anymore, you know? But you are, and I don't like to see you all worried, understand?

TRINI: Yes, papa.

JUAN: (*Perturbed.*) Look, back in the other room, there's a little money I've saved up by not having coffee or wine with the men from time to time.

TRINI: Papa!

JUAN: Don't say anything! Let me talk! Since coffee and wine aren't good for people over a certain age . . . I just put aside the money I don't spend. Understand that Rosa isn't important to me anymore. But if it will make you feel better . . . , you can give her that money.

TRINI: Oh, yes, papa, I will.

JUAN: I'll get it.

TRINI: You're such a good father!

JUAN: I'm doing this for you.

Very moved, she awaits her father's return as she anxiously glances toward door IV. JUAN *returns with a few bills, counts them out, and hands them over without looking up.*

JUAN: There you are.

TRINI: Yes, papa.

JUAN: (*Going toward door I.*) Give this to her, if you like . . .

TRINI: Yes, papa.

JUAN: . . . as something from you, of course.

TRINI: Yes.

JUAN: (*After knocking on door I with exaggerated authority.*) I don't want your mother to know anything about this!

TRINI: No, papa.

URBANO *opens the door to* JUAN.

JUAN: Oh! You're here.

URBANO: Yes, papa.

JUAN *goes in and closes the door.* TRINI *happily turns around and knocks insistently on door IV. Then she realizes that the door of her apartment is still open. She closes that door and returns to knock at IV. Pause.* ROSA *opens the door.*

TRINI: Rosie!

ROSA: Hello, Trini.

TRINI: Rosie!

ROSA: I'm glad you came. Sorry if I didn't open the door right away . . .

TRINI: That's not important . . .

ROSA: Don't hold it against me, what I did just now. I know I shouldn't have defended Pepe that way, but . . .

TRINI: Rosie! Papa gave me some money for you!

ROSA: What?

TRINI: Look! (*Showing her the bills.*) Here! They're for you! (*She thrusts the money into her hand.*)

ROSA: (*About to cry.*) Trini, no . . . It can't be . . .

TRINI: Yes, it can . . . Papa loves you . . .

ROSA: Don't lie to me, Trini. This is your money.

TRINI: Mine? Where would I get any money? He gave it to me! Papa gave it to me just now! (ROSA *cries.*) Let me tell you all about it. (*Taking her inside.*) First he started talking about you; then he said . . .

They go in and close the door. Pause. ELVIRA *and* FERNANDO *come up the stairs.* FERNANDO *carries the baby. They are arguing.*

FERNANDO: Let's go in for just a minute and say what we need to say when there's a death in the family.

ELVIRA: I've already told you: I'm not going.

FERNANDO: Well, you wanted to before.

ELVIRA: And you didn't.

FERNANDO: Yes, we should go. Try to understand.

ELVIRA: I'm not going.

FERNANDO: Then I'll go by myself.

ELVIRA: Oh, no! That's what you really want: to see Carmina and do your little routine with her . . .

FERNANDO: Elvira, don't start that. Everything ended between Carmina and me a long time ago.

ELVIRA: Don't pretend. You think I don't see those little glances you send her way and how you just happen to run into her by accident?

FERNANDO: You're making all that up.

ELVIRA: Making it up? You loved her a long time ago and never got over it.

FERNANDO: Elvira, you know that I . . .

ELVIRA: You never loved me! You married me for my father's money.

FERNANDO: Elvira!

ELVIRA: But I'm smarter than she is.

FERNANDO: Please! The neighbors will hear us!

ELVIRA: I don't care. (*They get to the landing.*)

FERNANDO: I swear to you that Carmina and I haven't . . .

ELVIRA: (*Stamping her foot.*) I don't believe you for a minute! And this has got to stop! (*She continues on toward their door while he remains close to door I.*)

FERNANDO: Let's offer our sympathy. Don't be stubborn.

ELVIRA: I told you I'm not going. (*Pause. He approaches her.*)

FERNANDO: Here; take the baby. (*He hands her the baby and prepares to open the door.*)

Story of a Stairway (Madrid, 1968), Act II, Carmina (Nuria Carreti), Urbano (Antonio Carreras), Fernando (Francisco Valladares), Elvira (Victoria Rodríguez), and Paca (Cándida Losada) (Courtesy, Basabe)

ELVIRA: (*In a low voice between clenched teeth.*) And you're not going either! You hear me? (*He opens the door without responding.*) Did you hear me?

FERNANDO: Go in!

ELVIRA: You first!

Door I opens. **CARMINA** *and* **URBANO** *emerge holding hands, making their new situation quite apparent.* **FERNANDO** *is stunned.* **ELVIRA** *closes the door and walks over to them, smiling.*

ELVIRA: What a coincidence, Carmina! We were just coming over to tell you how sorry . . .

CARMINA: Thank you so much. (*She tries to free her hand, but* **URBANO** *doesn't let her.*)

ELVIRA: (*Assuming the appropriate facial expression.*) What a terrible loss . . . I know how you must feel.

FERNANDO: My wife and I are so sorry. If there's anything we can . . .

CARMINA: (*Without looking at him.*) Thank you.

The tension mounts between the two couples.

CARMINA: Oh, please go on in. I'll be right back . . . (*Spiritedly.*) as soon as I say good night to Urbano.

ELVIRA: Shall we go in, Fernando? (*He makes no response.*) Don't worry; it's all right. (*To* **CARMINA.**) He's concerned because it's time to feed the baby. (*Looking tenderly at* **FERNANDO.**) He adores his family and would do anything for us. (*To* **CARMINA.**) I'll just nurse him in your house. You don't mind, do you?

CARMINA: Of course not.

ELVIRA: Look how beautiful my little Fernando is. (**CARMINA** *has been able to free herself and comes close.*) He's fast asleep. But it won't be long before he wakes up and begins to cry for his mommy's breast.

CARMINA: He's like a little doll!

ELVIRA: He looks just like his daddy. (*To* **FERNANDO.**) Yes, he does; even though you deny it. (*To* **CARMINA.**) He says he looks just like me. I say he's the image of Fernando. What do you think?

CARMINA: Well, I don't know . . . What do you say, Urbano?

URBANO: I don't know much about babies. They all look alike to me.

FERNANDO: (*To* URBANO.) Of course. Elvira always exaggerates. He could look like her . . . or anybody; he might even look like Carmina, for example.

ELVIRA: That's what you say now! But you're always saying he looks just like me!

CARMINA: Well, he could look like your side of the family, but to say that he looks like me! That's silly!

URBANO: Absolutely!

CARMINA: (*On the verge of tears.*) You're going to make me laugh, Fernando! And on a day like this . . .

URBANO: (*Very solicitous.*) Carmina, don't get upset. (*To* FERNANDO.) She's very sensitive! (FERNANDO *nods agreement.*)

CARMINA: (*With exaggerated tenderness.*) Thank you, Urbano.

URBANO: (*Pointedly.*) Please don't cry, Carmina. Think of happier times. I know you can . . .

FERNANDO: (*With the presumption of a former sweetheart.*) Carmina always was very sensitive.

ELVIRA: (*Trying to change the subject.*) She has good reason to be sad today. Shall we go in, Fernando?

FERNANDO: (*Tenderly.*) Whenever you like . . . , darling.

URBANO: Let them pass . . . , darling.

> URBANO *guides* CARMINA *out of the way with a proprietary air for* FERNANDO's *benefit.*

CURTAIN

ACT THREE

Twenty years have flown by, and it is now 1949. The stairway remains modest, despite the landlord's attempt over the years to disguise its shabbiness with minor improvements. Tinted glass has replaced the dingy windowpane, and on the wall of the upper landing, a metal plaque reads: "Fifth Floor." The walls have been whitewashed rather than painted, and each apartment now has a doorbell. A white-haired, obese, wrinkled, and stooped old woman laboriously climbs the stairs. As she reaches the lower landing, we see PACA *pulling heavily on the handrail with one hand and in the other carrying a basket of purchases.*

PACA: (*Breathless.*) I feel so old! (*Caressing the banister.*) I'm as old as you are, old friend. A-a-a-h-h-h . . . (*Pause.*) And just as alone. I mean nothing to my children or my granddaughter anymore. I'm just a burden! (*Pause.*) And I don't want to be a burden, darn it all! (*She pauses, puffing.*) Oh . . . These stairs . . . You'd think that stingy landlord would've put in an elevator by now. There's sure room for one! He just doesn't want to spend the money. (*Pause.*) I remember when my Juan took these steps two at a time, and he did it until the day he died. But I can't handle them anymore. Looks like Gabriel forgot to blow his horn for me. (*Pause.*) Well, now that no one is listening: do I really want to die? (*Pause.*) No. I don't. (*Pause.*) What I really want (*At the upper landing now and gazing at door I.*) is to sit down with Generosa and Juan and have one of our long talks. . . . (*Pausing before walking toward her door.*) Poor Generosa! I guess there's nothing left of her anymore, not even bones! (*She pauses before unlocking the door and entering.*) And I wish my granddaughter would pay more attention to me!

PACA *closes the door. After a short pause, door IV opens, and the* WELL-DRESSED OLDER MAN *emerges. On his way to the stairs, he passes door I as the* WELL-DRESSED YOUNGER MAN *emerges.*

YOUNGER MAN: Good morning.

OLDER MAN: Good morning. Going to the office?

YOUNGER MAN: Yes, sir. You too?

OLDER MAN: Yes, me too. (*They go down the stairs together.*) So how's business?

YOUNGER MAN: Pretty good! I've almost doubled my salary in the past couple of years, so I can't complain. How are things with you?

OLDER MAN: Going all right. I just wish some of these old-timers would get out of here so I can have an exterior unit. After fumigating and painting the place, I might even invite people over.

YOUNGER MAN: Yep. You want what we all want.

OLDER MAN: Besides, it's not fair for us to pay so much rent while we wait for a better place when those old people are paying at the old rate.

YOUNGER MAN: Since they've been here so long. . . . That's rent control for you.

OLDER MAN: Well, it's not fair. Is my money worth less than theirs?

YOUNGER MAN: You're right about that, and those old folks are a real eyesore.

OLDER MAN: You can say that again. If it weren't for them . . . Because even though the building is old, it's not bad.

YOUNGER MAN: That's right; and the apartments are spacious.

OLDER MAN: The only thing we don't have is an elevator.

YOUNGER MAN: Oh, they'll eventually put one in. By the way, have you seen the new Fiat?

OLDER MAN: Yes; outstanding.

YOUNGER MAN: Really! And did you notice how the chassis is completely . . .

> URBANO *and* CARMINA, *getting on in years now, emerge from door III.* CARMINA *takes her husband's arm familiarly and they start down the steps. When they are about halfway down,* FERNANDO *and* ELVIRA *come up the stairs. Showing signs of age,* ELVIRA *also holds* FERNANDO's *arm. As regards economic status, neither couple reflects change: one bears the stamp of the laboring class, and the other couple has the office-worker look. They greet each other perfunctorily as they pass.* URBANO *and* CARMINA *continue down as* FERNANDO *and* ELVIRA *arrive in silence at door II, and* FERNANDO *rings the bell.*

ELVIRA: Why don't you use the key?

FERNANDO: Manolin will open for us.

> MANOLIN, *a young boy of about twelve, opens the door.*

MANOLIN: (*Kissing his father.*) Hello, papa.

FERNANDO: Hello, son.

MANOLIN: (*Kissing his mother.*) Hello, mama.

ELVIRA: Hello.

MANOLIN *peeks around them both to see if they have brought anything.*

FERNANDO: What are you looking for?

MANOLIN: Didn't you bring me anything?

FERNANDO: You don't see anything, do you?

MANOLIN: Will you bring something later?

ELVIRA: Bring what?

MANOLIN: A cake!

FERNANDO: A cake? No, son. Cakes cost too much.

MANOLIN: But papa! It's my birthday!

FERNANDO: Yes, I know.

ELVIRA: We do have a surprise for you, though.

FERNANDO: But we couldn't afford a cake.

MANOLIN: I want a cake!

FERNANDO: Sorry; it can't be.

MANOLIN: What's the surprise?

ELVIRA: You'll see. Let's go inside.

MANOLIN: (*Going toward the stairway.*) No.

FERNANDO: Where are you going?

MANOLIN: Out to play.

ELVIRA: Don't be long.

MANOLIN: All right. See you later.

The parents close the door. MANOLIN *goes down the steps to the little clubhouse, muttering to himself.*

MANOLIN: Gee! Talk about stingy!

He shrugs his shoulders and, with a pleased expression, pulls out a cigarette. After a furtive glance in the direction of his door, he takes out a match, strikes it on the wall, lights up, and begins to smoke with obvious delight. Pause. ROSA *and* TRINI *come out of door III. Their faces, also aging, bear the stamp of life's disappointments and pain. Rosa carries a basket.*

TRINI: Why are you coming, too? I'll just be a minute!

ROSA: I need some fresh air. I'm suffocating in there. (*Picking up the basket.*) Besides, I can help you.

TRINI: I'm not like you. I'd rather stay home.

ROSA: It's just that . . . I really don't like staying home alone with mother. I don't think she loves me.

TRINI: That's ridiculous!

ROSA: She's felt that way about me . . . ever since . . . You know.

TRINI: Who thinks about that anymore?

ROSA: Everybody! We all think about it, even though we don't say anything.

TRINI: (*Sighing.*) Oh, don't worry about it.

> MANOLIN, *seeing them come down the stairs, steps out and greets them happily. The women stop.*

MANOLIN: Hi, Trini!

TRINI: (*Affectionately.*) You little rascal! (*He proudly exhales a big puff of smoke.*) My goodness! You, smoking? Put that filthy thing out this minute!

> *She tries to grab the cigarette, but he dodges.*

MANOLIN: Today's my birthday!

TRINI: My goodness! And how old are you?

MANOLIN: Twelve! I'm a man!

TRINI: If I give you a present, will you accept it?

MANOLIN: What is it?

TRINI: Money for a cookie.

MANOLIN: I don't want a cookie.

TRINI: You don't like cookies?

MANOLIN: I'd rather have a pack of cigarettes.

TRINI: Oh, no! And get rid of that one!

MANOLIN: No; I don't want to. (*This time, she gets the cigarette and tosses it away.*) Hey, Trini. You love me a lot, don't you?

TRINI: Of course I do.

Story of a Stairway (Tokyo, 1964), Act III, Rosa (Keiko Tamaki), Trini (Keiko Ishigaki), and Manolin (Tosiko Okabe)

MANOLIN: Well . . . I want to ask you something. (*He looks at* ROSA *out of the corner of his eye as he leads* TRINI *over to the clubhouse area.*)

TRINI: Where are you taking me?

MANOLIN: Come over here. I don't want Rosa to hear me.

ROSA: Why? I love you lots, too. Don't you love me back?

MANOLIN: No.

ROSA: Why not?

MANOLIN: Because you're an old grump.

   ROSA *bites her lip and steps aside toward the railing.*

TRINI: (*Reprovingly.*) Manolin!

MANOLIN: (*Pulling on* TRINI.) Come over here with me . . . (*She follows him, smiling. He stops and faces her mysteriously.*) Will you marry me when I get older?

TRINI: (*Smiling as she looks at her sister.*) Hey! A proposal!

MANOLIN: (*Flushing with embarrassment.*) Don't laugh! Answer me.

TRINI: Don't be silly! Don't you see I'm a much older woman?

MANOLIN: No.

TRINI: Well, I am. And by the time you're ready to get married, I'll really be an old lady!

MANOLIN: I don't care! I love you anyway!

TRINI: (*Very emotional and smiling, she cups his face in her hands and kisses a cheek.*) You sweet boy! But you're so silly! (*Kissing him again.*) Don't talk foolishness. (*Another kiss.*) You sweet kid! (*She draws away and, with a spring in her step, goes to join* ROSA.)

MANOLIN: But . . .

TRINI: (*Leading* ROSA, *who looks hurt.*) Hush, now. I don't know what I'll get you for your birthday, whether it'll be a cookie or a pack of . . .

   They exit quickly as MANOLIN *watches, apparently proud of himself. He then takes out another cigarette and lights it. Sitting on the floor of the little clubhouse, he smokes very leisurely, lost in youthful dreams. Door III opens and* YOUNG CARMINA, *the happy-go-lucky eighteen-year-old daughter of* CARMINA *and* URBANO, *emerges.* PACA *is saying good-bye to her at the door.*

YOUNG CARMINA: Bye, grandma. (*She walks along hitting the banister in time as she hums a tune.*) La, la, la, la, la . . .

PACA: Hey!

YOUNG CARMINA: (*Turning around.*) Yes?

PACA: Leave that handrail alone! You're going to break it! Can't you see it's old?

YOUNG CARMINA: They should put in a new one!

PACA: Put in a new one . . . You young people think when something's old, it's no good and should just be tossed out. Old things should be taken care of, understand?

YOUNG CARMINA: Since you're old, you like old stuff.

PACA: What I want is for you to show more respect for . . . maturity.

YOUNG CARMINA: (*Who comes back and kisses her effusively several times.*) Silly! You're a beautiful old lady!

PACA: (*Won over, but still protesting.*) Stop it, you little hypocrite! Now you're trying to butter me up! (**CARMINA** *shoves her inside gently and tries to close the door.*)

YOUNG CARMINA: Come on; go inside.

PACA: Who do you think you are, ordering me around? (*They push each other gently.*) Leave me alone!

YOUNG CARMINA: Well, go inside. (**PACA***'s resistance ends with a slight smile.*)

PACA: Don't forget the garlic!

> **CARMINA** *closes the door. As she goes down the stairs quickly, she continues to keep time on the banister as she hums a tune.* **YOUNG FERNANDO**, *the twenty-one-year-old son of* **FERNANDO** *and* **ELVIRA**, *opens door II and emerges in a short-sleeved shirt. He looks brash and immature.*

YOUNG FERNANDO: Carmina.

> *Still on the first steps,* **CARMINA** *pauses, stops singing, and vacillates, but does not turn around. He quickly joins her.* **MANOLIN** *hides and listens with childish curiosity.*

YOUNG CARMINA: Leave me alone, Fernando! Not here! They can see us!

YOUNG FERNANDO: So what?

Story of a Stairway (Madrid, 2003), Act III, Young Carmina (Barbara Goneaga) and Young Fernando (Nocolás Belmonte) (Courtesy, Chicho)

YOUNG CARMINA: Leave me alone. (*She tries to continue down the stairs, but he stops her brusquely.*)

YOUNG FERNANDO: Listen to me, I said! I'm talking to you!

YOUNG CARMINA: (*Taken aback.*) Please, Fernando.

YOUNG FERNANDO: No. I need to talk to you right now. You've got to tell me why you're avoiding me. (*With an anguished look, she glances up the stairwell.*) Come on! Tell me! Why? (CARMINA *looks up toward the door of her apartment.*) Don't look up there! Nobody's watching!

YOUNG CARMINA: Fernando, not now. This afternoon we can meet where we did last time.

YOUNG FERNANDO: All right. But you have to tell me now why you haven't shown up these past few days.

She descends a few more steps, but he stops her again and backs her against the railing.

YOUNG CARMINA: Fernando!

YOUNG FERNANDO: Say something! Don't you love me anymore? (*Pause.*) Or maybe you never did love me, is that it? You just wanted to play around with me; have some fun!

YOUNG CARMINA: No, no . . .

YOUNG FERNANDO: Yes; that's got to be it! Well, you're not going to get away with that!

YOUNG CARMINA: Fernando, I do love you, but it's no use. You know they'll never let us . . .

YOUNG FERNANDO: Why not?

YOUNG CARMINA: My parents won't allow it.

YOUNG FERNANDO: So what? That's just an excuse. And not a very good one!

YOUNG CARMINA: No, that's it, I swear.

YOUNG FERNANDO: If you really loved me, that wouldn't matter.

YOUNG CARMINA: (*Sobbing.*) But they . . . they threatened me. They even hit me!

YOUNG FERNANDO: What?

YOUNG CARMINA: Yes; and they say awful things about you . . . and about your parents, too. . . . Just leave me alone, Fernando. (*She frees herself, as he stands stunned.*) Forget about us; forget our plans. None of that can ever be. . . . I'm scared . . .

She exits quickly, crying. **FERNANDO** *looks over the railing, lost in thought, as he observes her progress down the stairs. When he turns around and catches sight of* **MANOLIN,** *his expression hardens.*

YOUNG FERNANDO: What are you doing there?

MANOLIN: (*Finding the situation amusing.*) Nothing.

YOUNG FERNANDO: Go home.

MANOLIN: What if I don't want to?

YOUNG FERNANDO: Get up there, I said!

MANOLIN: It's my birthday, and I'll do what I want. You can't tell me what to do! (*Pause.*)

YOUNG FERNANDO: If you weren't the family pet, I'd give you a very special birthday present! (*Pause. As he goes up the steps, he watches* **MANOLIN,** *who continues to chuckle.*)

MANOLIN: (*Boldly.*) Looks like you're pretty interested in Carmina!

YOUNG FERNANDO: Shut up!

MANOLIN: (*Enjoying himself.*) You two were just like a couple of lovers in the movies! (*In mock melodrama.*) Don't leave me, Nelly! I adore you, Bob!

FERNANDO *slaps him, and tears come to* **MANOLIN**'s *eyes. Angry,* **MANOLIN** *tries to kick his brother's shins and stomp his foot.*

MANOLIN: Meanie!

YOUNG FERNANDO: (*Holding him.*) What were you doing in there hiding?

MANOLIN: None of your business! You're mean, and stupid, and so mushy!

YOUNG FERNANDO: You were smoking, weren't you? (*Pointing to cigarette butts on the floor.*) Wait till I tell papa!

MANOLIN: I'll tell him you're still fooling around with Carmina!

YOUNG FERNANDO: (*Squeezing his arm.*) You really know how to get what you want out of our parents, you little hypocrite! But these cigarettes are going to cost you!

MANOLIN: (*Freeing himself and running up the steps.*) I'm not afraid of you! And I'm going to tell them about Carmina! I'm going to tell right now! (*He rings his doorbell repeatedly.*)

YOUNG FERNANDO: Get back here, you little tattletale!

MANOLIN: No! And besides, those cigarettes butts aren't even mine!

YOUNG FERNANDO: Come back here!

The elder **FERNANDO** *opens the door.*

MANOLIN: Papa, Fernando was kissing Carmina!

YOUNG FERNANDO: Liar!

MANOLIN: He was, too. I know, 'cause I was right there on the stairway!

FERNANDO: (*To* **MANOLIN.**) Get inside.

MANOLIN: Papa, it's true! Honest!

FERNANDO: Inside! (**MANOLIN** *sticks his tongue out at his brother as he goes inside.*) And you; get up here, too.

YOUNG FERNANDO: Papa, it's not so, what he says about kissing Carmina. (*He starts up the steps.*)

FERNANDO: Were you with her?

YOUNG FERNANDO: Yes.

FERNANDO: How many times have we told you not to have anything to do with her?

YOUNG FERNANDO: (*On the landing now.*) I know.

FERNANDO: And you disobeyed . . .

YOUNG FERNANDO: Papa, I . . .

FERNANDO: Get in there. (*Pause.*) Did you hear me?

YOUNG FERNANDO: (*Rebelling.*) I heard you, but I'm not going in, and that's that!

FERNANDO: That's what?

YOUNG FERNANDO: I'm not going in there! I've had it with all your stupid rules!

FERNANDO: (*Controlling himself.*) I really don't think you want to put on a scene out here for the neighbors . . .

YOUNG FERNANDO: I don't care. I've had it with all your fears. (**ELVIRA**, *probably alerted by* **MANOLIN**, *comes to the door.*) Why can't I talk to Carmina anyway? I'm an adult!

ELVIRA: (*Intervening bitterly.*) For Carmina, you're not.

FERNANDO: (*To* **ELVIRA**.) You stay out of this! (*To his son.*) And you get inside. We can't stand out here shouting at one another.

YOUNG FERNANDO: What do your old grudges have to do with me? Why can't Carmina and I be together?

ELVIRA: No! It's out of the question!

FERNANDO: Impossible.

YOUNG FERNANDO: But why?

FERNANDO: You wouldn't understand. Between that family and ours, there can be no marriages.

YOUNG FERNANDO: But you talk to them.

FERNANDO: We say good morning or good afternoon, and that's all. (Pause.) It really wouldn't matter so much to me, but your mother . . .

ELVIRA: And I say it can't be. There's no use talking about it!

FERNANDO: Her parents wouldn't hear of it either. You can be sure of that.

ELVIRA: You ought to back me and forbid it, too, rather than giving in with your stupid softness. That's wrong; all wrong.

FERNANDO: Elvira!

ELVIRA: All wrong! (*To her son.*) Come inside.

YOUNG FERNANDO: But mama . . . , papa . . . , I don't get it! You seem determined not to understand that I . . . can't live without Carmina!

FERNANDO: You're the one who doesn't understand. Let me explain some things to you.

ELVIRA: You don't need to explain anything! (*To her son.*) Come in here.

FERNANDO: But we do have to explain things to him. . . . (*To his son.*) Come on in.

YOUNG FERNANDO: I don't understand you. . . . I just don't understand you . . .

They close the door. **TRINI** *and* **ROSA** *return from the market.*

TRINI: Didn't you ever see him again?

ROSA: Oh, I saw him lots of times! At first, he didn't even say hello; he just avoided me. And since I was such a fool back then, I'd arrange to be wherever he might be. Now it's the other way around. . . .

TRINI: He tries to see you?

ROSA: He says hello to me, and I don't answer him. I know he's bad news. He led me on for years; then dropped me when no one else wanted me.

TRINI: Now he's old . . .

ROSA: Really old! And he looks awful; still drinks too much and carouses around till all hours . . .

TRINI: What a life!

ROSA: In a way, I'm glad we didn't have children. They wouldn't have turned out very well. But I did want a child, Trini! And I would have wanted him to look like Pepe but be different.

TRINI: Things hardly ever turn out the way we want.

ROSA: No, they don't. (*Pause.*) But having a child could have filled my life! (*Pause.*)

TRINI: And mine, too.

ROSA: What? (*Short pause.*) Of course. Poor Trini! What a shame you never married!

TRINI: (*She stops and smiles sadly.*) When all's said and done, you and I are a lot alike!

ROSA: Seems like all women have similar lives.

TRINI: Yes. You were the black sheep of the family, and I was the victim. You wanted to live your life on your own terms, and I sacrificed mine for others. You've lived with a man, and all I've ever known is family. . . . When all's said and done, we're both failures.

ROSA *puts an arm around* TRINI's *waist and presses softly.* TRINI *returns the gesture. They arrive at the door with their arms around each other.*

ROSA: (*Sighing.*) Unlock the door, will you?

TRINI: (*Sighing.*) All right. . . . Just a minute.

She opens the door with her key, and they enter. Pause. URBANO, CARMINA, *and their daughter come up the stairs. The father scolds his daughter as she listens, sad and submissive. The mother is out of breath and very tired.*

URBANO: And I don't want you even thinking about that Fernando! He's a lazy good-for-nothing, just like his father!

CARMINA: That's right!

URBANO: His father and I smoked many a cigarette down there (*Pointing toward the little clubhouse.*) when we were young. I remember it all very well. He was a dreamer; always had his head in the clouds. And his son is just like him: a lazy do-nothing. So I don't even want his name mentioned around here again. Understand?

YOUNG CARMINA: Yes, papa.

Out of breath, the mother leans on the railing.

URBANO: Are you tired?

CARMINA: A little.

URBANO: Don't give up. We're almost there. (*To his daughter, handing her the key.*) Here; you open the door. (*The daughter unlocks the door, goes in, and leaves the door ajar.*) Chest pains again?

CARMINA: Yes, a few.

URBANO: That weak heart of yours!

CARMINA: It's nothing. The pains will go away in a minute. (*Pause.*)

URBANO: Why don't you see a different doctor?

CARMINA: (*Dryly.*) Because I don't want to.

URBANO: You're so stubborn! Another doctor might . . .

CARMINA: It's no use; it's age . . . and life's disappointments.

URBANO: Nonsense! We could try . . .

CARMINA: No, I said! And leave me alone! (*Pause.*)

URBANO: Will we ever agree about anything?

CARMINA: (*Bitterly.*) Never.

URBANO: When I think about what you could have been in my life . . . Why did you marry me if you didn't love me?

CARMINA: (*Dryly.*) I never deceived you. You insisted.

URBANO: Yes, I thought I could make you forget . . . things. . . . And I hoped that in time you'd come to love me, and that you might . . .

CARMINA: Be more grateful?

URBANO: That's not it. (*Sighing.*) Oh well, I guess we just have to be patient.

CARMINA: Patient . . .

PACA *leans her head out of the door and observes the couple. Her voice, now weak, contrasts with the strength of her voice twenty years before.*

PACA: Aren't you coming up?

URBANO: Yes.

CARMINA: Yes; right now.

PACA *goes back inside.*

URBANO: Can you go on now?

CARMINA: Yes.

Urbano offers her his arm and they go up the steps slowly without speaking. With each step, CARMINA *breathes laboriously. Finally they arrive at their door and enter. As she is about to close the door,* URBANO *sees the elder* FERNANDO *emerge from door II and head toward the steps.* URBANO *hesitates a moment but decides to call him when* FERNANDO *has gone down a few steps.*

URBANO: Fernando . . .

FERNANDO: (*Turning around.*) Yes? What do you want?

URBANO: Just a minute of your time, please.

FERNANDO: I'm in a hurry.

URBANO: It won't take long.

FERNANDO: What is it?

URBANO: I want to talk to you about your son.

FERNANDO: Which son?

URBANO: Fernando.

FERNANDO: What about him?

URBANO: You'd be smart to keep him away from Carmina.

FERNANDO: You think I like the way things are between them? We've told him what he needs to know. That's all we can do.

URBANO: Then you knew about it?

FERNANDO: Of course I did. You'd have to be blind not to.

URBANO: You knew about it, and you were glad, weren't you?

FERNANDO: Me? Glad?

URBANO: Yes, I bet you were glad to have a son so like you; glad to see he's irresistible like you were thirty years ago . . . (*Pause.*)

FERNANDO: I have no interest in hearing what you have to say. Good-bye. (*He starts to leave again.*)

URBANO: Wait! We have to settle this. Your son . . .

FERNANDO: (*Coming up the steps and confronting him.*) My son is a victim, just like I was. My son likes Carmina because she's right here and catches his eye. She's the one tempting him. What you need to do is watch out for your daughter.

URBANO: Oh, you can be sure of that! I'd rather see her dead than involved with your Fernando. He's the one you have to watch and set straight, . . . because he's just like you were: a Don Juan, and lazy to boot.

FERNANDO: Me, lazy?

URBANO: Yes. What ever happened to all your big plans about work? The only thing you ever did was look down on everybody. You didn't free yourself or change anything! You're still stuck here in this same place (*Slapping the banister.*), just like I am; just like we all are!

FERNANDO: Yes, just like you. You were going to do great things with your union and all that solidarity. (*Ironically.*) You were going to make things better for everybody. . . . Even me.

URBANO: Yes, even the loafers and cowards like you!

The elder **CARMINA** *comes out on the landing and, after listening a moment, intervenes. The altercation will become increasingly tense and violent until it ends.*

CARMINA: That's exactly right! You're a coward! You've always been a coward! A loafer and a coward!

URBANO: You stay out of this!

CARMINA: I don't want to! I had to tell him that. (*To* **FERNANDO.**) You've been a coward all your life, even in the tiniest, most insignificant things . . . just like you were for the most important ones. (*Tearful.*) You were a weakling and a coward when you needed to be . . . strong and brave!

URBANO: (*Furious.*) Get inside!

CARMINA: No, I won't! (*To* **FERNANDO.**) And your son is just like you: a coward, a loafer, and a liar. He'll never marry my daughter. Understand that? (*Out of breath, she pauses.*)

FERNANDO: I'll certainly do everything I can to keep him from doing something so foolish!

URBANO: For you people, it wouldn't be foolish: she's a million times better than he is.

FERNANDO: A father's opinion, of course, and acceptable only as such. (*Door II opens.* **ELVIRA** *observes the scene and listens.*) Carmina is like her family; she takes after Rosa. . . .

URBANO: (*Approaching, flushed with anger.*) I'm going to . . . (*His wife restrains him.*)

FERNANDO: Yeah, toss me down the stairwell, right? Your favorite threat. That's something else you've never been able to follow through on.

ELVIRA: (*Advancing.*) Why do you argue with lowlife like that? (*Young* **FERNANDO** *and* **MANOLIN** *are standing in the doorway now, observing the scene in astonished disbelief.*) Just mind your own business.

CARMINA: A lowlife you have no right to address!

ELVIRA: And I don't.

CARMINA: You should be ashamed! What happened here is all your fault, anyway!

ELVIRA: My fault?

CARMINA: Yes! Always the schemer and busybody. Little Miss Tricky-Missy! That's you!

ELVIRA: And what about you? Little Miss . . . Mousy, but it didn't get you what you wanted!

FERNANDO: (*To his wife.*) Stop it! You're both talking crazy . . .

Young **CARMINA,** **PACA,** *and* **TRINI** *crowd into their doorway.*

ELVIRA: You shut up! (*To* **CARMINA,** *referring to* **FERNANDO.**) You think I took him away from you? Well, you can have him back anytime!

FERNANDO: Elvira! Stop it! This is embarrassing!

URBANO: (*To his wife.*) Carmina, don't argue with her!

ELVIRA: (*Ignoring her husband.*) You couldn't ever keep anybody . . . or inspire strong feelings . . . or even feel them yourself.

CARMINA: You, on the other hand, had all kinds of strong feelings at just the right moment! That's how you roped him in!

ELVIRA: You shut up! You have no right to say anything! Neither you nor anybody in your family has any right to talk to decent people. All her life, Paca has been a busybody and a weakling. (*To* URBANO.) And you're just like her! You give in to Rosa's every whim. And she's just a tramp! A prostitute!

ROSA: You shut up, you witch!

> ROSA *grabs her by the hair, and everybody begins to shout.* CARMINA *tries to hit* ELVIRA. URBANO *tries to separate them, and* FERNANDO *restrains his wife. The two men manage to separate the women.* YOUNG FERNANDO's *face shows bitterness and disgust as he walks slowly behind the group toward the stairway and descends with his back touching the wall. He continues to listen in desperation from the clubhouse to the feuding family members.*

FERNANDO: Enough! Enough!

URBANO: (*To his family.*) Everybody inside!

ROSA: (*To* ELVIRA.) Yes, I moved in with Pepe, and things didn't go like I wanted, but you trapped Fernando!

ELVIRA: I didn't trap anybody!

ROSA: You did too trap Fernando!

CARMINA: Yes! Fernando!

ROSA: And he stayed with you. So he's a parasite and a pimp, just like Pepe!

FERNANDO: What?

URBANO: (*Facing him squarely.*) Of course! She's right about that! You wanted money. When all's said and done, you're a leech, just like Pepe. No better, no worse! You never earned the money you got either!

FERNANDO: I'm not letting you have it because . . .

URBANO: Because you can't! You don't have the guts! But if that son of yours comes around Carmina again, he'll get his, I assure you!

PACA: Right! He'd better not touch my granddaughter!

URBANO: (*In a very loud voice.*) That's it! Everybody inside! (*He begins shoving people toward their doors.*)

ROSA: (*Before going in her door, addressing* **ELVIRA**.) Conniving bitch!

CARMINA: (*Also addressing* **ELVIRA**.) Scheming hussy!

ELVIRA: Oh, you people are so common . . . , so vulgar!

> **URBANO** *succeeds in getting his family inside before slamming the door noisily.*

FERNANDO: (*To* **ELVIRA** *and* **MANOLIN**.) Both of you get inside, too!

ELVIRA: (*After a moment's thought, scornfully.*) And you; get back to your own business, which you don't do very well, either.

> **FERNANDO** *gives her an angry look. She shoves* **MANOLIN** *inside and slams the door.* **FERNANDO**, *affected by the scene, goes down the steps with the slow gait of a person defeated.* **YOUNG FERNANDO** *watches in shocked silence as his father crosses and disappears. The stairway is now quiet.* **YOUNG FERNANDO** *hides his head in his hands. There is a long pause before* **YOUNG CARMINA** *sneaks out of her door and quietly closes it behind her. Her face shows no less distress than* **YOUNG FERNANDO**'s. *She looks down the stairwell and gazes anxiously at the little corner cubbyhole that serves as the clubhouse. She continues staring at that spot as she timidly goes down a few steps. Hearing her approach,* **YOUNG FERNANDO** *leans forward.*

YOUNG FERNANDO: Carmina!

> *Although she suspected he was there, she cannot repress a gasp of surprise. They look at each other a moment before she runs down the stairs and throws herself into his arms.*

YOUNG CARMINA: Fernando! You see . . . I told you it could never be.

YOUNG FERNANDO: Yes, it can! Don't be defeated by this sordidness and those disgustingly ordinary people. What do we have in common with them? Nothing! They are old and don't understand anything. . . . I'll work so hard for us, and I'll succeed. But you have to help me, Carmina. You have to trust me and believe in our love.

YOUNG CARMINA: I can't!

YOUNG FERNANDO: Yes, you can. You'll do it because I'm asking you to. We have to be stronger than our parents. They let life get them down. They've spent thirty years going up and down this stairway, day in and day out, becoming stingier all the time and more ordinary. But we won't let this atmosphere get us down. No, because we're leaving here. We'll stand by each other. You'll help me succeed and leave behind this miserable place with all its poverty and constant fighting. You'll help me, won't you? Tell me you will, please. Tell me!

YOUNG CARMINA: I need you, Fernando! Don't ever leave me!

YOUNG FERNANDO: My little sweetheart!

They stand there a moment, holding each other. Then he leads her to the first step, seats her against the wall, and sits down beside her. They hold hands and look ecstatically into each other's eyes.

YOUNG FERNANDO: Carmina, I'm going to start working for us right away. I have so many plans! (**CARMINA** *comes out of her door looking anguished. The young couple is not aware of her presence.*) I'm leaving here. I'm leaving my parents. I don't love them. And I'll take you with me. We're leaving this hornet's nest. We're leaving all that fighting and bitterness behind.

YOUNG CARMINA: Fernando!

The elder **FERNANDO** *goes up the steps and pauses in astonishment as he hears the conversation.*

YOUNG FERNANDO: Yes, Carmina. This building is full of ugliness and meanness. Nobody here understands us. Listen. With your love, I can do all kinds of things. First, I'll become a construction tech. That's not hard. In a few years, I'll be really good at it and earn a lot of money. All the builders will be after me. By then, we'll be married and have a wonderful little home, all bright and clean . . . far away from here. But I won't stop there. Oh, no! Then I'll become an engineer. I'll be the best engineer in the whole country, and you'll be my adored little wife . . .

YOUNG CARMINA: Fernando! We'll be so happy! So happy!

YOUNG FERNANDO: Carmina!

They look at each other adoringly and are about to kiss. The parents look at each other across the empty stairwell and then look back at their children. As their eyes meet again for a long time, their gaze over the dreaming couple below communicates infinite sadness.

CURTAIN

BEFORE DAWN

(*Madrugada*)

Dramatic Episode in Two Acts

By Antonio Buero-Vallejo

Translated by Patricia W. O'Connor

This play opened in Madrid's Alcazar Theater on December 9, 1953.

Characters

SABINA

NURSE

AMALIA

LORENZO

LEONOR

MONICA

DAMASO

LEANDRO

PAULA

Stage directions (left, right, etc.)
are from the audience's perspective.

ACT ONE

The action transpires before dawn on a spring day in the spacious suburban home of Mauricio, a well-known painter. The artist's studios occupy the entire upper floor, and the living space is on the main floor, site of the action. Occupying the entire left area of the stage is a luxurious, tastefully decorated living room, the rear part of which curves right to connect with a foyer leading to other rooms. Downstage right, there is a door, and downstage left, sliding double doors open onto the dining room. In the curve that defines the rear area are bookcases, and under a large picture window there is a sofa. Center stage, and around a table with magazines and smoking materials, are several comfortable chairs. A smaller table and other chairs close to the large window complete the furnishings. On the walls, and in more profusion and less order than contemporary decoration might dictate, the artist's paintings, drawings, and sketches bespeak boldness and honesty. Despite these qualities, the painter has successfully satisfied the whims of art collectors and made a very comfortable living. In the corner of the foyer visible to the audience, there are additional paintings and wood panels. A central chandelier, wall fixtures, and a lamp on the table to the right of the large window provide soft lighting for the living room. The drapes at the window are parted to reveal the dense dark of night. Between the window and rear door stands a large and very beautiful grandfather clock that will mark precisely the events of the evening. The silence of the house is underscored by the dull ticking of this clock, the hands of which indicate exactly four fifteen.

As NURSE *naps on the sofa, the lamp beside her illuminates a pale, weary face. Shortly,* SABINA, *the elderly housekeeper, enters from the rear. She observes the motionless figure and then approaches to look more closely. Appearing to sense her presence, the* NURSE *rouses and opens her eyes.*

SABINA: Tired?

NURSE: (*Smiling.*) A little. What time is it?

SABINA: (*Looking at the large clock.*) Four fifteen. Don't you have a watch?

NURSE: (*Looking at her wrist sleepily.*) No, I left it on the dresser with my cape.

SABINA: It'll still be there.

NURSE: Of course. It never crossed my mind it wouldn't be. (*Smiling.*) The lady of the house was kind enough to let me sleep here.

SABINA: Where would you go at three thirty in the morning? You certainly deserve to stay right here.

NURSE: What I did isn't important. It's my job. (*Getting up.*) I'm just sorry we couldn't save him. Have you worked here long?

SABINA: Many years.

NURSE: The doctor said he was an important artist. Are all these paintings his?

SABINA: Most of them, and there are a lot more upstairs. An important artist? You'll see when you read the morning papers.

NURSE: It's really sad . . . and so young; because he *was* still young.

SABINA: Forty-two years old. (*Sighing.*) Oh, well, I don't mean to waste your time. I have things do. When do you have to be at the hospital?

NURSE: At six thirty.

SABINA: The early bus comes by at six. If you leave a little before that, you can catch it on the corner. Until then, go ahead and sleep . . . (*Stammering.*) but not here. . . . I was going to tell you before when I was taking the dog out, but you were napping, and I didn't want to bother you. The lady of the house hopes you won't mind using the couch in the bedroom.

NURSE: (*Puzzled.*) In the same room with . . . him?

SABINA: It's the only other couch; we don't have one upstairs. (*Matter-of-factly.*) Now, if you don't mind . . .

NURSE: I was just wondering about her. I figured she'd want to spend time alone with him. I'm really fine here. (*Pointing to where she is sitting.*)

SABINA: Some relatives are expected. . . . Well, friends, actually. They'll need a place to talk privately, she thought . . .

NURSE: Oh, if that's the way it is, I don't mind. Shall I go there now?

SABINA: In a few minutes. She's changing her clothes right now.

NURSE: (*Surprised.*) She is?

SABINA: Yes, of course. She has those people coming.

NURSE: She seemed so upset by his death; I'm surprised she can think about clothes.

SABINA: She can do that and a lot more. (*The door on the right opens slowly.*) Here she is now.

AMALIA *enters slowly, eyes red and face showing strain. A beautiful woman with an imposing presence, she wears a tastefully elegant black outfit that suggests ostentation more than mourning. Her hair is carefully coiffed, and she wears a diamond necklace and earrings. The contrast of her attire with the sorrow apparent on her face makes her appearance even more striking. Having fully entered the living room now, she looks back at the darkened room she has just left with an expression of pain and bewilderment. Her gaze continues fixed on the room as she closes the door and slowly turns toward the two women.*

AMALIA: Did Sabina explain . . . ?

NURSE: Yes, ma'am.

AMALIA: I know it's not the ideal place. . . .

NURSE: Don't worry. I'm used to those things.

AMALIA: That's why I thought perhaps you wouldn't mind.

NURSE: Of course not. She told me you were expecting relatives . . . (*Noting Sabina's anxious gesture.*)

AMALIA: (*Hastily.*) Relatives? Oh, no; they're just friends.

NURSE: Oh, yes. I meant to say friends.

AMALIA: Yes, friends. They won't go in to see him, so you'll be able to rest just fine on that couch; it's quite large. And if you'd like to read, you'll find some books on the table. (*She steps aside, silently indicating the way to the bedroom through the foyer.*)

NURSE: Yes, ma'am. (*Preparing to go.*)

AMALIA: Oh! And if you want to sleep, please leave the lights on. I'd like to turn them out in the foyer.

NURSE: That'll be fine.

AMALIA: That way, I can see by the bedroom light, if you leave the door slightly open. . . . But I suppose you prefer it that way anyhow; you'll have better ventilation.

NURSE: As you wish. Anything else?

AMALIA: No, that's all, and thank you.

NURSE: Then if you'll excuse me . . . (*As she starts to leave,* AMALIA *and* SABINA *look at each other. With her hand on the doorknob, she pauses.*) Oh, by the way . . .

AMALIA: Yes?

NURSE: If you'd like to do anything in the bedroom . . . prepare it in some special way, it's no problem. I don't mind.

AMALIA: Oh, no. That won't be necessary. At six o'clock, people are coming from the Fine Arts Academy to set things up for the visitation. They'll bring funeral wreaths, stands, flowers, and all those things. Until then, it's better to leave the room as is. (*She turns away and sighs heavily as she looks off into space, and then returns abruptly to the business at hand.*) But I do appreciate your understanding. You can go in now if you like.

NURSE: All right, ma'am. (*She exits stage right and closes the door.* **AMALIA** *and* **SABINA** *breathe a sigh of relief.*)

AMALIA: I didn't think we could do it. (*Walking left.*)

SABINA: You probably should have explained part of it to her.

AMALIA: (*Pacing nervously.*) She might have suspected something and refused to help.

SABINA: What if somebody talks to her?

AMALIA: I'll just have to risk it. Did you telephone them?

SABINA: Yes.

AMALIA: Are they all coming?

SABINA: Yes.

AMALIA: Was Leandro at the newspaper?

SABINA: Yes. He's coming right over. It took a while to wake him. When he finally got to the phone and heard the news, he was very surprised.

AMALIA: Do you suppose he suspected?

SABINA: No . . . I don't think so.

AMALIA: That's good . . . That's good . . . (*Looking at her watch.*) Do you think they'll be here soon?

SABINA: In about ten minutes, I suppose.

AMALIA: Sabina, we've got to keep them from suspecting anything! I have an idea. . . . Look; they'll be here about four thirty. It won't take me long to say what I have to say. They'll probably want to think it over, so we may have to give them a nudge; a jolt, really! At about four forty-five, please arrange to be in the bedroom. You'll come in here and you'll say: "Mr.

Mauricio has stirred. I think he's trying to wake up." Understand what I need you to do?

SABINA: But what if they still refuse?

AMALIA: They'll have no choice! (*Pacing nervously.*) They must decide by six o'clock at the latest. That's when the nurse leaves, and they'll bring in all those awful things that will make it impossible to continue the pretense. (*Stopping.*) But if they don't decide, and if by five twenty, for example, they still haven't made up their minds, then you come in again and say the nurse wants to know if she should give him an injection to wake him up. (*She leans on the table, horrified by what she has just said.* SABINA *approaches her solicitously.*)

SABINA: You're exhausted. Can you really do this?

AMALIA: I have to. (*She collapses into one of the armchairs and leans her head back. Suddenly, from the garden comes the prolonged, pathetic howl of a dog.* AMALIA *straightens up, tense again.*)

SABINA: He tried to bite me when I tied him up out there. (*She goes to the large window and peers through the glass before drawing the heavy drapes.*)

AMALIA: I couldn't let Amigo stay in the house. They'd take one look at him and know . . . So I had to hurt him, too.

SABINA: (*Approaching to stand behind her chair and speaking tenderly.*) Why are you doing this?

AMALIA: (*Without turning around, she acknowledges the question with a grimace.*) I'd give anything to know that he's hearing me. Before, when I put on this jewelry . . . and this "costume," I leaned over him, and I cried and I kissed him several times . . . wondering if he understood I just wanted to impress these people with this false exterior. . . . I wondered if he knew how very much I've loved him . . .

SABINA: Maybe he heard you. . . . Maybe he's hearing you now.

AMALIA: But I can't be sure. And that doubt torments me, Sabina! Not to know what he really thought about me.

SABINA: I'm sure it wasn't anything bad, ma'am.

AMALIA: You can't possibly understand. . . . Mauricio kept everything to himself and taught me to do the same. . . . I never talked about our private life.

Maybe you didn't notice, but for some time, there had been a kind of tension; a distance between us.

SABINA: Yes, I did notice.

AMALIA You know how I started living with him. First, I was his model; then . . . (*With a fatalistic shrug of the shoulders.*) Then a miracle happened, Sabina! The miracle of love in me! He made it happen with his touch, with his gentleness, his goodness! He meant everything in the world to me! Everything! No man could ever compare to him! (*Lowering her head.*) But he knew all too well that before . . . before him, I had been the artist's model . . . and all the rest of it . . . of another painter, an awful man. (*Brief pause.*)

SABINA: We women are weak, sometimes. . . . Don't let grief get you down. Mauricio adored you. Forget the will, and also . . .

AMALIA: The will! (*Squeezing* **SABINA***'s hand on the table.*) Sit down. (**SABINA** *obeys.* **AMALIA** *speaks in a low voice.*) Wait a minute . . . Remember? You were here when the family stopped coming over. Why did he leave them out of the will without any explanation? Everybody is included, all but two; or really, everybody except him . . . Leandro. Do you think Mauricio heard rumors about Leandro's persistence? (*Darkly.*) If he did, the omission speaks for itself and explains those awful months when he was so distant. Nothing for Leandro! Nothing for the seducer, and nothing for the traitor's father either, just in case . . . But the fallen woman gets something. Is it benevolence, forgiveness, scorn? Maybe even payment? (*Getting up.*)

SABINA: How can you think that, after he . . . ?

AMALIA: Payment! Just payment! (*Turning around.*) How do you know whether or not I had an affair with Leandro? Do you think so? If you're not sure, maybe he wasn't sure either! (*She goes to the window as* **SABINA** *slowly stands up.*)

SABINA: I have faith in you, ma'am.

AMALIA: (*Her face relaxes. Sighing, she turns around.*) What about him? Do you think he had faith in me, too?

SABINA: I'm sure he did . . .

AMALIA: (*Walking slowly downstage, lost in thought.*) When we were alone, I tried to find out . . . But it was hard. . . . It takes more than a few minutes to thaw the ice that has built up over months. Besides, I was afraid; reluctant to broach a delicate subject. My stupid pride kept us from creating the trust we both needed. . . . In the end, all I said was something crazy; one of those things you just blurt out without thinking. I said: "You never loved me!" (*Brief pause.*) His answer was something terrible. He said: "It's too late to say so many things, my darling Amalia. But perhaps, just perhaps, in death, I'll win you back." (*With her gaze glued to the foyer door.*) I started crying, and I said, "But you never lost me!" And he said, "No, I never lost you, but maybe from that other shore I'll make you mine again." (*Transition.*) I put my arms around him and asked him what he meant . . . And he just died. (*Emotional.*) What do you suppose he meant?

SABINA: Maybe he suspected you had doubts and wanted to reassure you.

AMALIA: No. He meant something very specific. His voice had the sound of infinite kindness. . . . Forgiveness, perhaps? Forgiveness for something I didn't do? (*Bitterly.*) If that's what it was, he has lost me forever. (*Walking toward* SABINA.) But I can't stand to think that! I have to know what he meant! (*Her gaze seems to search for* MAURICIO *in the room.*) It's like he's telling me to search for the answer! And they're going to give it to me. I know they have it . . . (*Crossing stage left.*) I know he's referring to them without mentioning any name. And through them, we'll be joined forever, or separated forever.

SABINA: (*Fearfully.*) Maybe another day . . . Maybe when you're feeling better . . .

AMALIA: It's now or never! Today I can shock them; get them to tell me before they've had a chance to think about it. And besides, Sabina . . . I can't go on any longer . . . without letting him, as he said, "try to win me back . . . forever." (*The sound of the doorbell interrupts their conversation, and they separate quickly.*) They're starting to arrive! (*She rushes toward the foyer.*) Don't call me until they're all here! (*Looking at her watch.*) My goodness! It's so late! I haven't much time! Let them in! (*She leans against the foyer door as* SABINA *walks stage rear.*) Sabina! I'm scared!

SABINA: Be brave! With the two of us, it will be easier.

AMALIA: Thank you . . .

SABINA *exits.* AMALIA *opens the door to the foyer and pauses a moment, listening. Then she exits rapidly, closing the door behind her. Almost immediately* LORENZO *enters from the rear followed by* SABINA. LORENZO, *about sixty, is handsome, has a pleasant manner and is wearing, with studied carelessness, an inexpensive suit.* SABINA *turns on the overhead light.*

SABINA: I'll let madam know you're here. (*Walking right.*)

LORENZO: Wait. Don't you remember me? You were here in the old days, when we all used to visit.

SABINA: Yes, I remember you, Mr. Lorenzo. Won't you have a seat?

LORENZO: Yes, thank you. (*He sits down at the desk.*) I'm dead tired, and sleepy, too.

SABINA: I'll bring you some coffee.

LORENZO: Not a bad idea . . . And the lady of the house? How's she holding up?

SABINA: You can imagine. . . .

LORENZO: Yes, I can. She probably didn't have a chance to talk to him.

SABINA: Very little.

LORENZO: How did it happen?

SABINA: He had a heart attack about three thirty this morning.

LORENZO: Did he lose consciousness?

SABINA: Well, sort of. For a few minutes, he mumbled things and asked for pen and paper . . .

LORENZO: Yes . . .

SABINA: But she didn't have time to understand much of anything. He lapsed into a sort of coma and hasn't come out of it yet.

LORENZO: My, my! And what did the doctor say?

SABINA: There's no hope of recovery. (**LORENZO** *clucks his tongue and shakes his head sadly.*) If you'll excuse me, I'm going to let Miss Amalia know you're here.

LORENZO: Of course, of course; go right ahead. (**SABINA** *exits stage right and closes the door.* **LORENZO,** *curious, gets up and examines the room. He goes to the door on the right and listens. The doorbell rings again, and* **LORENZO** *rushes back to his chair. Brief pause.* **SABINA** *returns and closes the door behind her.*)

SABINA: Madam will be right down. Would you care for a cocktail or something else to drink before I prepare the coffee?

LORENZO: No, thanks. There's someone at the door.

SABINA: Yes, I'm going right now.

LORENZO: Maybe it's my brother.

SABINA: Or it could be your son.

LORENZO: (*Frowning.*) Of course; my son will be coming, too.

SABINA: Yes, sir, everybody. (**SABINA** *exits.* **LORENZO** *stands up and waits expectantly, facing stage rear. After a moment,* **SABINA** *returns.*) Your brother is here, Mr. Lorenzo.

Sabina stands aside as **DAMASO**, **LEONOR**, *and* **MONICA** *enter.* **DAMASO**, *about fifty-five, is tall and lean. He wears a worn dark suit, a starched white shirt, and on his lapel an insignia. His attire, voice, and gestures suggest a failed attempt to convey a position of great respectability. His wife,* **LEONOR**, *is quite overweight and looks much older than her forty years. At twenty, however, her vulgar full-bodied appearance may have attracted attention. She now wears a tasteless homemade dress meant to look elegant, and her numerous brass bracelets rattle as she moves her arms.* **MONICA**, *their daughter, not yet twenty, is slender and wears a simple outfit without accessories. For a long moment, the married couple regards* **LORENZO** *coldly.*

LORENZO: (*Approaching them amiably.*) How are you? (*Shaking* **DAMASO***'s hand.*) And you, Leonor?

LEONOR: (*Bitterly.*) We're fine and here for the same reason you came. (*She walks downstage and takes a seat right of the table.* **DAMASO** *also crosses toward the large window.*)

MONICA: Hello, Uncle Lorenzo. (*Standing on tiptoe, she kisses him.*)

LORENZO: Hi, little one. (*Kissing her.*) You should be in bed. This is nothing for you to be concerned about.

LEONOR: If we brought her with us, it must mean we don't see it that way, don't you think?

DAMASO: Mauricio said for her to come.

LEONOR: Sit down, Monica.

MONICA: Yes, mother. (*She sits on the other end of the sofa. The clock strikes the half hour.*)

DAMASO: Is he still living?

LORENZO: Yes. (*Pacing.*)

DAMASO: Have you seen him?

LORENZO: No. I just got here.

DAMASO: What about the Dragon Lady?

LORENZO: (*With a half smile.*) I haven't seen Amalia.

DAMASO: What did they say about what happened?

LORENZO: Same thing they told you, I suppose. It's serious, for sure. I tried to check it out in a book before I came. The doctor says it's hopeless.

LEONOR: Yes. (*Tapping her heel impatiently and rattling her bracelets as she looks at her husband.*)

DAMASO: (*Clearing his throat.*) It was quite unexpected. Do you know what time he had the attack?

LORENZO: At three thirty. I thought you knew. (**LEONOR** *and* **DAMASO** *look at the clock.*)

DAMASO: And ever since then, he's been . . . asleep?

LORENZO: (*Looking at them mockingly.*) I think he woke up a little at first . . .

DAMASO: (*Uneasy.*) Oh!

LEONOR: (*Likewise.*) Oh!

LORENZO: Then he drifted off again before saying anything.

DAMASO: (*Relieved.*) Ah!

LEONOR: (*Likewise.*) Ah! (**MONICA** *cries quietly and dabs at her eyes.* **LORENZO** *sits behind the table.*)

LORENZO: Actually, we've never known much about his health. When was the last time you saw him?

DAMASO: (*Pacing.*) At Mateo's farewell party.

LORENZO: That's the last time I saw him, too. By the way, have you heard anything from Mateo?

DAMASO: Only indirectly. Seems he's doing well over there, but he works hard.

LORENZO: He's going to be upset by all this. He has no idea of what's going on here!

DAMASO: But things will certainly go better for him, now.

LORENZO: You think so?

DAMASO: (*Coming closer.*) Yes, because if Mauricio hasn't written a will, Mateo stands to get a good chunk of the estate, and he also has profits from commissions these past few months on orders from New York and Paris. Didn't you know about that?

LORENZO: Yes.

DAMASO: (*Sighing.*) Poor Mauricio!

LORENZO: How much do you suppose he's worth?

DAMASO: Hard to estimate.

LORENZO: I don't think so. Sometimes I figure it couldn't be under . . . (**MONICA** *is sobbing openly now.*) Honey, what's the matter?

MONICA: (*Wiping her tears.*) Nothing, papa. (*She tries in vain to control the sobbing. The others look at her sympathetically.* **LORENZO** *goes over to pat her head.*)

LORENZO: It's all right, little one. . . . (*Speaking to the others.*) Poor Mauricio!

DAMASO: Yeah, poor . . . (*Sighing hypocritically as* **LORENZO** *begins to pace again.*)

LEONOR: (*Tapping her heel nervously.*) That tramp could at least come and greet us. Who does she think she is, anyway? You two are his brothers, and she's nobody in all this.

LORENZO: Well, she's not exactly nobody, you know . . .

LEONOR: (*Rattling her bracelets.*) Would you rather I used the right word?

DAMASO: (*Sarcastically.*) No! Monica is here.

LEONOR: Well, she's just a cheap . . . ! She's probably in there rehearsing her role as the tragic figure in this saga. Oh, maybe she will play the tragic part for real, now that she'll be penniless and out in the street.

DAMASO: Leonor . . .

LEONOR: You two will be prize fools if you let her take anything out of this house.

LORENZO: I don't think you want her walking out of here stark naked, do you? (*Sitting down.*)

LEONOR: No. I guess I wouldn't want that. She can take her stupid dresses . . . Well, some of them, anyway. But absolutely no jewelry, and no paintings!

DAMASO: Oh, calm down. At least she called us, and that shows she understands the situation. If Mauricio had left his estate to her, I don't think she would have bothered to call. . . . Rest assured that we'll do what's necessary about her. (*He stops his pacing beside* MONICA, *who continues upset as she listens. He puts a hand on her head.*) Monica, dear, now we can afford good schools for you and give you things you deserve. God knows, when they awarded me this medal . . .

LEONOR: (*Contemptuously.*) Oh, here we go again. (*Sitting down.*)

DAMASO: . . . I would gladly have exchanged that honor for a secure future for you. I've worked so hard all these years, and now comes the reward. God favors the good . . . (*He pauses, transported by his own words.* MONICA *bows her head, feeling sorry for him.*) Don't you have anything to say, honey?

MONICA: I feel sorry for her, papa. Amalia's really a good person.

LEONOR: (*Icily furious.*) If I ever hear you say anything like that again, I'll slap your face.

DAMASO: (*Conciliatory.*) That's enough, Leonor. Monica is young and doesn't know how to judge people yet. (*Short pause.*)

LEONOR: Why doesn't she come out?

DAMASO: (*Satisfied.*) She's afraid of us.

LEONOR: She's probably trying to look like some martyr. I'll bet she's putting spit on her eyelids so we'll feel sorry for her. . . . (*Tapping her heel on the floor.*) So don't get sucked in! You hear me, Damaso? She should know from the word go that we're in the driver's seat and aren't giving in to her. Understood?

DAMASO: Of course.

LEONOR: And what about you, Lorenzo?

LORENZO: We'll see.

LEONOR: (*Getting up.*) And just what might we "see"?

LORENZO: I told you we have to wait and see what happens! We don't really know anything yet.

LEONOR: We don't? I don't want us to "see" sometime in the future. I want to "see" everything right now. Where is she?

LORENZO: (*Pointing.*) In the bedroom.

LEONOR: Since she doesn't come out, I'll go in there. (*She walks toward the door.* **MONICA** *stands up, and* **DAMASO** *intervenes.*)

DAMASO: Wait a minute . . .

LEONOR: What for? This house is more ours than hers!

LORENZO: It will be ours . . . in time. (*Getting up.*)

LEONOR: That's the same thing! (*To* **DAMASO**.) Let me go!

LORENZO: Since you insist, let's see what happens. But don't you think it would be more appropriate for a relative to do that? Allow me. (*He goes to the door, turns the knob softly, and then stops to look back at the others, a serious expression on his face.*) It's locked. (**LEONOR** *approaches and tests the door. They all look at each other.*) I say we shouldn't do anything hasty. Let's just wait. (*He returns to the table and sits down behind her.* **MONICA** *sits down again.* **LEONOR** *and* **DAMASO** *look at each other, puzzled.* **SABINA** *enters from the rear and approaches the rear diagonal area.*) Did the others call?

SABINA: From the kitchen, I heard a car pull up. (*She exits.*)

LORENZO: (*Dryly.*) Probably my son.

With a great rattling of bracelets and attempts to strike a dignified pose, **LEONOR** *quickly sits down.*

DAMASO: Are you two . . . still on the outs?

LORENZO: I'm afraid it's inevitable. We just don't see eye to eye on anything.

DAMASO: Is he still at the newspaper?

LORENZO: (*Reluctantly.*) Yes.

SABINA *enters, followed almost immediately by* **LEANDRO**.

SABINA: Mr. Leandro is here.

Although **LEANDRO** *is perhaps forty years old, there is a youthful arrogance about him. His clothes, attractively simple and casual, suggest a man of action and hard work. For a moment, he looks around at everyone with open hostility.*

LEANDRO: Hello.

DAMASO: Hello.

LEONOR: Hello.

LORENZO *doesn't even look at him as he takes a cigarette from the table and lights it very deliberately.*

SABINA: I'll let madam know you're here.

DAMASO: I think the door . . . is locked.

SABINA: (*Surprised.*) Locked? (*To the surprise of those present, she opens the door easily, looks at them, and exits, closing the door behind her.*)

LEONOR: (*Intrigued.*) What does that mean?

LEANDRO: (*Irritated because no one has paid any attention to him.*) Could someone tell me how Mauricio is?

DAMASO: He's dying. (*He goes over to the table and also takes a cigarette and inhales its aroma before lighting up.*)

LEONOR: There's no hope of recovery, and he's dying without a will.

LEANDRO: You don't need to tell me that. It's written all over your faces. (*Looking at his father.*) You're certainly not doing a very good job of masking your joy.

LEONOR: And you're going to tell us you're sad, are you? Come on! We all know that . . .

LEANDRO: Watch what you say! No, I'm not going to say I regret my uncle's situation, because it would be a lie. But she's something else!

LEONOR: Of course! He's one thing, and she's another!

DAMASO: Leonor . . .

LEONOR: S-h-h-h! (*Pointing to the foyer door as it opens.* **SABINA** *enters and crosses the stage. Those present watch her in silence as she exits stage rear.*)

LEANDRO: (*To Leonor.*) What did you mean by what you said before?

LEONOR: Nothing you should find mysterious.

LEANDRO: I don't like your attitude. I want all of you to know that I respect Amalia's grief. We're in her home . . .

LEONOR: Oh, please!

LEANDRO: This is her home, and I don't want anyone insulting or humiliating her!

LEONOR: Well! I guess she didn't come out before because she was waiting for Sir Galahad, here, to come and take her away from all this. Right?

LEANDRO: Just a minute!

DAMASO: (*Eying the foyer door nervously.*) Watch out! (*They all look toward the door.* MONICA *stands up. As the door opens,* AMALIA, *with a finger pressed to her lips, asks for silence. Then with proud, self-assured composure and dry eyes, she emerges and closes the door behind her.* LORENZO *rises.*)

AMALIA: Hush! You're going to wake him!

MONICA: (*Hugging her impulsively.*) Aunt Amalia!

LEONOR: Sit down, Monica. She's not your aunt! (*Embarrassed,* MONICA *obeys.*) Amalia is just a . . . woman; a very well-dressed woman who wears expensive jewelry, but she doesn't seem to understand her role here. (*The rattle of her bracelets underscores her contempt.*)

AMALIA: (*Looking at her watch as she approaches* LEONOR.) And in your opinion, what is my role?

DAMASO: My wife is suggesting that perhaps your playing "lady of the house" is out of place. I think you know it and for that reason called us together.

AMALIA: Thank you for clearing up your wife's position. Is that how the rest of you feel? (MONICA *makes timid negative gestures that* AMALIA *pretends not to notice.*)

LEANDRO: No, Amalia, I don't feel that way, and everybody here knows it.

LORENZO: I don't have an opinion . . . yet. And I'm sorry about all this.

AMALIA: (*Dryly.*) Thank you. (*To* DAMASO.) Do you share your wife's opinion?

DAMASO: Since you're taking it like this, I'll tell you where I stand. I regret to remind you that we're here because, as family, we have a right to be. And that's not all: we're the only ones with any right to be at the dying man's bedside. Therefore, you'll have to leave.

LEONOR: In another outfit and no jewelry.

LEANDRO: Don't talk to her like that!

AMALIA: (*Dryly.*) Thank you anyway, Leandro, but I don't need help from anybody. (*To* LEONOR.) So you'd like to get rid of me, just like that?

LEONOR: You might put it that way.

AMALIA: Toss me out, like a piece of trash?

LEONOR: (*Viciously.*) My, my! You found just the word.

LORENZO: Well, there's no need to be nasty . . .

DAMASO: Of course not. (*To* AMALIA.) Now, will you please take us in to our brother?

AMALIA: Yes, come with me. (*As she approaches the foyer door, all follow.* SABINA, *standing by the door, exchanges with* AMALIA *a tense look unnoticed by the others.* AMALIA *boldly opens the door and watches the relatives closely as they gather around to observe in silence.*)

LEANDRO: Is that a nurse?

AMALIA: Yes.

LORENZO: She's looking at us.

DAMASO: She's getting up . . .

LEONOR: And waving to us . . . (*The group responds with a slight movement of hands.*)

MONICA: He looks very peaceful.

AMALIA: (*Bitterly.*) Yes, he's peaceful, now. (*She closes the door softly.*)

LEONOR: (*Raising her voice in anger.*) Why close the door? We're going in!

AMALIA: Please! Keep your voice down!

LEONOR: (*Speaking even louder.*) And why should I do that?

AMALIA: It's a delicate moment. You might wake him up.

LEONOR: And why not?

AMALIA: Because if he wakes up, he'll sign the will I've prepared. (*Silence.* LEONOR, *agitated, steps back as* SABINA *crosses in front of her.*)

AMALIA: (*Advancing.*) Would you all have a seat, please? I called you here to tell you something. (MONICA *sits on the couch while the others, listening carefully, take places around the table.*) Mauricio has been dying since three thirty. He awakened briefly, only long enough to say he wanted to make a will. The doctor had been very frank with him about his condition. . . . You're aware of the nature of his illness. Then he slipped back into a coma. The doctor said he can't possibly last another day, and he described that calm that you see as the worst possible sign. The doctor can bring him back briefly, but not save him. We might wake him up by speaking to him or touching him, but if that doesn't work, the doctor can give him an injection. (*Pausing briefly beside the table.*) Did any of you notice the paper with the pen on the nightstand beside his bed?

Before Dawn (Madrid, 1953), Act I, Damaso (Manuel Díaz), Leandro (Gabriel Llopart), and Amalia (María Asquerino)

MONICA: I did!

AMALIA: That's the will I personally prepared. I believe it represents what he wanted: everything for me and nothing for you.

LEONOR: That's outrageous!

AMALIA: Outrageous? No, I'm sure it's what he wanted. If he wakes up, all I have to do is read what I've written, and he'll sign it without hesitation.

LEANDRO: (*Softly.*) Won't you need a notary's signature?

AMALIA: With five witnesses, no notary is required. I'm well aware of my rights. You could be one witness, I suppose . . .

LEANDRO: Of course.

AMALIA: (*Glancing sharply at the others.*) If there aren't enough witnesses here, some neighbors will come in. Sabina knows who to ask. (*Brief pause.*) And now, if you would care to take your places at his bedside . . . running the risk, of course, of waking him up, go right ahead. There's the door. (*Absolute silence.*)

LEANDRO: I'm going in. (*Getting up and starting to walk.*)

LEONOR: (*Getting up almost simultaneously.*) Where are you going?

DAMASO: Stop right there, Leandro!

AMALIA: (*Smiling.*) Why don't you sit down, Leandro? We'll eventually wake him up, if that's what the others decide.

LORENZO: (*Who has not gotten up.*) Why didn't you wake him before?

AMALIA: Because I have a proposition to make. Everybody please sit down again! Please! (*They do so.*) You and Mauricio haven't been in contact for several years. Mateo was the only brother he still saw, and when Mateo decided to try his luck in America, Mauricio didn't hesitate to pay for the trip. He even gave him a little extra to get started. . . . He did that perhaps because Mateo never seemed to resent having a successful brother. (**LEONOR** and **DAMASO** *exchange uncomfortable glances.*) Six months ago, as a kind of farewell party, Mateo got you all together at his house. He invited all of you; just family. Mauricio felt obliged to attend. . . . At that gathering, one of you took him aside and told him something quite serious; something disturbing. (*Making an effort.*) Apparently, it was about me. (*As she looks at each in turn, they avoid her eyes, frightened, or perhaps puzzled. Only* **LEANDRO**

and MONICA *meet her gaze.*) And whoever that person was is going to repeat here and now word for word exactly what was said. . . . Otherwise, I'll awaken Mauricio, and he'll sign the will. But if that person does what I ask, I promise Mauricio will sign nothing. (*A long pause.*)

DAMASO: (*Clearing his throat and speaking with the affected sweetness and theatrical tremor of attempted conciliation.*) Couldn't you be mistaken? Perhaps you're imagining things. . . . That's understandable in your emotional state, and we all respect that. How else could you be so sure something happened at that gathering so many months ago?

AMALIA: I know.

LORENZO: Did he say something?

AMALIA: No.

DAMASO: You have no proof that anything happened. Don't you understand?

AMALIA: What was it you called Mauricio, Leonor? You were always so fond of creating nicknames that reflected your opinions. You dubbed him the "Silent One," didn't you? (*To* DAMASO.) But he's just shy and quiet, like good artists often are. But I know that someone said something!

LORENZO: I don't think so, Amalia. But let's suppose for a minute that someone did. What do you have to gain by finding out what it was now? Why do you put yourself through this needlessly?

AMALIA: (*Darkly resolute.*) That's my business!

LORENZO: (*He shrugs and stifles a yawn.*) I feel sorry for you. The stress of the past few hours has clouded your judgment.

AMALIA: (*Coldly.*) Is that what the rest of you think? (*Silence.*) Nobody is going to say anything?

LEANDRO: (*Getting up.*) Wake him up, Amalia.

AMALIA: All right, that's what I'll do. (*She walks slowly toward the foyer.*)

LEONOR: (*Getting up.*) You have no right to do that! (MONICA *gets up as well.*)

AMALIA: (*Turning around.*) So it was you? (*Walking toward* LEONOR.)

LEONOR: I didn't say anything! And you have no right! (*During this exchange,* MONICA *opens the foyer door and exits.*)

DAMASO: (*Getting up.*) Monica!

AMALIA: Monica! (*Rushing after her.*)

LEONOR: (*Her arms extended.*) No! (**LORENZO**, *who had nodded off, wakes up.* **AMALIA** *returns with* **MONICA** *and closes the door. Everybody except* **LORENZO** *gathers around them.*)

DAMASO: (*Furious.*) You wanted to wake him up, didn't you? Answer me!

MONICA: (*Softly.*) Yes. (**LEONOR** *has waited only long enough to hear the response; then, with ill-contained rage, she slaps* **MONICA**.)

LEONOR: Go back to your seat! (**MONICA** *obeys, but remains standing with her back turned as sobs shake her body.*)

AMALIA: (*Irritated.*) A fine example you set for your daughter!

LEONOR: She's my daughter!

AMALIA: And this is my home . . . still! Children aren't objects to slap around or kiss as the mood strikes! (**LEONOR**'s *only response is to rattle her bracelets and sit down.*)

MONICA: I only wanted to . . . help.

LEANDRO: Of course you did. Now come on; dry those tears. (*He hands her a handkerchief. She daubs at the tears and returns the handkerchief.*)

AMALIA: And I'm grateful, Monica. But you're not helping me that way, really. They're the ones who'll help by talking.

DAMASO: We've already told you we don't know anything.

AMALIA: Are you sure about that? (*Approaching them.*) It looks like you don't understand the situation. One of you has to confess right here, in front of everybody, and you must do it now! (*To* **DAMASO**.) It wasn't you? Congratulations. You, all of you, not I, will make the guilty party speak. You'll do it because it's in your best interests. . . . I'm asking that person, whoever you are, to speak up now. Save your relatives the trouble of telling me themselves. (*A pause, during which the relatives eye one another nervously.*) Come on! Speak up! Who is it?

No one speaks. Without taking her eyes off the family members, **AMALIA** *moves toward the foyer. Her expression clouds when she pauses to give them an inquiring look. All are quite attentive as she takes a few more steps. The tension mounts.* **DAMASO** *moves toward her, perplexed and wanting to stop her but not knowing how.* **LEONOR** *rises slowly.* **LORENZO**, *previously drowsy, is now alert.* **LEANDRO** *looks steadily at* AMALIA. MONICA *has turned around and moves forward slightly, seeming to indicate that she wants* AMALIA *to go in.* AMALIA *takes two or three more steps as* LEONOR *comes forward, her hands together.* LORENZO *gets up and makes a timidly pleading gesture.* AMALIA *is very close to the door now. She looks at the relatives and at the clock. Although the others don't know it, she is as nervous as they are. Suddenly, the doorknob turns, and* SABINA *emerges.* AMALIA *cannot repress a sigh of relief.*

SABINA: He's stirring, ma'am! He's trying to wake up! (*Her words have the desired effect on those present.* AMALIA *looks at them triumphantly and prepares to enter the foyer.*)

DAMASO: Please, Amalia, don't do that. I promise we'll help you find the answers you want. We'll tell you, really. But don't go in there.

AMALIA: You've taken too long. But I'll give you this much: if he isn't awake, I won't wake him. (*She exits, closing the door behind her.* SABINA *crosses toward the rear of the stage.* LEONOR *sits down.*)

LORENZO: (*Collapsing with a sigh on an armchair.*) When are you going to bring that coffee? I can't stay awake.

SABINA: Right away, Mr. Lorenzo. (*She exits, stage rear.*)

DAMASO: Monica, go along and help Sabina, will you?

MONICA: Don't you think it's a little late to get me out of the room, papa?

LEONOR: Do as your father says!

MONICA: (*Sadly.*) All right, mother. (*She follows* SABINA, *exiting stage rear. After a brief pause, all look at* LEONOR.)

LEONOR: Don't look at me like that! It wasn't me!

DAMASO: Nobody said it was. (*Anguished, he looks at his watch.*) But we have so little time. . . . Whoever said something had better speak up, and now. (*He looks steadily at* LEONOR.)

LEANDRO: (*Contemptuously.*) And why do you exclude yourself?

DAMASO: (*Irritated.*) Don't be silly. If it had been me, I wouldn't have let her go back in there. No, you let her go because you know she'll do what she says.

LEONOR: Well, I bet that witch has already tried waking him up!

DAMASO: (*Frightened.*) You think so? (*He goes to the door and listens.*) I don't hear a thing.

LEONOR: The bedroom is on the other side of the foyer. Open the door!

DAMASO: Shall I open it, Lorenzo? (**LORENZO** *has fallen asleep and does not respond.*)

LEONOR: (*Disdainfully.*) That zombie is out of it again! He's asleep.

DAMASO: All right. We need to come to an agreement here. (*He quickly goes over to* **LORENZO.**) Lorenzo! Wake up! How can you sleep through all this? (*He shakes him.*)

LORENZO: (*Becoming more alert.*) Because I'm sleepy.

DAMASO: Lorenzo, this is no time for jokes. We stand to lose a lot of money here!

Disgusted, **LEANDRO** *gets up and goes to the large window.*

LORENZO: Was it you? Come on, let's have it.

DAMASO: That's no way to solve anything.

LORENZO: Whether it was you or not is unimportant. It could have been your wife.

LEONOR: (*Enraged.*) Or it could have been the "financier with no finances."

LORENZO: (*Hurt.*) I thought it was strange you hadn't used that insult before. Thank you.

DAMASO: Looks like everyone wants Mauricio to sign that new will!

LEANDRO: That's my position, of course. And I'll go a step farther: if she doesn't wake him up, I'll do it myself.

LORENZO: (*Dryly.*) You wouldn't do that.

LEANDRO: Well, what do you know! My father is finally speaking to me. (*Stepping forward.*) And, yes, I'll do just that! I'm not going to be part of your dirty deals!

LORENZO: (*Harshly.*) You will do nothing of the kind!

LEANDRO: (*Exploding.*) Who are you to tell me what to do? I owe you nothing! You couldn't give me the position I should have had. You were only interested in your own projects, and even with those, you didn't waste what was yours! You wasted what was mine!

LORENZO: Son! (*Getting up and approaching him.*)

LEANDRO: Father!

DAMASO: All right, all right! Don't get into it, you two. This isn't the time . . .

LORENZO: Then you're going to wake him up?

LEANDRO: Rest assured!

LORENZO: Then do it now. (*Brief pause.*) What are you waiting for? The others can't stop you, and I'm not moving a finger. (**LEANDRO** *quickly takes a few steps toward the door.*)

LEONOR: (*Alarmed, she gets up.*) Are you out of your mind, Leandro?

DAMASO: Leandro! (**LEANDRO** *pauses.*)

LORENZO: (*Smiling.*) You're not going to do it?

LEANDRO: No. (**LEONOR** *sits down, exhausted.*)

LORENZO: I understand perfectly. (*Approaching him.*) You came here expecting to find a very different Amalia. She was a little cooler than you thought she'd be. Now it doesn't seem so certain that if she inherits Mauricio's money, you'll take his place. On the other hand, a father is always a father. I can take my share and waste it. But if I still have some money when my turn comes to pass it on . . . Eh? We understand each other, don't we, son?

LEANDRO: It's always been about money with you. Can't you understand that what I do is out of respect for Amalia's wishes?

LORENZO: (*Mockingly.*) What about the dying man's wishes?

LEANDRO: I don't care anything about that. (*Walking over to the picture window.*)

DAMASO: Well, that's very important; she's going to force him to sign!

LORENZO: (*Serious.*) I don't think so. She'll wait as long as she can to find out what she wants to know. And since you people don't seem willing to give her that information, this little tug-of-war is going to last a while. The longer it lasts, the better it is for you and the worse it is for her, because he can die any minute. It's a race against the clock. (*He indicates the clock with his head.*) She wishes the hands didn't move so fast, and you'd like to nudge them along. But it's a dangerous game you're playing. She's stretched to the limit. She could snap at any moment and decide to wake him up. (*Without looking at anyone.*) The one who has the information she wants shouldn't gamble much longer. Better yet, that person should just confess when she comes back.

LEONOR: Now you're excluding yourself.

LORENZO: (*Shrugging his shoulders.*) I never get involved in that kind of silliness. . . . (*He returns to his place and sits down.*) And since it looks like that coffee isn't ever coming, let me sleep. I can't stay awake. (*He leans his head on his hands and closes his eyes.*)

LEONOR: Oh, hurry up and die!

LORENZO: (*Ironically and without opening his eyes.*) Which one? Him or her?

LEONOR: Both of them! (*Brief pause.*)

> *Suddenly, from outside, comes a dog's long piercing wail.* **LEONOR**, *alert, gets up.* **LORENZO** *opens his eyes.* **LEANDRO** *takes a few steps toward the large window. All wait, their faces tense, until the wail dies down.*

LEANDRO: (*Serious.*) It's Amigo. He senses death in the air.

LEONOR: (*Increasingly upset.*) Do you suppose Mauricio's dying right now? (*She rushes to the right and tries to listen. Trembling, she straightens up slowly.*) I'm scared.

DAMASO: (*Rushing to her side.*) Calm down! It's only a howling dog!

> *The door to the foyer opens suddenly, and* **DAMASO** *stifles* **LEONOR**'s *moan with his hand.* **AMALIA** *appears and looks at them.* **LEONOR** *and* **DAMASO** *try to see around her into the bedroom.* **AMALIA** *stands aside so they can have a better look before closing the door.*

LEONOR: The nurse is very calm . . .

DAMASO: You can see that everything is all right.

AMALIA: (*Closing the door.*) At least there is nothing to be alarmed about right now. He's quiet. (*Coming forward.*) I'm waiting for your answer, Damaso.

DAMASO: (*Hesitantly.*) Actually . . . I tried to convince them . . . (**AMALIA**'s *look hardens.*)

LEANDRO: It's no use, Amalia. They refuse to talk. (*Sitting down.*)

DAMASO: It's not that. What you're asking is very strange. Maybe you're confused. Couldn't it have been something else that happened about the same time?

AMALIA: No.

LEONOR: Or perhaps somebody else . . .

AMALIA: (*Making the slightest concession.*) I don't think so. (*The doorbell rings.*

AMALIA *turns her head quickly and looks at the clock.*) Who can that be? . . . (*Curious, she walks to the rear of the stage.*) Where's Monica?

DAMASO: Helping the maid.

AMALIA: (*Walking to the foyer and opening the door.*) Oh, there you are! (SABINA *enters.*) Did you hear the bell?

SABINA: Yes, I looked out of the kitchen window to see who it was. It's a woman.

AMALIA: A woman?

SABINA: I think it's a woman. It's very dark out there. Shall I let her in?

AMALIA: (*Holding her by the arm.*) Wait . . . I don't feel like seeing anyone else. Just take a message. Do what you have to, and get rid of her.

SABINA: Yes, ma'am. (*She exits as* AMALIA *waits impatiently.* LORENZO *stirs and rouses slightly.*)

LORENZO: Isn't that darn coffee ready yet? (*No one answers. As all gaze stage rear, he wakes up completely.*) What's going on? (SABINA *returns and hesitates.*)

SABINA: She refuses to leave. I told her we have a sick person here. She claims to be a relative . . .

AMALIA: A relative?

SABINA: She says her name is Paula.

AMALIA: The fashion designer?

LEONOR: La-dee-da! The one who does the fancy *"robes et manteaux"*!

AMALIA: (*Irritated.*) What could she be thinking? Tell her I'm very sorry, but . . . No, I'll do it myself. (*Taking a few steps.*)

DAMASO: Don't you think it might be wiser to invite her in?

AMALIA: Why?

DAMASO: She's a family member, and it wouldn't be fair to dismiss her at a time like this. (*To the others.*) Don't you agree?

LEANDRO: If Amalia doesn't want to let her in, I see no reason why she should. Paula's only a distant relative.

DAMASO: Not so distant. She's your second cousin, and therefore she's related to Mauricio and the rest of us. (*He directs imploring glances all around.*)

121

AMALIA: That doesn't matter. (*Walking stage rear.*)

LORENZO: It just might matter to you. Don't you think it's strange that she should be coming here at this hour?

LEANDRO: They're trying to trick you! Ignore them! (**AMALIA** *looks from one to the other.*)

AMALIA: (*Her mind made up, she speaks to* **SABINA**.) Have her come in. (**SABINA** *exits, and there is a pause.*) Was she at the farewell party for Mateo?

LORENZO: No. (**SABINA** *enters and pauses.*)

SABINA: Miss Paula is here.

> **SABINA**, *stage rear, steps aside and observes curiously.* **LEANDRO** *and* **LORENZO** *rise as* **PAULA** *enters. Young and pretty,* **PAULA** *wears a low-cut and very elegant evening gown. Wishing to be pleasant without offending, given the circumstances, she smiles only slightly.*

PAULA: Good evening, everybody.

DAMASO: (*Expansively.*) Well, little Paula!

PAULA: (*To* **AMALIA**.) Perhaps you don't remember me. Uncle Mauricio introduced us a few years ago. (*Extending her hand.*)

AMALIA: (*Shaking hands with her.*) Won't you have a seat?

PAULA: Thank you. (*Accepting the chair that* **LORENZO** *courteously pulls out for her.* **LEONOR** *sits down and* **AMALIA** *remains standing.*) I came in case there's something I can do. (**LORENZO** *and* **LEANDRO** *sit down.*)

AMALIA: (*Puzzled.*) You knew . . . ?

PAULA: Well . . . yes. Actually, it was quite a coincidence. I was with some friends at a nightclub and, coincidentally, at the next table there was a sculptor I knew from the Fine Arts Academy . . . (**AMALIA** *and* **SABINA** *exchange alarmed glances.*) He had just found out. (**AMALIA** *trembles. She continues staring at* **PAULA**, *but her face betrays her anxiety.*) He told me what happened, and I got a taxi immediately.

DAMASO: It's strange how the news gets around . . .

LORENZO: But understandable in the case of a famous person. What did your friend tell you, Paula? (**AMALIA** *closes her eyes, almost hopeless now. Not knowing what to do,* **SABINA** *takes a few steps forward.*)

PAULA: It was disturbing. I guess he exaggerated.

AMALIA: (*Breathing heavily.*) What was it he exaggerated? (**LEANDRO**, *perturbed, watches her.*)

PAULA: He told me that . . . he was dying. I hope it isn't that serious.

AMALIA: (*Opening her eyes now and fixing her gaze on* **PAULA**.) He told you he was dying? (*She seems not to understand. Puzzled, she looks at* **SABINA** *as everyone else watches her.*)

LORENZO: Are you all right, Amalia?

AMALIA: (*Without taking her eyes off* **SABINA**, *she reacts.*) I'm fine. I was just thinking . . . Sabina, would you bring the coffee as soon as possible? And bring another cup.

SABINA: Yes, ma'am. (*She exits, stage rear.*)

AMALIA's *expression changes. She now knows that* PAULA *lied, but she doesn't know why. Recovering her composure, she regards* PAULA *coldly.*

PAULA: I'm assuming now that it isn't so serious . . .

AMALIA: It's true; he's dying.

PAULA: I'm so sorry.

AMALIA: (*Coldly.*) Thank you. (*Pacing.*) Your devotion to the family is very moving, especially considering that you and Mauricio hardly ever saw one another.

PAULA: That's unimportant. He's my uncle and . . .

AMALIA: A distant uncle.

PAULA: But still my uncle.

AMALIA: Perhaps. Tell me this: did you see him by any chance about six months ago?

PAULA: Me?

AMALIA: Yes, you.

PAULA: I don't think I've seen him for at least two years.

AMALIA: You don't think? Is that just a guess?

PAULA: (*Coldly.*) Why do you use that tone with me?

AMALIA: I find your devotion to the family intriguing. Six months ago, another uncle of yours, Mateo, left for America. Did you say good-bye to him?

PAULA: Yes, he called on the telephone and . . .

AMALIA: Oh; you said good-bye on the telephone. Perhaps you didn't love him as much as you loved Mauricio.

PAULA: I loved them both equally. Can I see him?

AMALIA: No.

PAULA: (*Hearing the insult implicit in the response and getting up.*) I see I'm not welcome here. I'm sorry.

AMALIA: (*Rapidly.*) On the contrary, Paula . . . Please stay. You got here just in time to take part in a curious little game. I have a feeling it will interest you.

PAULA: What are you talking about?

AMALIA: Mauricio didn't make a will. I can bring him out of the coma and get him to sign one before he dies. And I'll do just that, unless the people in this room tell me what I want to know. All that is unimportant to you, I suppose, because in either case, you won't inherit anything.

PAULA: That's right, and I don't need anything, either.

AMALIA: So you're neutral. (*Sharply.*) It looks that way, anyhow. You can be the impartial observer in this take-no-prisoners war. (*Raising her voice as she speaks to all present.*) The battle continues!

DAMASO: Don't get all excited again!

AMALIA: Before that clock strikes five, I demand that the guilty party come forward. (*Silence.*) Well? (*She goes to the door of the small foyer.*) Nobody wants to say anything. You think I want this so much that I'll be patient until time runs out. But I warn you: don't push me. (*She laughs.* **LEONOR** *and* **LORENZO,** *disconcerted, stand up.*) Because I *am* upset! I could tire of this game at any minute and just wake him up. . . . You idiots! Did you think I wasn't going to listen? War is war! (*She goes to the door and, with a sudden movement, puts her hand on the knob.*) Am I at the end of my rope? Think carefully, now. (*With an absolutely resolute tone.*) For the last time: what will it be? Are you going to talk or not? (**SABINA** *enters from stage rear carrying the coffee service on a tray.* **MONICA** *follows with a tray of cups.* **AMALIA** *looks at them with enormous* *irritation.* SABINA *stops, hesitates, and starts to go back.* AMALIA's *voice breaks as she speaks.*) No. Don't go. Leave those things on the dining room table. (LORENZO *rushes to open the folding door on the left and turns on the light in the dining room.* SABINA *and* MONICA *enter with the coffee.*)

DAMASO: (*To* AMALIA.) Please . . . Give us the time to have coffee. . . . Just a few minutes . . .

LORENZO: It's to your advantage, believe me.

AMALIA: (*Exhausted, pointing to the door.*) Go ahead . . . (LEONOR *and* DAMASO *enter.*)

LORENZO: (*From the door of the dining room.*) Aren't you coming, Paula?

PAULA: After you, Uncle Lorenzo. (*Approaching the dining room and waiting in the doorway.*)

LORENZO: How about you, Amalia?

AMALIA: I'll join you in a minute. (LORENZO *goes into the dining room. Exhausted,* AMALIA *leans against the foyer doorway.* LEANDRO *takes a few steps toward her.*) Please go in! (LEANDRO *turns and enters the dining room under* PAULA's *watchful eye. After a brief pause,* AMALIA, *on the verge of collapse, closes her eyes before painfully making her way toward the dining room. Before she arrives, the clock begins to strike five o'clock.* AMALIA, *stunned and full of dread, looks at the clock as she listens to the five chimes.*)

CURTAIN

ACT TWO

Someone has turned off the ceiling light. The clock now indicates exactly five fifteen, but probably nothing of interest has happened since five o'clock, as all have simply had coffee in the dining room, spoken little, and dealt with superficial matters as they prepared to continue the struggle. PAULA *may have learned another detail or two, and perhaps* AMALIA *has needed to repress womanly impatience and tears bordering on hysteria. None of this, however, is particularly important. The living room is empty, and through the half-open door stage left, a steady stream of light from the dining room is broken by a figure furtively sneaking away. It is* MONICA, *who slips silently into the living room without taking her eyes off the dining room as she tiptoes across the stage. As she approaches the foyer, she continues to make sure that no one is watching. She then quickly opens the foyer door and, without closing it, disappears inside. Shortly later,* MONICA *reappears, gruffly propelled by* SABINA *who holds in her left hand an empty cup and saucer.* SABINA *closes the door and confronts* MONICA.

MONICA: I want to see my uncle!

SABINA: Just see him, that's all? (MONICA *lowers her eyes.*) I've been watching you, and I don't like what I see. You're up to no good. Aren't you ashamed? You want to know what you're going to get, just like when you came around here before. You want to know what's in it for you!

MONICA: Please keep your voice down.

SABINA: (*Putting the cup and saucer on the table and grabbing her by the arm.*) I know you! Many a time I got rid of you before anybody knew you were here. Sabina wasn't born yesterday! And she's not blind, either! (AMALIA *comes out of the dining room and looks at them for a moment.*)

AMALIA: What's going on here?

MONICA: (*Throwing herself into* AMALIA's *arms.*) Aunt Amalia!

SABINA: Ask her why she tried to sneak into the bedroom again! (AMALIA *steps away from* MONICA *brusquely and looks at her, controlling the impulse to hug her again.*) If I hadn't been watching, she'd have gone in, the little . . .

AMALIA: That's enough, Sabina. Leave us alone here.

SABINA: (*Disgusted, she picks up the cup and saucer.*) Be on guard with her! Tonight, you shouldn't trust anyone. . . . Anyone! (*She exits stage rear.*)

AMALIA: Did you mean to wake him up? (*Lifting* MONICA's *chin.*)

MONICA: (*In a low voice.*) Yes.

AMALIA: (*Sweetly.*) Why? (*Taking her by the hand, she leads her silently to an armchair.*) Sit down. (*Sitting beside her.*) It's because of your parents, isn't it? You know they're the ones who spoke, and you're trying to save them the embarrassment of saying so. But a moment of shame isn't all that important. I'll keep my word. If they speak up, it will mean a comfortable future . . . for them and for you.

MONICA: No, no! I don't want to hear those things!

AMALIA: You're defending them, and that's not so bad. They're your parents, after all. (*Getting up.*) Go back with them.

MONICA: (*Begging her.*) Aunt Amalia . . .

AMALIA: I'm not really your aunt. (MONICA *begins to cry.* AMALIA *shivers a little. She approaches her and smoothes her hair, but* MONICA *rebelliously jerks her head away.*) Why are you crying?

MONICA: (*Choking back her tears.*) He's going to die. Don't you understand that? Maybe it's true, what they say, that you don't care. . . . My uncle is in there all alone, and here you are, talking to us instead of being with him, holding him. . . . That's awful! (*Calming slightly.*) What do I care about money! I hate money! My father is always talking about dignity, about not owing anybody anything . . . But when my mother made me come . . . to ask Uncle Mauricio for a little money, my father pretended not to know anything about it. Then at night, I'd hear them arguing about how much each of them was going to get. But if I refused to come, it was worse. . . . Then my mother would hit me and threaten to make me work as someone's servant. And now, my uncle is dying, and you won't even let me kiss him good-bye.

AMALIA: (*Touched.*) You loved him that much?

MONICA: And I loved you, too. It was embarrassing to come here for money, but at the same time, I liked it, because you two were so different from the others. You were . . . so nice to me. That's why I wanted to call you Aunt Amalia . . . because lots of times I felt like . . . I really didn't have a family.

AMALIA: (*Leaning affectionately toward her.*) Monica . . .

MONICA: (*Getting up.*) Don't touch me! It kills me to tell you this, because I don't want to love you anymore. (*Retreating.*) You offer money, you get dressed up, you put on jewelry, and you're determined to find out I-don't-know-what! All that means you don't love him.

127

AMALIA: Monica, my child . . .

MONICA: Don't call me that! I'm not your child! (*Brief pause.*)

AMALIA: (*Very serious.*) I've cried, I swear I have. And when this night is over, I promise I'll cry again. I'll cry and grieve for him the rest of my life, but not right now.

MONICA: (*Beside herself.*) Why not?

AMALIA: (*Stammering.*) You wouldn't understand. I'll tell you . . . (*In a confidential tone.*) something you don't know . . . (*Looking toward the dining room.*)

MONICA: (*Encouraging her, in tone and gestures.*) What, Aunt Amalia? What? (*Brief pause.*)

AMALIA: (*Her expression hardens.*) No. I can't tell you yet. Because I don't trust you either! (*Agitated and turning away abruptly.*)

MONICA: (*Sadly.*) It's no use. I'm so alone.

AMALIA: (*Harshly, and without looking at her.*) So am I. And so is he. We'll all be terribly alone until this night is over. Perhaps then we can find the love we need, or perhaps we'll lose it forever. (*Turning toward her.*) Meanwhile, we're surrounded by suspicion and deceit. Loneliness is our lot in life. Now, go splash some cold water on those eyes. They look awful.

MONICA *sighs and walks stage rear. Before exiting, she makes a subtle gesture of conciliation that* AMALIA *chooses to ignore.* AMALIA *stands lost in thought for a moment before reacting. After a nervous glance at the clock, she goes toward the dining room. Before she gets there, however, the door opens and* LEANDRO *emerges, closing the door behind him.*

AMALIA: Open the door. It's time for them to come back.

LEANDRO: I want to talk to you.

AMALIA: Do you know something?

LEANDRO: Maybe.

AMALIA: All right. What is it?

LEANDRO: I know that you should wake him up now, because they're not going to tell you anything.

AMALIA: Why not?

LEANDRO: You're chasing phantoms! They'll tell you any little trivial thing to stall! Save yourself the agony!

AMALIA: That's my business.

LEANDRO: Don't you see they don't deserve your patience?

AMALIA: Your father is one of those people, Leandro.

LEANDRO: (*Darkly.*) My father . . . You know how my father is.

AMALIA: Was he the one?

LEANDRO: You're obsessed! I'm not talking about that right now. I'm referring to what you're about to do, which is give Mauricio's fortune to my father and the others, and they never loved him.

AMALIA: And what about you? Did you love him? (*Brief pause.*)

LEANDRO: (*Lowering his eyes and standing back.*) At first, I did. We were friendly, because we were about the same age. He was successful, and I was just a hack writer. That's hard for a man to take, Amalia. It's something you couldn't understand.

AMALIA: I've lived around artists. . . . I do know about those things.

LEANDRO: I'm not complaining about his success. I consider it deserved. What hurts . . . the thing I can't stand . . . is that I don't deserve failure. I've been pushed aside, looked down on by all those pedantic types who don't know how to put two sentences together, but they're novelists, playwrights, and newspaper editors! And here I am, assigned to weddings and baptisms! And I know I'm a better writer than any of them! (*Slowly.*) And then . . . , and then . . . , fate smiles on Mauricio. He gets everything, and I get nothing. Why is that?

AMALIA: Hush. You're hurting me.

LEANDRO: He even got you. Why?

AMALIA: Don't talk about that!

LEANDRO: How can I not talk about it? It's an open wound that won't heal, Amalia. Let me air it, even though you refuse to help me . . .

AMALIA: (*Agitated.*) Please . . . Leandro.

LEANDRO: I'm sorry. I just wanted to support you; be your ally against them, and against him, too. (*Pointing toward the foyer.*)

AMALIA: What are you saying?

LEANDRO: (*Coming very close to her.*) Did the "Silent One" have the right to be silent with you, too? Can a man really keep things from the woman he loves? And if he does, why? Because he's shy, you say. But I have a feeling it's distrust; maybe indifference. I have just bared my soul to you, because I love you. Yes, I love you.

AMALIA *moves away quickly and goes toward the foyer, looking emotionally at the door. When she looks at* LEANDRO, *her expression softens almost automatically.* LEANDRO *follows her, takes her hand, and brings his face very close to hers; to kiss her? Perhaps this idea crosses both their minds. But* AMALIA *recovers her composure, and her mouth tightens with decision. A furtive glance in the direction of the foyer suggests the presence of Mauricio in her thoughts.*

AMALIA: I was just thinking that two people have declared their love for me tonight.

LEANDRO: What?

AMALIA: And you're the second one to ask me to wake him up. Please let go of my hand.

LEANDRO: Amalia!

AMALIA: Let go of me! (*He does so.*) I'd like to know which one of you is trying to deceive me.

LEANDRO: (*Hurt.*) You don't believe me.

AMALIA: I can't trust anybody!

LEANDRO: (*Walking stage left.*) I'll remind you of just one thing: I never asked Mauricio for a penny. (*The dining room door opens slightly as* PAULA *enters, eying them suspiciously.*)

PAULA: Am I interrupting?

AMALIA: On the contrary. You got here just in time to offer an opinion. Leandro thinks I should awaken Mauricio immediately. What do you think?

PAULA: It's none of my business.

AMALIA: Even so, give me your . . . neutral position.

PAULA: (*After a slight hesitation.*) Perhaps you shouldn't wake him up right away. Perhaps not.

AMALIA: And why do you say that?

PAULA: Because you have to finish what you started.

LEANDRO: Amalia really doesn't know what she wants!

PAULA: (*Coldly.*) I don't agree. I think she knows very well what she wants.

AMALIA: Do you always finish what you start?

PAULA: Just like you do.

AMALIA: No matter what?

PAULA: No matter what! (*A brief pause.* AMALIA *approaches the dining room and abruptly opens the door.*)

AMALIA: (*Dryly.*) Would everyone come in, please? (PAULA *drifts toward the rear as* LEANDRO *watches her with open hostility.* LORENZO *is the first to enter, bringing with him a cup of coffee.* LEONOR *and* DAMASO *follow, the latter with a glass of wine.*)

LORENZO: (*Affably.*) This is my third cup of coffee, Amalia. But it's no use. Forgive me if I get sleepy. Coffee doesn't wake me up or steady my nerves anymore. (*He sits down in a comfortable chair behind the table, savoring the coffee. As they enter,* LEONOR *and* DAMASO *sneak glances at the clock.* SABINA *enters stage rear and turns on the overhead light.* LEONOR *takes her seat.*)

SABINA: Shall I take the coffee away, ma'am?

AMALIA: Wait a little while. Did you take some in to the nurse?

SABINA: Yes, ma'am. She asked about giving Mr. Mauricio that shot. (*A general reaction among those present as* DAMASO *crosses right and stops short.*)

AMALIA: No, not just yet.

SABINA: That's what I told her.

DAMASO *fairly gulps his wine before leaving the glass in the closest place as he takes a seat downstage near the foyer.*

LEONOR: (*Sweetly, trying to change the subject.*) Where's Monica? I don't see her.

AMALIA: (*Smiling.*) She's washing up. (*To* SABINA.) Ask her to join us.

LEONOR: I don't need her . . . I was just wondering . . .

SABINA: Yes, ma'am. (*She exits stage rear.* PAULA *sits down at the table, while* LEANDRO *takes a seat near the large window.*)

AMALIA: (*Looking around at everyone.*) Five people. It's not so hard. All you have to do is remember who took Mauricio aside and talked to him alone. Do you remember, Leandro?

LEANDRO: It's not all that simple, Amalia. I'd have to think about it.

LEONOR: Could Leandro be one of those people?

LEANDRO: (*Forcing a smile.*) I was just going to say that, Leonor. Naturally, I spoke to Mauricio a minute alone.

LEONOR: For quite a while, I'd say. (**MONICA** *enters stage rear and sits on the end of sofa opposite* **LEANDRO**.)

LEANDRO: (*Dryly.*) It was only a few minutes. Saying good-bye to Mateo had made us all nostalgic, and we started talking about old times. That's all. (*Pause.*) Believe me, Amalia. (**AMALIA** *looks at him without speaking.*) I wasn't the only one who took him aside.

AMALIA: Who else did?

LEANDRO: (*Gesturing toward the married couple.*) They spoke to him, too, now that I think of it.

DAMASO: But not alone! We spoke to him in the group . . .

AMALIA: And what did you say to him?

DAMASO: (*Looking at his wife, who avoids his eyes.*) That we were sorry to see Mateo leave; that it was a pity . . . (**MONICA**, *intrigued, gets up and approaches.*)

AMALIA: That's a lie.

DAMASO: (*Getting up.*) Just a minute! That's an offensive word. You forget that I'm a respected person. I've even been decorated.

AMALIA: (*Sternly insistent.*) What did you talk to him about? (*Walking over to him.*) You're not telling me anything.

DAMASO: (*Walking downstage.*) You've insulted me.

AMALIA: Or is it that you just don't want to tell me? (**DAMASO** *crosses his arms in dignified fashion.*) Or should I tell the nurse to do what she just asked about? (*Approaching* **LEONOR**.) You're the losers if I do. Think of those millions in commissions that just came in from New York and Paris. That's a pretty good amount of money. (*Thoughtfully.*) Perhaps it's silly to wait around any longer . . . in exchange for a few words.

Before Dawn (Madrid, 2001), Act II, Leandro (Francisco Rojas), Monica (Victoria Alvas), Lorenzo (Manuel de Blas), Damaso (Mariano Vanacio), Leonor (Sonsoles Benedicto), and Amalia (Kitti Manver)

LEONOR: (*Getting up, excited.*) Go ahead and tell her, Damaso!

AMALIA: (*Going rapidly over to her.*) You tell me yourself!

DAMASO: Don't say anything! (*To* **AMALIA.**) It's not what you're looking for. We told Mauricio that his attitude toward Mateo was admirable; that the generosity he showed his family honored him. That's all.

LEONOR: That's a pretty way of saying (*To* **AMALIA.**) we asked him for money! We asked him for money one more time!

DAMASO: You're the one who asked! (*Agitated.*) I don't stoop to that kind of thing!

LEONOR: Of course not! Why should you, when you have your daughter—and me, too—to do it for you? You just mention helping the family, and out go our hands!

MONICA: Mama!

LEONOR: We're beggars! That's what you have turned us into!

DAMASO: Leonor!

LEONOR: (*Going toward him.*) Beggars and slaves! Slaves to take care of you and your clothes; even lie for you! (*Speaking to everybody.*) He honors us by making us his servants. And we're supposed to be grateful, because he's from a good family. He's a gentleman who even has a medal. (*Furious, she points to her husband's lapel.*) A medal you bought at the flea market! You started wearing it fifteen years ago when you were turned down for a real one! (*She pauses, exhausted.* **DAMASO** *clenches his fists and looks at her with infinite anger. He raises an arm, about to strike her.*)

MONICA: (*Anguished.*) No . . . no . . .

AMALIA: (*Standing between them and taking them both by the arm.*) Very edifying, but not enough. Did either of you say anything about me? (**LEONOR** *takes a step back, disconcerted. Without letting go of her wrist,* **AMALIA** *steps back with her.* **DAMASO,** *humiliated, slumps into a chair.*)

LEONOR: No. We left then, and . . .

DAMASO: And you stayed behind a few minutes, talking to him.

LEONOR: (*Pointing to her husband.*) He told me to! See if he denies it!

AMALIA: (*Shoving her toward a chair and making her sit down.*) And then you told him something about me, didn't you?

LEONOR: No. I tried to get some more money . . . , but it was no use.

AMALIA: You lied then, just like you're lying now!

LEONOR: All right! He did give me a little money that I didn't tell you about!

DAMASO: That's nothing new!

LEONOR: If I'd given you the money, what would we have eaten the next day?

AMALIA: And after that, you talked to him about me.

LEONOR: (*Getting hysterical.*) Leave me alone! I didn't tell him anything! Are you trying to drive me crazy? (*She rattles her bracelets, and* AMALIA *takes up a position behind her, which alarms her even more.*)

AMALIA: (*Softly.*) This is like chasing a little fish in a tank with my bare hands. I've almost trapped what I want, here or there, in words of one or the other, and then it slips away. Then suddenly, I have it cornered again, and it's almost mine. (*Placing her hands solidly on* LEONOR'*s shoulders.*) Speak up, Leonor. It's not hard, and it's going to be so rewarding. You'll have a nice home, maids, things you've wanted all your life. Then you can stop ruining your hands with all that washing and sewing. Look at my hands. (*Holding a hand up to her face.*) Clean, soft, manicured. Yours could be just like that.

DAMASO: (*Looking nervously at his wife.*) Remember your promise, Amalia!

AMALIA: I'll keep my promise. (*To* LEONOR.) And you can have clothes like mine. You can take care of your skin and nails, damaged by slaving over the stove and sink. . . . (*Bringing her face very close to hers.*) Look at the jewels in my earrings, my necklace. You like my necklace, don't you? It'll be yours. You'll have jewels; fine, expensive ones. Then you can get rid of all those ugly brass bracelets and that cheap costume jewelry. (*The clock strikes the half hour.*)

LEONOR: (*Angry, she gets up and faces her.*) Yes! I'm the one who did it!

AMALIA: (*Triumphant.*) Now we're getting somewhere!

PAULA *has gotten up, as has* LORENZO. MONICA, *exhausted, sits down on the sofa.*

LEONOR: (*Furious, rather than fearful now,* AMALIA, *still looking triumphant, goes back toward the large window followed by* LEONOR.) I said things to him about you; yes, about the things you just mentioned! I talked about your clothes, your jewels, and all the things you've taken—stolen, really—from the rest of us! I talked about the things you dared to insult me with just now! Yes, insult!

Who do you think you are, anyway? You're just a common . . . (AMALIA, *who had encouraged her to talk, now winces;* LEONOR *has touched a nerve.* DAMASO *gets up.*)

AMALIA: Don't say that!

LEONOR: Yes! A common whore! That's what you are! And that's what I told Mauricio! I said he wouldn't help his own family, but he bought jewels for his whore!

AMALIA: Don't say that!

LEONOR: You wanted to know, didn't you? So now you know! He laughed when I said that, but I could tell it got to him. And what about you? Are you going to laugh, too? I don't think so! (*Laughing.*) I'm the one laughing! You see? I'm the one! (*Striking her chest, she lets out a discordant laugh.*) Because I'm respectable! A lady! (*After giving* AMALIA *a triumphant look,* LEONOR *returns to her place with a great rattling of bracelets.* AMALIA *needs to sit down.* MONICA *runs to the dining room.*)

DAMASO: (*To* AMALIA.) Are you happy now? Did you get what you wanted?

AMALIA: (*Darkly.*) I don't know.

DAMASO: What do you mean, you don't know? (AMALIA, *sad and deep in thought, makes no reply.* MONICA *comes out of the dining room, stirring a cup of coffee.*)

LEONOR: (*Bitterly.*) I don't recall asking for a cup of coffee, Monica. But that's very thoughtful of you. Bring it here.

MONICA: (*Nervously.*) It's not for you, mama . . . (*She approaches* AMALIA *rapidly and holds the cup out to her.*)

LEONOR: (*Furious.*) I said bring it here!

MONICA: (*Not daring to look at her.*) Wait, mama. (AMALIA, *grateful, sips the coffee.*)

LEONOR: Monica! (MONICA *ignores her.*)

AMALIA: (*Timidly.*) You didn't say anything else to Mauricio?

LEONOR: (*Disdainfully.*) Wasn't that enough? (*To her daughter, who now removes* AMALIA's *coffee cup.*) Would you bring your mother a cup of coffee now, please?

MONICA: (*Hastily.*) Of course, mama! (*She rushes to the dining room. During a brief pause,* DAMASO *furtively removes the medal from his lapel and, after looking at it bitterly, slips it into his pocket.*)

PAULA: (*Getting up, she approaches* LEONOR *as she keeps her eyes on* AMALIA.) Would you allow me to help you? Perhaps I can find the question you don't dare ask.

AMALIA: (*Shocked.*) You?

PAULA: Yes, me. (MONICA *returns with the cup of coffee she offers her mother.*)

LEONOR: (*Sipping the coffee and then making a face.*) You didn't put any sugar in it!

MONICA: Oh, I'm sorry, mama. (*She rushes back to the kitchen with the cup and returns shortly, stirring the coffee.*)

PAULA: (*To* LEONOR.) What you told Uncle Mauricio about Amalia wasn't important. He already knew how you felt. You must have told him about something new; something he didn't know.

LEONOR: What do you mean?

PAULA: Perhaps some sexual indiscretion that you attributed to Amalia?

AMALIA: But there hasn't been anything like that!

PAULA: (*Dryly.*) I would expect you to say that.

LEONOR: If I had said such a thing, I wouldn't mind admitting it. (*Taking the cup of coffee from* MONICA *and drinking it without protest this time. Relieved,* MONICA *approaches* AMALIA.)

PAULA: (*Looking at* AMALIA *with a malicious smile as she takes out a cigarette.*) So you mentioned no name. Would you give me a light (*Pointedly, as she directs the question.*), Leandro? (AMALIA *looks at* LEANDRO, *who rushes to light the cigarette.*) Thank you. Who could she have mentioned, do you suppose, Amalia? (AMALIA *does not respond.*) Who?

DAMASO: (*Authoritatively.*) How is that important? The fact is that Leonor has spoken up, and Amalia now knows what she wanted to know.

AMALIA: (*Suspiciously, to* LEONOR.) Did you mention someone's name?

LEONOR: No!

DAMASO: (*Impatiently.*) And that's that! Now you have to keep your word. (*As he speaks,* AMALIA *turns to look at the clock.* MONICA *timidly whispers something in her ear.*)

AMALIA: What's that? (*Flustered,* MONICA *repeats the message.* AMALIA *moves forward and stares fixedly at* LORENZO.) You were the one?

LORENZO: I was the one who what?

AMALIA: Monica says you also took Mauricio aside. (*All look at* **LORENZO,** *who smiles as he stands up slowly.*)

LORENZO: Who saw me, Monica? Were you the only one?

MONICA: (*Taking refuge behind* **AMALIA.**) You stopped him in the hall when everybody else was in the foyer or the living room! You took him into the bedroom and whispered something to him. That's what happened! It's true! (*A general reaction among those present.* **AMALIA** *places her coffee cup on the table.*)

LORENZO: All right. I guess I'll have to tell you.

AMALIA: Yes, please do!

LORENZO: It's all pretty clear, Amalia. I . . . asked for money, too. (**AMALIA** *seems disappointed.*) But not like **LEONOR.** I didn't talk about putting food on the table. I had bigger plans. Of course, he didn't give me what I wanted. We walked out of the bedroom (*Looking at* **MONICA.**), and there was the kid, spying on us. I was perfectly aware of it. I left Mauricio then and went into the living room with the others. . . . Meanwhile, Monica went up and talked to him. (*As he stops speaking,* **LEONOR** *and* **DAMASO** *exchange a nervous glance.* **AMALIA** *turns around and looks steadily at* **MONICA,** *who hangs her head.* **LEONOR** *starts to say something, but changes her mind.*)

PAULA: (*Breaking the stark silence.*) That's very interesting. (*Taking a seat near the large window.*)

AMALIA: Can it be? Are you that little fish that keeps slipping away? (*Taking* **MONICA** *by the arm.*) Speak up!

LEONOR: (*Taking a few steps toward her.*) No!

MONICA: (*Trying to free herself.*) You're hurting me!

AMALIA: (*Spinning her around impatiently.*) Are you going to tell me or not?

DAMASO: Wait, Amalia.

LEONOR: Go ahead! Spit it out!

MONICA: No! I don't want to!

AMALIA: Tell me!

MONICA: (*Bowing her head.*) Mama told me to . . . ask him for more money. And he said I had a lot of nerve! (**DAMASO** *and* **LEONOR** *lower their eyes, ashamed.*

LEANDRO *walks toward the hall as he takes out a cigarette.* LORENZO, *fatigued, rubs his face and eyes as he sits down.*)

AMALIA: (*Emotionally.*) Forgive me! (*She embraces the young girl, but* MONICA *squirms free, blushing with shame. Hiding her eyes with the back of her hand she escapes to the dining room.* AMALIA *tries but fails to stop her and stands with an expression of pity and frustration.*)

PAULA: And the slippery little fish wiggles free again. (DAMASO *sits down at the table.*)

AMALIA: Yes, leaving behind only a money trail. That demon money. (*She turns around slowly, lost in thought.*) Could I have been mistaken? (AMALIA *walks slowly stage right as* LEONOR *approaches the dining room and peeks in.*)

MONICA: (*Her voice, offstage.*) Go away! I don't want to see anybody! (LEONOR, *disconcerted, steps back and goes to where* LORENZO *is sitting and leans on the back of his chair.* AMALIA *turns her head in the direction of the dining room.*) Wake him up! Ask him! Don't torture me anymore!

AMALIA: (*Turning her head slowly and talking to herself.*) Ask him. (*She approaches the foyer and looks at the door in anguish.* DAMASO *straightens up nervously.*)

PAULA: (*Standing up and approaching, with apparent nonchalance, the foyer door.*) You ought to get to the bottom of this.

AMALIA: I've reached rock bottom already. As you see, it's no use.

PAULA: Don't give up. (*Everyone observes nervously the look of concentration on* AMALIA's *face as her eyes remain glued to the door.* DAMASO *finally stands up.*)

LEANDRO: (*Imperiously.*) Go in!

PAULA: (*Going rapidly to the door and protecting it with her body.*) No!

DAMASO: What? (AMALIA *looks at* PAULA *in surprise.* LEANDRO *represses a gesture of impatience.*)

AMALIA: Why not?

PAULA: (*Repentant and biting her lip.*) Because you've got to get to the bottom of this!

AMALIA: What if I don't want to?

PAULA: (*Nervously.*) Do it anyway!

AMALIA: (*Confronting* PAULA.) Your role in all this has never been clear. And now I know I was mistaken when I thought of only five people. Because there are six people here, not five! And all of you have come for some reason. (*Her question resembles the cracking of a whip.*) Why? (PAULA *remains silent as* AMALIA *approaches her.*) Get out of my way!

PAULA: You're not going in there!

AMALIA: (*Struggling with her to get her to talk.*) Get out of the way!

LEANDRO: (*To* PAULA.) Are you crazy?

PAULA: Crazy? I've been watching you people all night! I've seen your little glances and heard your mutterings. (AMALIA *releases her and listens attentively.*)

LEANDRO: Hush!

PAULA: And just what should I hush? Your lies? Your selfishness? Your double dealing? Oh, I understood everything when I called the newspaper.

LEANDRO: You called the paper?

PAULA: (*More and more agitated.*) I called at four AM. They told me not to worry, that you'd be here shortly, that you were already on the way. They confused me with someone here who had called you before. They told me what had happened. . . . I know you! You got over here right away to get as much as you could! Paula was unimportant! The big moment had come, and it was time to sacrifice Paula. (*To* AMALIA.) But I don't let people walk all over me! Absolutely not!

AMALIA: (*Offended.*) Why are you telling me this? Why?

PAULA: You think I don't know what you two were doing behind his back?

AMALIA: That's not true!

PAULA: That's what you were afraid somebody had told Mauricio!

LEANDRO: Will you shut up? . . .

PAULA: Go ahead! Hit me! You've done worse things.

LEANDRO: Amalia, I swear to you, I . . . (*Irritated,* AMALIA *turns her back on him.*)

PAULA: Aren't you going to tell her you love her; that I was just a little fling, and that she should believe you? Go ahead and say it! And I have other things to tell her, too.

LEANDRO: (*Serious.*) You're making me do this, because I would never offend you voluntarily. Consider it said, Amalia. (*Depressed and retiring toward the rear.*)

PAULA: (*Approaching* **AMALIA**.) But you'll never take him away from me! He won't marry you without your money, and you won't ever get that money, because you won't wake him up. (**AMALIA** *turns around to look at her.*) Go on; I dare you to go in there. (*Pointing toward the foyer.*) Shall I open the door for you? (*Going to the door and putting her hand on the doorknob.*)

DAMASO: (*Nervously.*) Paula . . .

PAULA: (*Laughing.*) Don't worry! Haven't you people caught on yet? I just did! She doesn't do it because she's afraid that he really might not sign a will that gives her everything! Because she doesn't know whether he believed she was unfaithful or not! (*Defiantly.*) Well? Shall I open the door, Amalia? (**SABINA** *enters from the rear and stands by the door.*)

AMALIA: (*Imploring, almost defeated now.*) I swear to you that between Leandro and me, there has never been anything!

PAULA: How valuable is the word of a whore?

AMALIA: (*Her face loses composure.*) Don't say that!

PAULA: (*Merciless.*) Leonor got that one right: a whore. (**AMALIA** *seems to wilt under the insult.* **SABINA** *goes quickly to her side.*)

SABINA: Please come with me a moment, ma'am. I need to consult with you. (**AMALIA**, *distressed, leans on her shoulder.*) Come this way. (*She leads her stage rear as* **MONICA** *appears in the doorway of the dining room.*)

AMALIA: They're getting the better of me, Sabina.

SABINA: Don't say that!

LEANDRO: (*Approaching.*) Don't give up. I'm coming with you. (**AMALIA** *motions him away sadly.*) Please let me come with you!

SABINA: You stay here with the others! You're one of them!

MONICA: (*Running to* **AMALIA**.) But I'm not like them, Sabina! Let me be with her! (**AMALIA** *now leans on her as well.*)

LEONOR: (*To* **DAMASO**.) Do you see what our daughter is doing?

DAMASO: Leave her alone.

LEONOR: (*To* **MONICA**.) Go back to your place!

AMALIA: (*Exhausted.*) Let her come with us, Sabina. I want her with us. (**SABINA** *grumbles as the three get to the door.*)

SABINA: (*Glancing critically at all before exiting.*) When you come back, don't give it any more thought. Have them give Mr. Mauricio that shot. He loves you. He can't possibly believe those awful lies. (**AMALIA** *casts a desperate look at the clock as the three exit. Pause.* **LORENZO** *nods off again.*)

LEANDRO: (*To* **PAULA.**) I'll never forgive you for this!

PAULA: I'll never forgive you either!

LEONOR: (*Suddenly optimistic.*) Let's celebrate! Everything seems to work out in the end. We're the winners here! (*Going over to* **LORENZO** *and rattling her bracelets in his ear.*) Wake up, you zombie! We've beaten her out! (**LORENZO** *rouses slightly.*) We're going to be rich, Damaso!

DAMASO: (*Serious.*) When she comes back, they're going to wake him up. You heard Sabina.

LEANDRO: (*Maliciously.*) Maybe she won't have to; what with all the shouting around here, maybe he's awake.

LEONOR: (*Alarmed.*) What? No, that can't be. The nurse would have said something. And if she wakes him up, we'll all tell him about her!

LORENZO: (*Calmly.*) And she'll tell him about us.

DAMASO: Then you think the way I do.

LORENZO: (*Getting up and speaking solemnly.*) Yes, she's going to wake him up; no doubt about it. She's not getting anywhere here, and in there she can win it all. She'll do it, that is, if what she says is true.

DAMASO: What do you mean?

LORENZO: For the past hour, I've been wondering about Mauricio's true condition.

LEONOR: He's dying!

LORENZO: That's what she tells us. But the nurse seems awfully calm. . . . Looks like she's planning to spend some time here. Maybe he just has a bad cold or something. (*Looking at them.*) I think we ought to talk to her, now that Amalia is out of the room.

LEONOR: I'll do it!

LORENZO: No. You stay here and keep watch. (*Pointing to the rear door.*) If we're really going to do this, that is.

DAMASO: Let's do it right now!

LORENZO: Are you with us, Paula?

PAULA: Of course! (*Sitting down comfortably by the large window.*)

LORENZO: Aren't you going to open the door, Damaso?

DAMASO: You do it.

LORENZO: I suppose my dear son is also interested in knowing what's going on.

LEANDRO: (*Disdainful.*) Go ahead and open the door. Maybe that will wake him up. (*He goes to the table and leans against it with crossed arms.*)

LEONOR: (*Stage rear.*) Hurry up!

DAMASO: Do you hear anything?

LEONOR: No. (LORENZO *opens the foyer door.*)

DAMASO: (*In a low voice.*) You won't call her, will you?

LEANDRO: No. (*He pauses. Then he signals for the* NURSE *to approach. He makes an affirmative gesture with his head and repeats it, as though the* NURSE *had asked him a question using sign language. All wait nervously.*)

LEONOR: (*In a choking voice.*) Hurry!

DAMASO: S-h-h-h! (*The* NURSE *appears at the door of the foyer.*)

NURSE: Did you want to see me?

LORENZO: (*Through the half-open door of the foyer.*) Excuse us. . . . We just wanted to ask you a couple of questions . . .

NURSE: Yes?

LORENZO: Was the attack really serious?

NURSE: Extremely serious. Hardly anybody survives something like that. (*The brothers look at each other, relieved.*)

LORENZO: Isn't it possible to prolong life a little by combining stimulants with other medications?

NURSE: We always do everything possible, but unfortunately, in this case, nothing worked.

LORENZO: Yes, of course, what a pity. (*Clearing his throat.*) But I guess we should never give up hope of saving a dying person. (*Intrigued by the conversation,* **LEONOR** *moves away from her post and edges closer and closer.*) Isn't it possible even for a hopelessly ill person to recover miraculously and live many more years?

NURSE: Those things do happen, but unfortunately not here. (*Considering the fact obvious.*)

LORENZO: Are you sure about that? (*Brief pause.*)

NURSE: (*Offended.*) I'm sorry if you doubt it. All I can say is that the doctor did everything he could to save him. (*From the rear,* **AMALIA,** **SABINA,** *and* **MONICA** *enter.* **AMALIA** *almost faints from fright on seeing the* **NURSE.** **PAULA** *sees her and gets up.* **LEONOR** *turns around, frightened.*) Quite frankly, it bothers me that you could think otherwise.

DAMASO: Oh, no, you misunderstood.

NURSE: And I prefer it that way. Now if you'll excuse me. (*She returns, almost slamming the door behind her. Wide-eyed,* **AMALIA** *comes forward hesitantly.* **SABINA** *follows her closely.*)

LORENZO: Forgive us. As you will understand, we wanted to confirm that what you said about his condition was accurate.

AMALIA: (*Speaking with difficulty.*) Yes.

LORENZO: But you don't look any better. You're still very pale.

AMALIA: It's nothing.

DAMASO: You should get some rest. What's the point of going on with this?

AMALIA: (*Believing that they know everything.*) I suppose there isn't any. (*They look at one other, happy with this sudden change.*)

LEONOR: (*Almost kindly, now.*) You're exhausted. Why don't you lie down?

AMALIA: Not yet. I understand that I've lost the battle. I couldn't think of everything. (*With a tearful voice.*) All I can do now is appeal to your compassion . . . compassion you may find hard to give. I'm begging you now to tell me what was said.

DAMASO: But there's nothing to tell . . .

AMALIA: Out of pity, then. (*Joining her hands in an imploring gesture.*)

LEONOR: (*With a dismissive rattle of bracelets.*) Are we going to start that again? We thought you had given up the idea of waking him up.

AMALIA: (*Blinking.*) What?

LEONOR: I get it! The little drama is still on, isn't it? After the threats come the tears, right?

LORENZO: (*Doubtful.*) Leonor, listen . . .

LEONOR: (*Trying a trick.*) It's no use. The nurse said . . . (AMALIA *looks at her in alarm.*) giving him a shot wasn't a good idea! That could kill him!

LEANDRO: She said nothing of the kind. You can still revive him, and you should! LEONOR *puts her hand over her mouth, regretting having forgotten about* LEANDRO. LORENZO, *annoyed, shakes his head.* AMALIA *takes a deep breath. Her face reflects tremendous relief. She looks at* SABINA, *who has had a similar reaction, and then looks at the clock. She walks toward* LEONOR *and is about to say something when suddenly her knees buckle under her.* SABINA *and* LEANDRO *keep her from falling.*

LEANDRO: Amalia!

MONICA: (*Rushing toward her.*) Aunt Amalia!

SABINA: Bring her this way! Into the dining room! (*Assisted by others,* LEANDRO *carries* AMALIA *to the dining room.* LORENZO *stands apart downstage right, lost in thought.*)

LEANDRO: Call the nurse. (MONICA *runs to obey.*)

SABINA: (*Stopping her.*) No! She'll be all right with a little brandy. (MONICA *stops.*)

LEANDRO: Is there any ammonia?

MONICA: I'll look for some! (*Running stage rear.*)

LEONOR: (*To* DAMASO, *before going into the dining room.*) Well, we finally won.

LEONOR *and* DAMASO *exit, leaving* LORENZO *alone.* LORENZO'*s expression changes completely now, becoming hard and determined. He goes to the dining room door and closes it softly before crossing stage right. Halfway there, he stops, and the door opens.* DAMASO *comes in and looks at him.*

DAMASO: Aren't you coming?

LORENZO: (*With a negative gesture.*) No. Do you want something?

DAMASO: No. (*He goes to the table and takes out a cigarette.* LORENZO *taps his foot impatiently.*) What's the matter with you? (LORENZO *seems to decide something.*

He goes to the dining room door and closes it without making a sound.) What do you want?

LORENZO: Can't you guess?

DAMASO: (*Putting out the cigarette.*) Huh?

LORENZO: (*Approaching him.*) We have very little time. As soon as she revives, she'll wake Mauricio. Then there's no way out.

DAMASO: (*Trembling without knowing why.*) She said she wasn't going to do that. . . .

LORENZO: But she will, the minute she comes to! You think I'm stupid? I've had my eye on her all night. I can see she's reached her limit and is about to snap. A little more, and millions fly out the window and away from us, unless . . .

DAMASO: Unless what?

LORENZO: Unless he just doesn't wake up, if you get my drift.

DAMASO: I don't want to hear anything like that. I'm leaving.

LORENZO: (*Turning him around furiously.*) Idiot! We're not young anymore. What else is there in life if we don't get this? It's ours, and you're just going to toss it away because you're scared?

DAMASO: It's better just to confess . . .

LORENZO: Confess? Who should confess?

DAMASO: (*Timidly.*) You.

LORENZO: I didn't say anything! Besides, she's going to wake him up anyway. Do you really trust her?

DAMASO: (*Dejected.*) I wouldn't dare do what you're thinking.

LORENZO: You're not going to do anything. None of us will do anything. He's going to die, that's for sure. What it comes down to is . . . just speeding the process up a little. If he couldn't breathe for a few seconds, he'd die right away. (**DAMASO** *looks at him terrified.*) Come on! Get your act together and help me! There's no time to lose. The clock is running out for us, too. Look, Damaso, we're talking about a lot of money here. Everything will be possible again. We might even turn that lie about your medal into the truth!

DAMASO: I won't know what to do!

LORENZO: Of course you will. (*Taking him by the arm.*) Listen. While I go in there, you keep watch from the foyer. I'll keep the bedroom door slightly open. If something happens, scratch on the door.

DAMASO: What about the nurse?

LORENZO: That's easy. The lady of the house has gotten sick, so she's busy. (**DAMASO**, *defeated, lowers his head.*) Ready? (**DAMASO** *nods weakly.* **LORENZO** *releases him and walks quickly toward the foyer. Suddenly, he stops.*) S-h-h-h! S-h-h-h! (*The door opens and the* **NURSE** *enters. She zips up a small cosmetics bag as she prepares to leave.*)

NURSE: (*Glancing in a routine manner at the clock.*) Where's the lady of the house?

LEONOR: In the dining room.

NURSE: I wanted to tell her I'm leaving. It's late, and I'd like to freshen up . . .

LORENZO: (*Quickly.*) Oh, that's fine. (*Looking at his brother.*) Don't worry. We'll tell her.

NURSE: Thank you. Then if you'll excuse me. (*Returning stage rear where she had entered.*)

LORENZO: The hell with it! Let's go. (*They go into the foyer, leaving the door ajar. No one is onstage for a few moments. Then* **MONICA** *enters stage rear with ammonia and rushes toward the dining room. Before she gets there, a natural curiosity makes her glance into the foyer. Surprised to see the door ajar, she approaches and cautiously peers in.*)

MONICA: Papa . . . (**DAMASO**, *extremely nervous, emerges from the dark foyer.*)

DAMASO: What do you want?

MONICA: What are you doing in there? It's all dark.

DAMASO: I stuck my head in for a minute . . . just to see . . . Go back to the dining room.

MONICA: That door is open. Is somebody in there with him now?

DAMASO: Of course. The nurse.

MONICA: (*Stepping back, shocked.*) No! She's in the bathroom!

DAMASO: (*After a moment's hesitation.*) Oh, yes, she did leave for a minute. I forgot. (*Wide-eyed,* **MONICA** *takes another step back.* **DAMASO** *responds brusquely.*)

Well. So what? Why are you looking at me like that? (*Pale and highly agitated,* LORENZO *enters suddenly and closes the door behind him.*)

LORENZO: What's she doing here?

DAMASO: I don't know. (*To* MONICA.) Go back to the dining room, Monica. (MONICA *rushes to the dining room door.*)

LORENZO: Wait!

MONICA: (*Alarmed.*) No! (*She struggles with the door as* LORENZO *comes quickly after her.*)

DAMASO: Lorenzo! (MONICA *is able to slip through the door and close it quickly.* DAMASO *collapses into a chair.*) She's going to tell them!

LORENZO: (*Panting.*) She can't say anything. . . . (DAMASO *hides his face in his hands.* LORENZO *goes over and roughly pushes* DAMASO's *clenched fists away from his face.*) Listen, Damaso! When I got in there, he was . . . already dead.

DAMASO: They'll never believe that!

LORENZO: I'm telling you the truth, you idiot! (*Lowering his voice.*) I didn't do anything.

DAMASO: (*Remorseful.*) But Lorenzo, that can't be. . . . The nurse said . . .

LORENZO: It must have happened after she left!

DAMASO: And before you went in?

LORENZO: (*Furious, shaking him.*) Don't look at me like that! I didn't kill him!

DAMASO: (*Whimpering.*) What's to become of us now?

LORENZO: You fool! You're going to sell out! And if you don't believe me, at least act a little calmer!

DAMASO: (*Ignoring him.*) And now, when the nurse comes back . . .

LORENZO *ignores him, too. Turning his head rapidly toward the dining room, he rushes back to his armchair and sits down.*

LORENZO: If anybody asks, just say we stuck our heads in there for a minute. You understand? We've got to be convincing. (*He rests his forehead in his hand, pretending to be asleep.*)

DAMASO: (*Going over to his chair.*) Don't leave me like this! Help me!

LORENZO: (*Glaring at him.*) Pretend! (*Putting his head down again.* DAMASO *goes toward the dining room and suddenly stops when he sees the door open.* LEANDRO *enters, looks at them and steps aside. Behind him comes* AMALIA, *exhausted but proudly erect. She looks at the motionless* LORENZO, *who pretends to sleep, and at* DAMASO, *who doesn't know what to do with himself. Behind* AMALIA, SABINA, LEONOR, *and* PAULA *enter.* MONICA *is not with them.*)

AMALIA: (*After looking at the clock.*) Ten minutes of six. I can't waste any more time . . . not a single minute more. You people asked for it! (*Going toward the foyer.*)

DAMASO: (*Panicked.*) No! (LORENZO *does not move, but his absolute stillness suggests close attention to what is being said. All eyes are on* DAMASO.) I mean, there's no use anymore! I'm leaving! Let's go, Leonor! Come on, Monica! (MONICA *enters with downcast eyes and walks around the perimeter of the room before peering through the door stage rear.*)

AMALIA: (*Harshly.*) You're leaving? Why is that?

DAMASO: Because I don't want to play this horrible game anymore! (*He looks at* LORENZO, *and then at his daughter. The latter, terrified, does not take her eyes off him.* AMALIA, *finding the situation very strange, turns rapidly toward the foyer.*)

MONICA: (*Impulsively.*) Aunt Amalia, don't go in there!

AMALIA: (*Shocked.*) Why not?

MONICA: I'm afraid . . . something . . . might have happened.

AMALIA: (*Frowning.*) The nurse would have told us . . .

MONICA: But she's not in there. She left for a few minutes . . . (*Terrified.*) and I don't think she's back yet.

AMALIA: What? (SABINA *walks rapidly stage rear.*) Wait, Sabina. (*Taking a few steps with her eyes focused on* DAMASO.) You were here?

DAMASO: (*Pointing nervously at* LORENZO.) With Lorenzo! Both of us were here! (*Suddenly* LEANDRO *grabs him by the shoulders, making him moan.*)

LEANDRO: Did the two of you go in there? Answer me! (AMALIA *looks at* DAMASO *and then at* LORENZO. *The immobility of the latter begins to frighten her.*)

DAMASO: (*Exploding.*) I didn't want to! All we meant to do was see how he was! I swear to you, Amalia! But I didn't go in!

LEONOR: (*Horrified.*) Damaso!

MONICA: (*Extremely worried.*) Papa didn't go in! I saw what was going on! It was just Uncle Lorenzo!

AMALIA: (*Through clenched teeth as she imagines, with repugnance, the scene.*) No!

DAMASO: It was just him! He's the only one! (**LEANDRO** *shoves him, as though he were a rag doll, against a chair.* **AMALIA** *stares steadily at* **LORENZO** *as though he were a scorpion. The others observe him in similar fashion with growing repugnance.*)

PAULA: (*Instinctively moving away from* **LORENZO**.) How awful! (**LEONOR** *looks at her husband and then at* **LORENZO**. **LEANDRO** *turns to his father with a terrible look on his face, and* **DAMASO** *grabs him roughly by the arm, forcing him stand up.*)

LEANDRO: Stop this pretense! You make me sick! You've been able to block the will, but you can't wiggle out of the confession. He was the one, Amalia! He told me about it a few days later, laughing, because, according to him, he'd spoiled my plan!

LORENZO: (*Struggling.*) Let go of me!

LEANDRO: (*Releasing him with disgust.*) He wanted money if you and I got married! And because I turned him down, he lied to Mauricio about us that afternoon!

AMALIA: (*Crushed, she looks toward the foyer.*) Oh, no!

LORENZO: A bad mistake, you idiot! But I never tell everything! I told you only what I said to Mauricio about the two of you. . . . What I didn't tell you was what he said to me about you.

LEANDRO: (*Livid.*) There's nothing he could have said about me!

LORENZO: (*To* **AMALIA**.) He had received an anonymous letter that day. He mentioned it to me not appearing to give it much importance, just to see my reaction. Then he said he wouldn't give me any money. That upset me, so I told him about you two; yes, I did. . . . And he said: "Looks like both father and son are trying to make trouble today. Leandro just warned me to keep an eye on Amalia."

AMALIA: (*To* **LEANDRO**.) You said that? (*Her face reflects tremendous hope.*)

LEANDRO: (*To his father.*) You're lying!

LORENZO: (*Raising his voice.*) You told him what he was afraid to hear! You simply confirmed his doubts, because you wrote the anonymous letter!

LEANDRO: That's a lie!

LORENZO: Mauricio can clear that up! You think he's dead? That idiot (*Pointing to* **DAMASO** *who stands up when hearing his name.*) has lost his mind and is about to drive the rest of you crazy, and all because I simply stuck my head in the door to see Mauricio for myself. (*Pointedly.*) He's still in a coma, Amalia.

MONICA: (*As though someone had just lifted a great burden from her shoulders.*) He's alive! (*She opens the foyer door and exits.*)

LEONOR: Monica!

DAMASO: Honey!

AMALIA: Stop her, Sabina! (*Looking at* **LEANDRO**.) Stop her so she won't wake him up! (**SABINA** *runs after* **MONICA**.) And now, Leandro, it's all up to you. Are you going to confess, or shall I ask Mauricio?

LEANDRO: (*Stammering and bowing his head.*) I wanted something to come between you two, because I wanted you for myself. But I didn't write any letter!

PAULA: (*Coming forward angrily, holding a piece of paper she has taken out of her pocket.*) You did write it! Here it is! (**AMALIA** *snatches it out of her hand and reads it feverishly.* **LEANDRO** *steps back as though someone had hit him.*) The letter was returned to you without a word, because he knew you lied. . . . I took it out of your pocket.

LEANDRO: That letter doesn't say anything about Amalia!

PAULA: You mean, it doesn't mention her by name.

LEANDRO: It was a stab in the dark to return it to me! I didn't write it!

PAULA: This letter was written on your office typewriter.

AMALIA: And it sounds like you. It has the ring of some cheap novel written by a mediocre writer like you. You knew perfectly well that the other painter was the mistake of my life. I never wanted to see him again. . . . And you told Mauricio that I did see him; that I went to his wild parties and, by doing so, sullied the love and trust that he so honored me with. You're despicable! (*She wads up the letter and throws it in his face.*)

LEANDRO: Amalia, I was in love with you, and . . . (**AMALIA** *cuts him short with a slap.* **LEANDRO** *shudders slightly before rushing at* **LORENZO**.)

LEONOR: No!

DAMASO: Leandro! (**LORENZO** *and* **LEANDRO** *struggle briefly.*)

151

LORENZO: (*Freeing himself with a hard shove.*) Get your hands off me! (**SABINA** *and* **MONICA** *enter.*)

AMALIA: Monica! Tell me what you saw in there!

MONICA: (*Looking at her father.*) I don't know. . . . Uncle Mauricio is . . . asleep. . . .

AMALIA: No! Tell the truth!

MONICA: (*Lowering her head.*) He's dead.

DAMASO: Oh, my God!

LEONOR: Damaso! (*Everybody looks at* **LORENZO**, *terrified.*)

LEANDRO: (*Spitting out the word.*) Murderer!

>The **NURSE** *enters from the rear wearing her cape and carrying a small satchel. She looks around at everyone inquisitively.*

NURSE: Excuse me, ma'am, but it's almost six o'clock, and I want to get to the hospital on time. If there's nothing else you need . . .

AMALIA: No, nothing. Thank you for everything. Sabina, show her to the door, please. (**SABINA** *approaches the* **NURSE**, *who turns to go.*)

LORENZO: (*Smiling.*) Just a moment, miss. Exactly what time was it when he died?

NURSE: It was three thirty, sir.

LORENZO: Thank you so much. (*He looks at everyone triumphantly.*)

NURSE: You're welcome. (*To everyone.*) Good night. (*She exits stage rear accompanied by* **SABINA**.)

MONICA: Papa! (*Rushing into her father's arms, sobbing. Moved, he strokes her hair sadly. Emotionally spent,* **LEONOR** *needs to sit down.*)

LORENZO: Congratulations, Amalia. You fooled us all. What were you trying to do?

AMALIA: (*Smiling.*) What was I trying to do? (*Walking center stage.*) I wanted to understand the meaning of those six awful months of silence you caused between us. I wanted to know if Mauricio despised me, or if he was paying me, as one does some prostitute, or whether he was proving his love and faith by . . . making me his wife. (**SABINA** *returns.*)

LORENZO: (*Roaring.*) By doing what?

DAMASO: You're married?

LEONOR: Then we don't get the money!

AMALIA: Some will; Mateo has a share. (*After a pause, to* **LEONOR** *and* **DAMASO**.) And you do, too. "So that Monica will have the kind of future her parents couldn't provide her otherwise." That's how the will reads . . . (*Turning to* **LORENZO** *and* **LEANDRO**.) And for the two people who have told such horrible lies about me, nothing! No mention at all! (*Going toward them.*) Only silence. And that silence doesn't mean distrust, as I feared at first. It's not a silence because the son wanted to seduce me, but because the two of you insulted me! It's a saving silence that brings him back to me! (*She walks downstage and, after a furtive glance toward the foyer and feeling deep emotions, closes her eyes.*) It's a silence that brings him back . . . from the other shore. (*After a brief pause, she turns around and, trembling with emotion but resolute, speaks.*) And now, get out of my house!

MONICA: No! Don't make me go away, too! (*Running to his side.*) Papa! Let me stay here with her!

DAMASO: Yes, honey. You can stay, if it's all right with her.

LEONOR: Absolutely not!

DAMASO: Be quiet! She'll stay, because I say so! And I hope this night teaches us something, Leonor. . . . That's what I hope. (*Taking her by the arm.*) Let's go. (*Walking with her stage rear, where he pauses.*) Good-bye, Amalia. Please don't judge us too harshly. . . . Perhaps our greatest sin was . . . being poor.

AMALIA: No. I mustn't judge. He just judged for me. I hope you'll forgive me these hours I had you on trial. Open the door, please, Sabina. See them out, will you, Monica? (**LEONOR** *and* **LORENZO** *exit stage rear, followed by* **SABINA** *and* **MONICA**.)

LORENZO: All right. I suppose I should leave, too. It's been a difficult, wasted night. And you won. But with money on your side, it wasn't so hard.

AMALIA: It wasn't just money I had on my side.

LORENZO: (*Sardonically.*) Really? What else was it then?

AMALIA: (*Very softly.*) Love.

LORENZO: (*His face clouding, as though the mention of the word displeases him.*) I can't say otherwise. You are one of the few people in the world who think some things are more important than money. (*With ill-disguised sarcasm.*) Aren't you the lucky one? (*Walking stage rear and turning around with a cynical smile.*) Good-bye. (*No one responds.*) You're not going to tell me good-bye, Amalia?

AMALIA: (*After a pause.*) Murderer! (LORENZO *winces and exits quickly.*)

LEANDRO: My battle wasn't about the money, Amalia! (PAULA *walks toward the rear.*)

AMALIA: (*Quietly.*) No, yours was about envy. You've envied him all your life, and in the end, you even envied his having my love.

LEANDRO: Please . . .

AMALIA: (*Boldly.*) Why don't you rush down to the newspaper and write your little piece about the death of an artist? You could have a scoop if you hurry!

LEANDRO: (*Pleading.*) Forgive me!

AMALIA: Don't you understand that you've lost the battle? He won everything forever just now, in there!

PAULA: Good-bye, Amalia.

AMALIA: Good-bye, Paula. And thank you. (LEANDRO *looks at* PAULA, *humiliated.*)

PAULA: (*To* AMALIA, *without looking at* LEANDRO.) We both know what it's like to fight for a man . . .

LEANDRO: (*Hopefully.*) Paula . . .

PAULA: You, at least, can go on loving yours. (*She turns around and exits.*)

LEANDRO: (*Demoralized, he approaches* AMALIA.) Amalia . . .

AMALIA *doesn't even look at him. Then he exits slowly, stage rear.* AMALIA *stands motionless. Her beautiful expression reflects a superhuman calm and limitless love.* MONICA *enters slowly from the rear and looks at her in silence. Then she turns off the overhead light, goes to the large window, and opens the drapes. The clean clarity of dawn floods the room, and* AMALIA *receives it with a long sigh of relief.* MONICA *approaches her timidly but dares not touch her. She finally speaks very sweetly.*

MONICA: Aunt Amalia . . . (*Brief pause.*)

Long-repressed grief wells up uncontrollably inside AMALIA, *and she breaks into heart-wrenching sobs. Calming herself, she looks toward the foyer. Very slowly, and looking steadily at the motionless figure in the bed not visible to the audience, she takes a few steps.)*

AMALIA: (*Her voice breaking with emotion.*) Mauricio! Mauricio!

The clock is about to strike, but AMALIA *no longer pays any attention to time, nor does she fear it. All her attention now has a single focus. As she enters the foyer, the clock strikes six.*

CURTAIN

THE BASEMENT WINDOW

(El tragaluz)

An Experiment in Two Parts

By Antonio Buero-Vallejo

Translated by Patricia W. O'Connor

This play opened in Madrid's Bellas Artes Theater on October 7, 1967.

PART ONE

This experiment involves projected images, at times vague, of the places described. The living room of a modest basement apartment occupies the right two-thirds of the stage, and at stage rear, a short hall leads to the front door. When the front door is open, light shines in. On the hall's right wall is the parents' bedroom door, and on the left wall is the kitchen door.

The left living room wall, not completely visible, extends only to the upper edge of the back wall, and the living room floor extends forward on a rectangular platform approximately four feet high. The furniture is sparse, cheap, and old. On the left, a small round table covered with a floor-length tablecloth is surrounded by two or three chairs. Downstage right against the wall are a chair and a coffee table on which there are papers, an ashtray, and a couple of books. Against the left wall stand a dilapidated old couch and a few more chairs. Against the right rear wall, there is a small cabinet for dishes and utensils on which there are glasses, a pitcher, fruit bowl, and breadbasket, thus suggesting that the cabinet doubles as a serving table. Thumb-tacked to the wall, postcards of artworks and magazine pictures of famous paintings, artists, and writers share space with old family photographs.

On the invisible fourth wall between stage and audience is a large, street-level barred window that allows some light to enter. When the characters go through the motions of opening and closing this basement window, the bars cast their shadows on the back wall.

The left third of the stage, an office, is on a raised platform. The right wall of this office is the left wall of the living room. The back wall is the only one clearly visible and, unlike the other walls, extends upward fully. Toward the right against this rear wall, a desk and chair face the audience. On the left stands a file cabinet, and between the desk and the file cabinet is the office door. Downstage left, a small typewriter table and chair stand in profile. On the rear wall above the desk, a large poster advertises a publishing house and shows clearly in large letters "New Literature." Displayed less clearly on the poster are book covers and photographs of authors, some of which also adorn the living room wall.

In front of the office platform are the small table and two chairs of a sidewalk café. On the other side of the stage and forming an angle with the right living room wall is a part of the building's dingy, peeling exterior. Downstage left and right are spaces for entrances and exits.

In the set's general structure, ceilings are not visible. Lighting effects as well as the quality of the building materials render imprecise the separation of the spaces described, and frequently their forms and outlines are blurred and hazy.

Spotlights on the researchers are white and steady; lighting for the other scenes and places is dim and suggests unreality.

When the house lights go down, SHE *and* HE, *a young couple wearing garments appropriate to a distant future, enter from the rear of the theater as spotlights illuminate their deliberate, graceful movements. When they reach the stage, they turn and look at the audience for a few seconds before speaking in calm, firm voices.*

SHE: Welcome. Thank you for wanting to see our experiment.

HE: We don't know if the one assigned us will interest you.

SHE: We find it fascinating. (*She looks at her partner, smiling.*) Did people say "fascinating" in those days?

HE: Yes, they did. (*Addressing the audience.*) There's a reason for my partner's doubt. If our way of speaking sounds strange, it's because we are new at these things. The council decided that we researchers should use the vocabulary of the period under reconstruction. We are speaking to you, then, in the language and style of the twentieth century, specifically, the second half of that now-remote period. (*Both go onto the stage by way of a small stairway and turn again to the audience.*) My partner and I believe that we are very fortunate to work on this particular experiment. The story line we recovered illustrates that *the question,* perfectly formed, existed even then.

SHE: As you know, *the question* was hardly ever found in the case histories our detectors reconstructed over the years. In this one, however, you will find that *question* articulated in a most surprising way.

HE: The person who asks *the question* was neither well-known nor considered important. He was an obscure person with health problems.

SHE: This case history is, like many others, uniquely clarifying as well as mysterious; centuries ago, we relearned the monumental importance. . . . (*To her partner.*) Is "monumental" the right word?

HE: Yes, monumental.

SHE: (*Continuing.*) . . . the monumental importance of each individual. When the men and women represented by these images lived, people said they couldn't see the forest for the trees. For long periods of time, they forgot to look at trees one by one so that their vision of the forest would not become impersonal. In order to survive, they learned this lesson, and they haven't forgotten it.

Raising a hand, HE *surveys the audience as oscillating lights sweep over the couple and across the curtain.*

HE: Since sounds cannot be recaptured, dialogue has been added by transcribing lip movement. When the figures had their backs to us, the electronic brains . . . (*To his partner.*) Is that what they were called then?

SHE: I think they were more commonly called computers.

HE: Yes; our computers deduced even unobserved words and have supplied natural sounds.

SHE: Certain words coming through the basement window have also been inferred by means of this same technology.

HE: But the accuracy of these communications as actual phenomena is, of course, less certain.

SHE: (*A gesture of her hand asks for patience.*) You will understand all this very soon . . .

HE: Also, from time to time, you will hear a strange noise; it's the only sound that we have added on our own.

SHE: It is the sound of a primitive form of locomotion called the train. We use it to express invisible anxieties that, in our opinion, should be underscored. You will hear, therefore, a train; in other words, an intense thought.

As the curtain goes up, ENCARNA *sits at the office typewriter.* VICENTE, *seated behind the office desk with papers in front of him, looks at her. In the living room, the* FATHER *sits at the table, holding a pair of scissors as he looks at an old magazine.* MARIO *is seated at the small table to the right with galley proofs and a ballpoint pen. All four are motionless as lights flash over the office and the living room.*

HE: As a basis for our experiment, we use a few places that the space projectors make visible simultaneously. (*Pointing to the stage.*) At this moment, the figures are functioning in a minimal way and appear motionless. They will perform in normal rhythm when their turn comes. (*The flashing lights diminish gradually, and those in the office are replaced by the steady, bright light of day. The other areas of the stage remain in semi-darkness. Slowly and hesitantly,* ENCARNA *begins to type.*) This case history took place in Madrid, capital of an ancient country known as Spain.

SHE: It is the story of a few trees, long gone, that once lived in an immense forest.

> **HE** *and* **SHE** *exit on opposite sides. The sound of the typewriter normalizes, but the typist is neither quick nor sure of herself. In the shadowy living room, the* **FATHER** *and* **MARIO** *move very slowly from time to time.* **ENCARNA**, *twenty-five years old, types from a paper beside the typewriter. Ordinary looking but not unattractive,* **ENCARNA** *wears simple, inexpensive clothes.* **VICENTE**, *nice looking and well-dressed, appears to be about forty. His clothes, well kept, are of good quality, and on one hand he wears a heavy gold ring. Perplexed,* **ENCARNA** *glances at* **VICENTE**. *He smiles at her, and she begins to type again.*

ENCARNA: I think I did it right.

VICENTE: That's good.

> **ENCARNA** *types enthusiastically for a few seconds. The telephone rings.*

ENCARNA: Should I answer it?

VICENTE: I'll get it. (*Picking up the telephone.*) Hello. Oh, hello, Juan. (*Putting his hand over the receiver.*) Go on, Encarna; you don't bother me. (*She resumes typing.*) Letterhead? Until the contract is signed, I don't think we should change the name of the publishing house. . . . What? I thought we still had a week. (**ENCARNA** *takes the paper out of the typewriter carriage.*) Of course I'm happy about it! Now we can really do big things. . . . No, the best-selling item in the new collection is Beltran's book. And we already have three translations under contract for him. . . . Sure; Beltran's other novel goes to press right away. He signs the contract day after tomorrow. I haven't mailed the manuscript yet; Encarna's reading it now. (*Showing great surprise.*) What? . . . Yes, I'm listening; I'm listening! . . . (*Frowning, displeased.*) Yes, yes. I hear you . . . But listen . . . Listen to me a minute, please. (*Covering the receiver.*) Hey, Encarna, did you get those magazines and postcards ready for me?

ENCARNA: It'll just take a minute . . .

VICENTE: Do it now, will you? (*Looking at his watch.*) We need to leave right away; it's time to go. (*She exits.*)

VICENTE: (*Into the telephone.*) Listen, Juan. It's one thing for the new people to intervene in the business operation, but something quite different for them to impose their literary or political tastes, prejudices, obsessions, or whatever you want to call them. . . . You know very well what I'm talking about! What do you mean, you don't know? It's obvious they have it in for Beltran! . . . (*Getting excited.*) Juan! We have binding contracts in place and others about to be signed! Listen! (*Reluctantly.*) Yes, yes; I hear you . . . (*His face changes expression and his tone softens.*) I don't know why you have to put it that way. . . . Of course I'm aware nobody's indispensable; I don't pretend to be. . . . Sure, I have as much to gain with the new group as you do . . . (*Displeased.*) Okay. (*Pounding the desk angrily.*) Well, you tell me what to do then! All right. I'll think up something to tell him. (*Bitterly.*) I got it straight, Juan; got it: Beltran is out, the new group is in, and long lives the business! . . . Oh, no; you're wrong about that. I like Beltran, but I recognize that he's a little old-fashioned; certainly not in sync with the people who matter today. Too bad. (**ENCARNA** *returns with a stack of magazines, postcards, and an envelope and places everything on the table. They look at each other.* **VICENTE**'s *tone becomes firm and determined.*) I agree with you. Count me in. We're not in this just for the money. We have to monitor what passes for literature these days. . . . Let me know if I can do anything else for you. . . . Talk to you tomorrow, then. (*He hangs up and sits deep in thought.*) Tomorrow the company contract will be signed, Encarna. The new group is going to give us good financial support. Everything is going to get better; a lot better.

ENCARNA: Will they make changes in the office staff?

VICENTE: You won't be leaving; I told you that already.

ENCARNA: But now others will have as much say about the office as you do. Suppose they decide to get rid of me?

VICENTE: In that case I'll find you something else.

ENCARNA: (*In a disappointed tone.*) A job at another office?

VICENTE: Why not?

ENCARNA: (*After a pause.*) So I can sleep with another boss?

VICENTE: (*Dryly.*) I can get you a job without any need of that. I have friends.

ENCARNA: Who'll get rid of me, too.

VICENTE: (*He sighs and looks at the papers in front of him.*) That's ridiculous. You're not going to leave here. (*Looking at his watch.*) Did you finish that letter?

ENCARNA: (*Sighing.*) Yes. (*She goes to the typewriter, picks up the letter and hands it to him. He looks it over.*)

VICENTE: Oh, oh! (*Picking up a red pen.*) That word is spelled with an "x"!

ENCARNA: But excellent has an "s"! I'm sure!

VICENTE: Right; just like "explain"!

ENCARNA: Esplain?

VICENTE: The way you say it, it sounds like an "s"; but you say it wrong. (*Marking the error.*)

ENCARNA: (*Humbly.*) I'll retype it.

VICENTE: Do it tomorrow. Have you finished Beltran's novel?

ENCARNA: Yes. I left it here for you. (*She goes to the file, picks out a manuscript, and takes it to him.*)

VICENTE: (*Leafing through the manuscript.*) I'll bet you thought it was excellent, with an "x."

ENCARNA: Yes; excellent, with an "x."

VICENTE: I'm not surprised you liked it. He goes overboard on the sentimental stuff.

ENCARNA: But . . . I thought you liked his novels . . .

VICENTE: He's our best writer, but in this last work, he went too far. (*He sits down and puts the manuscript in the drawer.*) Good literature isn't easy, Encarna. Writers must reflect life, but without all its triviality. (*As he prepares to pick up the magazines, he notices the envelope.*) What's this?

ENCARNA: Galley proofs for your brother.

VICENTE: Oh, yes! Just a minute! I want to look over the articles for the next issue of the magazine. (*He removes proofs from the envelope as* ENCARNA *sits down.*) Yes, Encarna; literature's not easy. Beltran, for example, writes that one of his down-and-out characters thinks this or that . . . An outmoded technique. But this idiot (*Pointing to the proofs.*) praises him. . . . You can only justify that kind of writing when one character asks another "What's on your mind?" (*She looks at him quizzically as he concentrates on reading. She then looks off into the distance, lost in thought. The lights gradually dim downstage. A woman in her forties with the unmistakable air of a cheap* **PROSTITUTE**

enters stage right and approaches the table at the sidewalk café. She sits down and takes out a cigarette. A thin, aging waiter with a laconic air appears from the left; he shakes his head and wags a finger at her, indicating that she is unwelcome. She looks at him provocatively, pointing toward the table in a gesture that says she'd like something to drink. The WAITER *repeats the negative gesture. She sighs, puts away the unlit cigarette, gets up, and walks right. After a pause and with a bored look she leans against the peeling wall.* VICENTE *looks up at* ENCARNA.)

VICENTE: What about you? What's on your mind? (*Lost in thought,* ENCARNA *makes no response.*) Huh? (ENCARNA *continues oblivious to him. Intrigued,* VICENTE *observes her closely as he lights a cigarette. The* WAITER *then signals for the* PROSTITUTE *to leave with even more forceful gestures and an inaudible, but clearly mouthed, "Get out!" With a grimace of scorn, she exits stage right. The* WAITER *wipes the table and also exits stage right. The downstage lights dim slightly. With some irony,* VICENTE *persists.*)

VICENTE: What's the lady . . . thinking?

ENCARNA: (*Startled.*) Lady . . .

VICENTE: Right now, you were just like a character in a novel. You were certainly thinking something.

ENCARNA: No . . . Nothing . . .

VICENTE: (*As he continues going over the proofs.*) Shall we grab a bite?

ENCARNA: You know I always have dinner with a girl from my hometown on Thursdays.

VICENTE: Oh, yes. Today's Thursday. Remind me to call Moreno first thing tomorrow. I need him to write an article for the next issue. This one won't do. (*He removes the article he was reading and puts it away.*)

ENCARNA: (*Covering the typewriter.*) Which one is that?

VICENTE: The Torres piece.

ENCARNA: About Beltran?

VICENTE: Yes. Well, can I drop you off somewhere?

ENCARNA: No, thanks. Are you going by your parents' place?

VICENTE: Yeah, and with all this stuff. (*He taps the pile of magazines and smiles as he picks up the postcards.*) My father will like this picture. You can see people walking along the street, and he'll love that. (*He leafs through the cards as the lights come up slowly on the living room. It is daytime. The movements of the occupants normalize. The* FATHER, *seated at the table, cuts something from an old magazine. He is white-haired and looks older than seventy-five. His son,* MARIO, *about thirty-five, is correcting galley proofs. Both wear old clothes: the* FATHER, *a worn-out suit under a threadbare bathrobe;* MARIO, *dark trousers and a sweater.* VICENTE *leans on the edge of the table.*) It's a good thing the old guy has gotten funny in his old age. (*He chuckles as he looks at the postcards.*) Did I tell you what happened with the priest?

ENCARNA: No.

VICENTE: One day, he ran into the priest, who was walking along with a parishioner. And my father, very politely, asked him: "Is this your wife?" (*They laugh.*) He was out with Mr. Anselmo; he's a lot of company and never crosses him on anything.

ENCARNA: But . . . is your father mentally ill?

VICENTE: No. It's just old age . . . senility, I guess. He'll be less trouble at home now, because last month I gave them a TV set. (*He laughs and tosses a postcard on the table.*) He won't like this card. No people. (*He becomes lost in thought.*)

The sound of a train, barely audible in the distance, swells as it starts up, whistles, and rapidly gains speed. This noise is very loud for a few seconds before drifting off into the distance as the FATHER *mutters to himself in the living room.*

FATHER: (*Holding up a paper figure.*) This one can get on, too.

MARIO: (*He stops his work and looks up.*) Get on what?

FATHER: The train.

MARIO: What train?

FATHER: (*Pointing straight ahead at the audience.*) That one.

MARIO: That's a window.

FATHER: That's what you think . . . (*Leafing through the magazine.*)

ENCARNA: (*Disconcerted by* VICENTE's *silence.*) Aren't we leaving? (*Lost in thought,* VICENTE *does not respond. She looks at him curiously.*)

MARIO: (*Observing his father closely.*) Vicente's coming today.

FATHER: What Vicente?

MARIO: Don't you have a son named Vicente?

FATHER: Yes; the older boy. I don't know if he's still alive.

MARIO: He comes every month.

FATHER: And you. Who are you?

MARIO: I'm Mario.

FATHER: You have the same name as my son?

MARIO: I am your son.

FATHER: Mario was smaller.

MARIO: I've grown up.

FATHER: Then it'll be easier for you to get on.

MARIO: On what?

FATHER: The train! (*He begins to cut out another figure.* MARIO *looks at him intrigued and then goes back to his work.*)

VICENTE: (*Coming out of his reverie and picking up the pile of magazines and post-cards.*) Shall we go?

ENCARNA: That's what I asked you.

VICENTE: (*Laughing.*) I was daydreaming, just like some character out of a Beltran novel. (*He puts the magazines in his briefcase and the postcards in an envelope.* ENCARNA *takes her purse, goes toward the table, and picks up the discarded postcard. At the door,* VICENTE *turns to look at her.*) Ready?

ENCARNA: (*Looking at the card.*) I'd like to meet your parents sometime.

VICENTE: You've told me that before.

ENCARNA: I'm not insinuating anything. I guess I shouldn't mention it again. (*With difficulty.*) But . . . if I got pregnant, what would you do?

VICENTE: (*Coming close and regarding her coldly.*) Are you pregnant?

ENCARNA: (*Avoiding his eyes.*) No.

VICENTE: It would certainly be stupid to get careless now . . .

ENCARNA: Even if we didn't get married, would you help with the child?

VICENTE: (*Dryly.*) If you're not pregnant, there's no use talking about it. Let's go. (*Turning toward the door.*)

ENCARNA: (*Sighing before speaking listlessly.*) I thought your father would like this card. It has a funny-looking train, like the ones they had thirty years ago.

VICENTE: It doesn't have any people.

ENCARNA *drops the postcard on the table and leaves, followed by* VICENTE, *who closes the door. The sound of the train returns, and the light goes out on the office.* MARIO *interrupts his work to look fixedly at the* FATHER, *who in turn meets his gaze. The sound of the train ceases. The* FATHER *gets up and takes his two paper figures to the cabinet in the rear.*

FATHER: (*Muttering as he opens the drawer.*) These two have to stay behind in the waiting room. (*He puts the figures down and rummages in the drawer before taking out a couple of postcards.*) I'm going to cut out this pretty little lady. (*Singing as he returns to the table.*) Rosita's a beauty, and Maria's a cutie . . . (*He sits down and starts to cut out the figures.*)

MARIO: Isn't she safer in the postcard?

FATHER: (*Without looking at him.*) Only if there are lots of people, because then you destroy them if you try to cut them out. I have to watch out for everybody, and I save the ones I can.

MARIO: From what?

FATHER: From the postcard. (*As he cuts, the door opens and the* MOTHER *enters with a package. She has a pleasant, lively manner and appears to be about sixty-five. The* FATHER *pauses.*) Who just came in?

MARIO: It's mama. (*She goes into the kitchen.*)

FATHER: (*Humming and singing as he resumes cutting.*) Maria's a cutie . . .

MARIO: Father . . .

FATHER: (*Looking at him.*) Huh?

MARIO: What train are you talking about? And what waiting room is that? You've never talked about any train before . . .

FATHER: About that one. (*Pointing straight ahead.*)

MARIO: There's no train there.

FATHER: You must be crazy, young man. Can't you see the window of that train? (*The son looks at the basement window and returns to his work. The* MOTHER *comes out of the kitchen with the package and enters the living room.*)

MOTHER: I'm heating the milk. Vicente won't be long. (*She goes to the sideboard and opens the package.*)

FATHER: (*Getting up and bowing.*) Madam . . .

MOTHER: (*Bowing teasingly.*) Sir . . .

FATHER: Make yourself at home.

MOTHER: (*Containing her laughter.*) Thank you, kind sir.

FATHER: If you'll excuse me, I have work to do.

MOTHER: Of course. (*They bow to each other again. The* FATHER *sits down and continues cutting. Not finding the scene amusing,* MARIO *lights a cigarette.*) These sweet rolls are like the ones we used to get. Your brother still likes them. In case he wants something to eat . . . (*Putting the pastries on a tray.*)

MARIO: Did you know that he has a car now?

MOTHER: (*Happily.*) He does? Have you seen it?

MARIO: I heard about it.

MOTHER: Is it big?

MARIO: I don't know.

MOTHER: I bet he'll bring it today!

MARIO: I don't think he'll drive it here.

MOTHER: You're right. He wouldn't want to park it out front. (MARIO *looks at her in slight surprise and returns to his work.*) It might be embarrassing. (*She comes close to him and lowers her voice.*) Mario, are you going to tell him what your father did?

MARIO: Maybe he won't ask.

MOTHER: He'll miss it.

FATHER: (*He gets up and goes toward the sideboard.*) The pretty young lady is ready now. But I don't know who she is.

MOTHER: (*Laughing.*) She's just a pretty young lady. Isn't that explanation enough?

FATHER: (*Suddenly irritated.*) No, that isn't enough! (*He opens the cabinet drawer brusquely and stores the paper figure.*)

MOTHER: (*Whispering.*) He's been impossible for days.

FATHER: Goodie! Pastry! (*He starts to take a sweet roll.*)

MOTHER: Don't start until Vicente comes.

FATHER: But *I'm* Vicente!

MOTHER: You'll eat later. (*Leading him away.*) Go back to your postcards. You're just like a child.

FATHER: (*Resisting.*) Wait . . .

MOTHER: Come on! Come one!

FATHER: But I want to kiss you.

MOTHER: (*She laughs.*) Oh! Look what the old gentleman is up to now!

FATHER: (*Taking her face in his hands.*) Just a little kiss . . .

MOTHER: (*Laughing heartily.*) Stop it, silly!

FATHER: Pretty thing! (*Kissing her.*)

MOTHER: You're awful! Aren't you ashamed, at your age? (*She pushes him away, but he rests his head on her bosom. She looks at her son with a helpless gesture.*)

FATHER: Sing me a song, pretty lady . . .

MOTHER: What song? When did I ever sing anything to you?

FATHER: When I was little.

MOTHER: That must have been your mother. (*Pushing him away.*) And stop it! You're choking me!

FATHER: Aren't you my mother?

MOTHER: (*Laughing.*) Yes, dear. Go ahead; sit down and clip out your paper dolls.

FATHER: (*Obediently.*) All right. (*He sits down and becomes absorbed in his magazines.*)

MOTHER: And be careful with the scissors. I don't want you to get hurt.

FATHER: Yes, mama. (*He tears out a page and begins to cut.*)

MOTHER: Huh! "Mama," he calls me. Next thing you know, I'll be Queen Elizabeth. (*The doorbell rings.*) Vicente! (*She hurries stage rear as* **MARIO** *gets up and approaches his father.*)

MARIO: It's Vicente, father. (*The* **FATHER** *ignores him.*)

MOTHER: (*Opening the door and throwing her arms around her son.*) Vinny! Son!

VICENTE: Hello, mother. (*They greet each other affectionately with kisses on each cheek.*)

MOTHER: (*She closes the door and hugs her son again.*) Vicente, dear.

VICENTE: (*Laughing.*) Come on, mama; you'd think I'd been to the moon!

MOTHER: It's just that I haven't gotten used to your not living with us. (*She takes his arm, and they both come into the living room.*)

VICENTE: Hi, Mario.

MARIO: How's everything? (*The brothers pat each other affectionately on the arm.*)

MOTHER: (*To the FATHER.*) Look who's here!

VICENTE: How's it going, father?

FATHER: Why do you call me that? I'm no priest.

VICENTE: (*Laughing.*) I see that he's the same as ever! But I think he'll like the pretty things I brought him. (*He opens his briefcase.*) Magazines and post-cards. (*He puts them on the table.*)

FATHER: Very nice of you, sir. I was almost out of people, and it's not good to be alone. (*He leafs through one of the magazines.*)

VICENTE: (*Smiling.*) Well, now you have company. (*He goes over to the sideboard.*) Great! Sweet rolls!

MOTHER: (*Happily.*) I'll make the coffee! It'll just take a minute. Can you stay for supper?

VICENTE: I can't stay long! I have a thousand things to do. (*He sits down on the sofa.*)

MOTHER: (*Disappointed.*) You can't stay today either?

VICENTE: I'm really sorry, mama.

MOTHER: I'll start the coffee. (*She starts to walk away.*)

VICENTE: (*He gets up and takes out a blue envelope.*) Before I forget, I brought this for you.

MOTHER: Thanks, son. It comes just in time, you know? Tomorrow the install-ment on the washing machine is due.

VICENTE: You can go ahead and order a new refrigerator now.

MOTHER: No! Not just yet . . .

VICENTE: But it's no problem! You have me, and I can afford it! (*The* MOTHER *looks at him, moved. Suddenly she kisses him again and hurries to the kitchen.*) I brought some proofs for you, Mario. (*He takes the envelope out of his briefcase.*)

MARIO *takes the envelope without saying a word and drops it on the coffee table. Meanwhile, the* FATHER *has gotten up and observes his sons thoughtfully. He takes a few steps and points to the postcard on the table.*

FATHER: Who is that person?

VICENTE: What?

FATHER: That one . . . the one in the derby.

VICENTE: What's he saying? (MARIO *has understood. The* FATHER *tugs at him, takes him to the table and puts his finger on a postcard.*)

FATHER: Here.

VICENTE: (*Coming close.*) That's Opera Square in Paris. Everybody wore derby hats back then. It's an old picture.

FATHER: But who is this person?

VICENTE: You can hardly see him. That's someone who just happened along when they took the picture. He's nobody special.

FATHER: (*Energetically.*) You're wrong about that!

VICENTE: How are we supposed to know who he is anyway? He wasn't anybody important.

FATHER: (*Forcefully.*) Yes he was!

MARIO: (*Softly.*) I'm sure he's probably dead by now.

FATHER: (*Looking at him, shocked.*) What are you saying? (*He searches among the magazines and picks up a magnifying glass.*)

VICENTE: A magnifying glass?

MARIO: I had to buy it for him. It's not the first time he's asked that question. (*The* FATHER *is seated and looks at the postcard with the magnifying glass.*)

VICENTE: (*In a low voice.*) Is he getting worse?

MARIO: I don't know.

FATHER: That person isn't dead. And the woman crossing the square, who is she? (*He observes them.*) Of course. You two don't know. But I do.

VICENTE: You do? And what about the man in the derby?

FATHER: (*Serious.*) I know who he is, too.

VICENTE: If you know who they are, why do you ask?

FATHER: To test you.

VICENTE: (*Turning his back and trying not to laugh.*) He thinks he's God . . . (*The* **FATHER** *looks at him a second and concentrates on the postcard.* **MARIO** *makes a slight gesture of agreement.*)

MOTHER: (*Coming out of the kitchen with a tray of coffee cups and speaking as she walks along the hall.*) When are you going to get married, Vicente?

FATHER: (*Looking at the postcard.*) I got married once already.

MOTHER: (*As the older son laughs.*) Of course. So did I. (*The* **FATHER** *looks at her.*) I wasn't talking to you, silly! (*She puts the tray down and places the cups on the table.*) And put your paper dolls away! It's time for coffee. Here. But not much for you; milk doesn't agree with you. (*As she puts a cup in front of him, she takes the magnifying glass and the postcard away. He looks at her but does not object. She gathers the postcards and magazines and takes them to the sideboard.*) Sit down, Vinny. I'll sit with the little boy, because if I don't, he's going to make a mess. (*Taking the sweet rolls to the table.*) Have a roll!

VICENTE: Thanks. (*He takes a roll and begins to eat.* **MARIO** *takes one too.*)

MOTHER: (*Sitting beside her husband and handing him a roll.*) Here! Don't you want one? (*The* **FATHER** *takes it.*) Why don't you dunk it in the coffee? (*The* **FATHER** *dunks the roll as she turns to* **VICENTE**.) You didn't answer me, dear. Isn't there some girl you like?

VICENTE: Too many!

MOTHER: You're awful!

FATHER: How do I eat this?

MOTHER: Take a bite right there; right where you dunked it.

FATHER: What do I eat it with? (*Raising the roll to his eyes.*)

MOTHER: With your mouth! Your mouth! You're impossible. (*She takes away the roll and begins to feed him as though he were a child, touching his lips with each bite so he will open his mouth.*) Here!

VICENTE: Is he really that bad off?

MARIO: Sometime he knows what to do, and other times he forgets.

MOTHER: Have another roll, Vicente.

FATHER: Your name's Vicente?

VICENTE: Yes.

FATHER: What a coincidence! We have the same name! (**VICENTE** *laughs.*)

MOTHER: (*To the* **FATHER.**) Eat some of this, and be quiet. (*Offering him another bite.*)

FATHER: I don't want any more. Who's going to pay the bill?

MOTHER: (*As* **VICENTE** *laughs again.*) It's already paid. Here . . .

FATHER: (*He rejects the bite and gets up, irritated.*) I don't want any more! I'm going home!

MOTHER: (*She gets up and tries to stop him.*) But you're already home!

FATHER: We're in a restaurant! (*He tries to push his wife away.* **VICENTE** *gets up.*)

MOTHER: Listen . . .

FATHER: I have to go back to my parents! (*He walks stage rear.*)

MOTHER: (*As she follows him, she speaks to* **VICENTE.**) Excuse me. He can't be left alone.

FATHER: (*In the hallway.*) Where is the door? (*He opens the door to his room and goes in. The* **MOTHER** *enters behind him, closing the door.*)

VICENTE: (*He takes a few steps toward the hall and then turns toward his brother, who has remained seated.*) He never used to get so angry before.

MARIO: (*Casually.*) But he gets over it quickly. (*Finishing his coffee and wiping his mouth.*) How's your car?

VICENTE: Oh! You know about that? It's not much, even though it looks pretty good. These days, a car's an absolute necessity . . .

MARIO: (*Serious and ironic.*) Of course; economic development and all that . . .

VICENTE: Right. (*Going over to his brother.*) And what about you? How are things going?

MARIO: I'm doing all right. I've just been assigned several books to edit.

VICENTE: Have you got a girl?

MARIO: No.

ENCARNA *enters downstage left.* VICENTE *picks up another sweet roll and, as he takes a bite, goes toward the hall to listen.* ENCARNA *looks at her watch and sits down at the sidewalk café. She looks toward the right as though expecting someone.*

VICENTE: He seems quieter now.

MARIO: I told you that's how it would be.

VICENTE: (*He looks at his watch, returns to the living room, and closes his briefcase.*) I didn't realize how late it was . . . (*The* WAITER *enters stage left, exchanges some words in a low voice with* ENCARNA, *and then leaves.*) I've got to go . . . (VICENTE *starts walking toward the hall.*)

MARIO: How do you find our father?

VICENTE: (*He turns, smiling.*) He gives me a few laughs, like just now about the restaurant. (*He approaches* MARIO.) Hasn't he thought up anything funny to do about the TV set?

MARIO: As a matter of fact . . . (VICENTE *looks around.*)

VICENTE: Where did you put it? They installed it here . . .

ENCARNA *looks at her watch, takes a book out of her purse and begins to read.*

MARIO: Didn't you notice how angry he got? Lately he does that a lot . . .

VICENTE: He does?

MARIO: When we first got the TV, he sat in front of it and every once in a while looked at mama, who made comments about various things she saw. She was delighted, you know. At times he seemed nervous; he'd go to his room without saying anything. . . . But one night, they put on one of those miracle plays, and that seemed to interest him. But they kept interrupting with all those commercials for washers, soft drinks, detergents . . . Before we knew what was happening, he'd gotten up and smashed the set with a chair. Mother didn't dare tell you.

VICENTE: What?

MARIO: There was a huge explosion. He wasn't hurt, but the TV was a total loss.

A moment of silence. The **WAITER** *returns to the table and serves* **ENCARNA** *a cup of coffee.*

VICENTE: (*Thoughtfully.*) Well, he never was very religious . . .

MARIO: No. (*Silence.*)

ENCARNA *drops two sugar cubes into the cup, takes a sip, and goes back to her book.*

VICENTE: (*Reacting.*) When all's said and done, he doesn't know what he's doing.

MARIO: You will admit, though, that what he did does make sense.

VICENTE: In another person, it might, but not in him.

MARIO: Why not? You yourself have said he thinks he's God . . .

VICENTE: I was joking!

MARIO: You're not around to see him like I am.

VICENTE: Are you going crazy too, Mario? He's senile!

MARIO: He's not so senile.

VICENTE: I don't understand what you're getting at.

MARIO: The doctor recently said something about a possible precipitating factor for his condition.

VICENTE: That's new. What kind of precipitating factor could that be?

MARIO: I don't know . . . Because of his general good health, the doctor was surprised at the advanced state of his condition. Our father is seventy-six now, and he's been like this for four years.

VICENTE: Other people get that way even earlier.

MARIO: It first started a long time ago. But you had already left home.

VICENTE: What happened?

MARIO: He got up one night and wandered around, talking incoherently . . . And he was only fifty-seven then. Mother was asleep, but I was awake.

VICENTE: You never said anything.

MARIO: Since it didn't happen again for so many years, I forgot about it. (*Silence.*)

VICENTE: (*Pacing back and forth.*) Maybe he has something hereditary. Anyway, I don't see that his reactions mean anything. He's like a child babbling nonsense.

MARIO: I don't know. And now he's got some new obsessions. . . . You saw one of them: wanting to know who everybody is in those postcards. (*He gets up and walks downstage where the invisible basement window is.*)

VICENTE: (*Laughing.*) He's testing us, he says. That's funny.

MARIO: Yes. Very strange. Remember the game we played as kids?

VICENTE: What game?

MARIO: We used to open this window to see the legs of the people as they passed by, and we imagined who they might be.

VICENTE: (*Laughing.*) The guessing game! I'd forgotten.

MARIO: Since he demolished the television set, he wants us to open the window so he can watch the people . . .

VICENTE: (*Pacing.*) It's like he's watching a movie.

MARIO: (*Without turning around.*) He calls it something else. Today he said the window was a train. (**VICENTE** *stops short and looks at him. Brief silence.*)

MOTHER: (*Coming out of the bedroom and returning to the living room.*) I'm sorry, dear. Now he's quiet.

VICENTE: I've got to go, mama.

MOTHER: So soon?

VICENTE: So late! I'm running behind!

MARIO: (*Turning around as the* **MOTHER** *enters.*) I'm leaving, too.

VICENTE: Can I drop you somewhere?

MARIO: I'll walk as far as the corner with you. I'm going some place close by.

MOTHER: I'd like to see your car, too. I heard about that! These things get around . . .

VICENTE: It's no big deal.

MOTHER: That's what you say. Next time, park out front. You don't have to be so cautious . . . And you hardly touched the sweet roll.

VICENTE: Next time I'll do better! (*Pointing toward the hall.*) Should I say good-bye to him?

MOTHER: Not now. He might want to go out again. (*Laughing.*) You know, the other day he tried to leave the house through the closet door!

VICENTE: (*Laughing, to his brother.*) Didn't I tell you? He's just like a child! (*He picks up his briefcase and walks toward the door.* **MARIO** *picks up his cigarettes and walks behind* **VICENTE** *and the* **MOTHER**.)

MOTHER: Please come back soon!

VICENTE: (*In the hallway.*) I will. I promise! (*He opens the door, touches his mother affectionately under the chin, and leaves.*)

MARIO: (*Walking out behind his brother.*) I won't be long, mother.

MOTHER: (*From the doorway.*) Bye . . . (*She closes the door with a sigh and returns to the living room, collecting what is left of the coffee and rolls before disappearing into the kitchen.*)

The light fades on the living room. As the **MOTHER** *takes her final steps, the young researchers reappear.* **ENCARNA** *looks at her watch impatiently and takes another sip of coffee.*

HE: The image of the person she was waiting for will be along in a minute.

SHE: We'll use that time to comment on the experiment.

HE: Have you seen only realities? Or have you also seen thoughts?

SHE: As you know, for some time the detectors have been able to capture intensely visual thoughts that could then be produced as images. The present experience is apparently one of those. Some of the scenes you have viewed, however, might really have happened, even though Encarna and Vicente imagined them at the same time in the office. Remember that some of these scenes continued even when those who imagined them had stopped thinking them.

HE: Did they simply stop thinking those scenes? We don't know. We'll never be able to gauge—nor could they—the power of their deepest feelings.

SHE: Did they think these thoughts with such intensity that they appear real to us without actually being real?

HE: Or did they perceive them as they were happening, believing they were imagining them?

SHE: Where is the dividing line between what we do and what we dream?

HE: You are witnessing here an experience of total reality: events and thoughts, impossible to separate.

SHE: Events and thoughts that ceased to exist centuries ago.

HE: But they never cease to exist completely, for we can retrieve them. (*Gesturing toward* **ENCARNA**.) Look at that image. How very alive and real she seems to us!

SHE: (*With a finger to her lips.*) S-h-h-h-h! Here comes the other image. (**MARIO** *appears behind them on the right and takes a few steps, looking at* **ENCARNA**.) They do look real, don't they?

The researchers exit. The lights downstage brighten. **ENCARNA** *raises her eyes and smiles at* **MARIO**. *When he reaches her, they touch hands. Without letting go of her hand,* **MARIO** *sits beside her.*

ENCARNA: (*Gently.*) You're a little late . . .

MARIO: My brother was at home.

ENCARNA: I know. (*She gently pulls her hand away. Slightly disturbed, he smiles.*)

MARIO: I'm sorry.

ENCARNA: Why did it take us so long to get to know each other? The few times you came by the office, you didn't look at anybody, and you always left right away. . . . We hardly know anything about each other.

MARIO: (*Overcoming her resistance, he takes her hand again.*) But we said we were going to tell each other things, so we would know.

ENCARNA: People never tell each other everything. (*When the* **WAITER** *reappears, she pulls her hand away again.*)

MARIO: Bring me a beer, please. (*The* **WAITER** *nods and leaves.* **MARIO** *smiles, but his voice trembles slightly.*) He probably thinks we're a couple of lovebirds.

ENCARNA: But we're not.

MARIO: (*Looking at her curiously.*) Just friends who tell each other things . . . for now. So tell me more about yourself.

ENCARNA: Do I have to?

MARIO: (*Smiling at her.*) You have to.

ENCARNA: I'm from a really small town. My mother died when I was little. My father worked in construction, doing whatever he could. But there were hardly any jobs, so we came to Madrid six years ago.

MARIO: Like so many others in those days . . .

ENCARNA: My father used to tell me I'd get ahead. He got a job here first as a bricklayer. He worked day and night at all sorts of jobs. He bought me a typewriter, a user's manual, and other books. And when he'd see me building a fire or sweeping or carrying water—we lived in a kind of shantytown outside the city—he'd say: "I'll do that. You study!" And he wanted me to dress nicely, and he wanted me to read a lot, and . . . (*Her voice breaks.*)

MARIO: And he got what he wanted.

ENCARNA: But it killed him. He always went to work dead tired; half asleep, really. Then three years ago, he slipped off some scaffolding . . . (*She is quiet for a moment.*) After that, I was completely alone. And so scared! I spent a whole year looking for work. I went from one boardinghouse to another. I learned how to look out for myself, that's for sure . . . (*In a small voice.*) until I started working here at the office, anyway. (*She looks at him out of the corner of her eye.*)

MARIO: You didn't just learn to look out for yourself; you did things the right way, the decent way. You studied and prepared yourself to hold a job. You have reason to be proud.

ENCARNA: (*Suddenly uncomfortable.*) I don't want to talk about that anymore. (**MARIO** *looks at her, intrigued. The* **WAITER** *returns with a glass of beer, places it in front of* **MARIO**, *and is about to leave.*)

MARIO: Take everything out of this. (*He holds out a bill. The* **WAITER** *makes change and leaves.* **MARIO** *takes a sip of beer.*)

ENCARNA: And what about you? Why didn't you go to college? You and your brother seem so cultured . . . You could have done a lot of things.

MARIO: (*Ironically.*) Cultured? My brother almost finished high school, but I never even started. The war ended when I was ten. My father worked in a government office, so he lost his job when Franco took over. . . . We came back to Madrid and had to take the first place we found. We moved into this basement apartment . . . and have never gotten out. And years later, when the laws changed and my father could ask for his old job back, he refused. I went on reading and studying on my own, but somebody had to take care of the family.

ENCARNA: And what about your brother?

MARIO: (*Coldly.*) He only lived with us only until he got drafted. When he got out of the army, he decided to live on his own.

ENCARNA: And he helps the family . . .

MARIO: (*Taking a sip.*) Yes.

ENCARNA: You might have done as well as he did . . . Maybe by coming into the publishing house you could . . .

MARIO: (*Dryly.*) I don't want to work there.

ENCARNA: But . . . you have to live . . .

MARIO: That's the problem: we have to live.

ENCARNA: (*She nods. After a moment, she speaks.*) Today, for example . . .

MARIO: What?

ENCARNA: I'm not sure . . . But you know about the new group investing in the business . . .

MARIO: Yes.

ENCARNA: I don't think they want to publish Beltran's new novel. And it's wonderful! Your brother liked it, too!

MARIO: (*Intrigued.*) What happened?

ENCARNA: Vicente was talking to Juan on the telephone, and he made me leave. Later he said Beltran was off base in that novel, and then he took out an article that praised him from the package of proofs he gave you today.

MARIO: The new group is behind that. They have it in for Beltran.

ENCARNA: They used to praise him.

MARIO: That was just to create an alibi . . . And my brother, mixed up in that dirty business . . . (*Thinking.*) Listen, Encarna. Be on guard there. Tell me what you find out about that deal. We've got to help Beltran!

ENCARNA: You're a lot like him.

MARIO: (*Incredulous.*) Me? Like Beltran?

ENCARNA: You don't ask for favors; everybody else comes around with their hands out, looking for favors . . .

MARIO: He's been able to succeed without resorting to dirty tricks or favors. Occasionally it does happen . . . (*He smiles.*) But I don't have his talent . . .

(*Turning serious.*) and probably not his integrity, either. Let me tell you what I dreamed last night. There was a deep chasm . . . I was on one side, correcting proofs . . . On the other side, someone I couldn't make out was running along with a rope tied to his waist, and I was holding the end of that rope. I didn't stop working, but I kept tugging on the rope . . . pulling him closer and closer. When he was running along the very edge of the precipice, I gave another pull and made him fall in. (*Silence.*)

ENCARNA: You're a decent person. That's why you told me this.

MARIO: I told you because I have something to ask you. (*They look at each other nervously. He gathers his courage.*) Will you marry me? (*She looks away.*) You didn't expect that? (*She nods, and he smiles.*) I'll never make a lot of money. If you marry me, it's a good deal for me.

ENCARNA: (*Sadly.*) Don't joke about things like that.

MARIO: (*Seriously.*) Encarna, in many ways, I'm a broken man. I've been buried in that pit we call home ever since the war. But if your sadness and mine join forces, perhaps we'll find some kind of strange joy.

ENCARNA: (*On the verge of tears.*) What sadness are you talking about?

MARIO: Don't pretend.

ENCARNA: What do you know?

MARIO: Nothing. But I know. (*She looks at him nervously.*) Would you like to come home and meet my parents? (*She looks at him with a mixture of joy and anguish.*) Before you decide about marrying me, you should meet them.

ENCARNA: I know a lot about them already. I collect magazines and postcards for your father . . . The more people there are in the pictures, the better he likes it, right? (*She smiles.*)

MARIO: (*He nods, pensively.*) And frequently he asks who this person or that person is.

ENCARNA: Your brother took a postcard out of the package today because it didn't have any people in it. That way I learn things about your parents.

MARIO: He likes pictures without people too. What was in it? Some monument?

ENCARNA: No. It was an old train. (**MARIO** *straightens up, looking at her intensely. Without looking at him, she continues after a short pause.*) Mario, we can go to your house if you like, but not as sweethearts!

MARIO: (*Cold and distant.*) Let me think. (*She looks at him, disconcerted.*)

> The **PROSTITUTE** *enters from the right and stops a moment, looking for a potential client.* **ENCARNA** *becomes quiet when she sees her.*

MARIO: (*Getting up.*) Shall we go home, then?

ENCARNA: All right; just not as your girlfriend or anything.

MARIO: (*Coldly.*) I'll simply introduce you as a friend. (**ENCARNA** *goes to his side. The* **PROSTITUTE** *gives a sad, ironic smile and crosses slowly in front of them.* **ENCARNA** *takes* **MARIO**'s *arm when she sees her approach.* **MARIO** *starts to walk, but she fails to move.*) What's the matter? (*The* **PROSTITUTE** *exits stage left, swinging her hips.*)

ENCARNA: You're not just playing around with me, are you?

MARIO: (*Irritated.*) Why would you ask something like that?

ENCARNA: (*Lowering her voice.*) Let's go.

> *They exit stage right. As the* **WAITER** *enters to clear and wipe the table, the lights go down. The researchers reappear from opposite sides of the stage. Separate spotlights illuminate them, and when the* **WAITER** *exits, they speak.*

SHE: The scene you are about to witness took place seven days later.

HE: It was impossible to reconstruct completely what happened during those days; the machines captured such intensely radiant fields that we were able to retrieve only fragmentary apparitions.

SHE: We researchers are all too familiar with these flashing images. They have caused many a scholar to give up this work, disheartened by the immensity of it all.

HE: Sometimes the machines project bizarre visions: birds flying, hands waving, cities burning, ants on dead bodies, frozen wastelands.

SHE: I saw what looked like apes goose-stepping in formation, and children behind a barbed-wire fence . . .

HE: And we saw other mysterious scenes we couldn't make out, probably images from distant galaxies or forgotten civilizations; innumerable presences whose decay forms part of all of us, even today. We sent them back to the void so as not to lose the thread of our story, which may be more valuable.

SHE: The most hidden or insignificant action can be discovered some day, for the all-mysterious cosmos preserves everything.

HE: Even the minutest event can be perceived from somewhere.

SHE: And at times, even without machines, by means of some acutely sensitive mind.

HE: The experiment continues.

Oscillating lights flash over the office area. **HE** *and* **SHE** *exit on opposite sides. The light becomes steady. The typewriter in front of* **ENCARNA** *has a sheet of paper in the carriage. The door opens and* **MARIO** *enters.* **ENCARNA** *turns around, suppressing a sigh.*

MARIO: I came to drop off some proofs. Before I go, I thought I'd say hello . . . to my brother.

ENCARNA: (*Nervously.*) He's been in a meeting with the new board for a couple of hours now.

MARIO: Well, what about his secretary? Is she seeable?

ENCARNA: (*Without smiling.*) Apparently so.

MARIO: (*Closing the door and coming in.*) Am I in the way?

ENCARNA: I have work to do.

MARIO: Are you upset about something?

ENCARNA: I'm worried about my job.

MARIO: Huh! I don't think you have anything to be concerned about.

ENCARNA: Well, I *am* concerned. And I'd appreciate it if . . . you didn't stay long.

MARIO: (*Frowning, he takes a chair and sits down near* **ENCARNA**, *staring at her. She does not look at him.*) I haven't seen you for three days.

ENCARNA: We've been busy with the reorganization . . .

MARIO: People can always find time . . . (*A brief pause.*) if they want to, that is.

ENCARNA: I . . . needed time to think.

MARIO: (*He takes her hand.*) Encarna . . .

ENCARNA: Please, Mario!

MARIO: You know you love me!

ENCARNA: No, I don't!

MARIO: I think you do!

ENCARNA: (*She gets up, nervously.*) No!

MARIO: (*He gets up almost at the same time and takes her in his arms.*) Why do you say that?

ENCARNA: Let me go! (*He kisses her hungrily. She struggles free and looks toward the door.* MARIO *approaches her again and takes her by the arms.*)

MARIO: (*Softly.*) What's the matter?

ENCARNA: We have to talk. (*Upset, she goes to the desk and leans against it.*)

MARIO: Maybe you didn't like my parents.

ENCARNA: I do like them, really.

MARIO: And they like you.

ENCARNA: (*She walks away, trying to think of something to say.*) Your father called me Elvira . . . Why?

MARIO: That was our baby sister who died. She was two years old when the war ended.

ENCARNA: He confused me with her?

MARIO: If she'd lived, she'd be about your age.

ENCARNA: What did she die of?

MARIO: When the war was over, it took us six days to get back to Madrid. It was so hard to get a train. They were packed with soldiers trying to get home . . . And it was even harder to find food; especially milk. We traveled in trucks, wagons, any way we could . . . Elvira had so little to eat . . . We didn't have anything either. She died of starvation four days later. (*Silence.*)

ENCARNA: (*She presses his shoulder tenderly.*) We have to forget those things, Mario.

MARIO: (*Closing his eyes.*) Help me, Encarna. Will I see you later at the café?

ENCARNA: (*On the verge of tears.*) Yes. I have to talk to you.

MARIO: (*His tone and facial expression change. He looks at her curiously.*) About my brother?

ENCARNA: And other things, too.

185

MARIO: Did you find out anything? (*She looks at him, disturbed.*) Did you?

ENCARNA: (*Rushing to the office door, she opens it and looks out a moment. Relieved, she closes the door and picks up her purse.*) Look what I found in the wastebasket. (*She takes out torn bits of a letter and pieces them together on the table.* **MARIO** *bends over to examine them.*) Do you know French?

MARIO: A little.

ENCARNA: They're talking about Beltran, aren't they?

MARIO: They want the translation rights for *Secret Story,* his third novel. And since that publishing house no longer exists, they're writing to see if you people hold the rights. . . . In case you don't, they want the letter forwarded to the author . . . (*Pause. They look at each other.* **ENCARNA** *hurriedly gathers up the scraps of paper.*)

MARIO: Don't throw those pieces of paper away, Encarna.

ENCARNA: No, I won't. (*She puts them back into her purse.*)

MARIO: I'll wait around for Vicente. I want to talk to him about this.

ENCARNA: No!

MARIO: We can't keep this to ourselves! It's about human decency and Beltran!

ENCARNA: (*Discouraged, she sits down in her chair.*) I'm the one who found the letter. Let me see what I can do on my own.

MARIO: It will be easier if I'm with you!

ENCARNA: Please!

MARIO: (*He looks at her insistently for a few moments.*) I'm not asking if you dare, because you have a moral obligation to do it. You know that.

ENCARNA: Give me a few days . . .

MARIO: No, Encarna! If you don't promise me you'll do it now, I'm going to stay and talk to Vicente myself.

ENCARNA: (*Quickly.*) All right, all right! I promise! (*She lowers her head. He touches her hair with sudden tenderness.*) He'll fire me for this.

MARIO: You don't have to accuse him of anything. Make him think it was something he did by accident.

ENCARNA: Can I do that?

MARIO: (*Harshly.*) When the moment comes to speak clearly, I'll do it. Be brave, Encarna. I'll see you at the café.

ENCARNA: (*Frowning, she looks at him.*) Yes. We'll talk there.

The door opens, and VICENTE *enters holding a folder. He seems very satisfied.* ENCARNA *gets up.*

VICENTE: What are you doing here?

MARIO: I just came by to say hello. I was about to leave.

VICENTE: Don't go yet! (*He leaves the file on the table and sits down.*) Look, Mario. I am going to make you a great offer.

ENCARNA: Shall I leave?

VICENTE: That's not necessary! (*To* MARIO.) Encarna should hear this, too. Listen. How about becoming my editorial assistant as of right now? (ENCARNA *and* MARIO *look at each other.*) I have some good news for you, too, Encarna: a raise! It's a small one, but it's something. You'll stay on at your typewriter and your files. But I need an assistant with a good literary background. You understand . . .

ENCARNA: Of course. (*She sits down in her chair.*)

VICENTE: It's just the job for you, Mario. And it has a great future. For starters, you'll get about three times what you're making now. What do you say?

MARIO: Look, Vicente . . .

VICENTE: Before you say anything . . . (*Affectionately.*) I can do this today. Later, maybe I can't. Imagine how happy this will make mama. . . . I can tell you now; she asked me to do this several times.

MARIO: I'm not surprised.

VICENTE: I'd be glad about it, too . . .

MARIO: (*Softly.*) No, Vicente. But thanks anyway.

VICENTE: (*He represses a gesture of irritation.*) Why not?

MARIO: I wouldn't be good at it.

VICENTE: (*Getting up.*) I know better than you what you're good at! And this is a wonderful opportunity! You're nuts to refuse! Think of the wife and children you'll have someday! (ENCARNA *and* MARIO *look at each other.*) Encarna, you're a woman; you understand these things. Talk to him!

ENCARNA: (*Very nervous.*) Yes . . . Really . . .

MARIO: I'm very grateful to you, believe me . . . But no.

VICENTE: (*Irate.*) This is getting embarrassing . . . and ridiculous. Anybody else would jump at the chance . . . and be grateful.

MARIO: I know, Vicente, I know . . . I'm sorry.

VICENTE: What does that "I'm sorry" mean? Is it yes or no?

MARIO: (*Forcefully.*) It's no. (ENCARNA *sighs, disappointed.*)

VICENTE: (*After a moment, dryly.*) It's your call. (*He sits down.*)

MARIO: Good-bye, Vicente. And thanks. (*He exits and closes the door.*)

VICENTE: (*After a pause.*) I gave up trying to understand him a long time ago. All I can say is that he's not just proud; he's stupid. (*He sighs.*) They'll stick someone else in here. But don't worry; you'll stay on, and with a raise to boot.

ENCARNA: I thank you.

VICENTE: (*With a gesture of irritation.*) He doesn't know how generous my offer was. Because that wasn't exactly true what I said. I'm not really all that eager to have him around here. With all those strange ideas of his, it could be uncomfortable. Well! I don't want to think about it right now. Anything to sign?

ENCARNA: No.

VICENTE: No unfinished business? (*Silence.*) Huh?

ENCARNA: (*With difficulty.*) No. (*She begins to cry.*)

VICENTE: What's the matter?

ENCARNA: Nothing.

VICENTE: Nerves . . . Finding out your job is secure . . . (*He gets up and approaches her.*)

ENCARNA: I guess so.

VICENTE: (*Laughing.*) Well, that's nothing to cry about! That's something to celebrate! (*Insinuatingly.*) Got any plans for tonight?

ENCARNA: It's Thursday . . .

VICENTE: (*Annoyed.*) Oh, yes; your girlfriend.

ENCARNA: Yes.

VICENTE: I thought we'd spend the evening together.

ENCARNA: It's too late for me to cancel.

VICENTE: Let's go where you're supposed to meet her. You can make excuses, and I'll wait in the car.

ENCARNA: That wouldn't be right. How's tomorrow? (*Silence.*)

VICENTE: (*Irritated.*) All right. Go ahead. (ENCARNA *gets up and takes her purse. Undecided, she turns around in the doorway.*)

ENCARNA: See you tomorrow . . .

VICENTE: See you tomorrow . . .

ENCARNA: And thanks again . . .

VICENTE: (*Ironically.*) It's nothing! Nothing!

> ENCARNA *exits. In a gesture of fatigue,* VICENTE *rubs his eyes. He looks over some papers, lights a cigarette, and leans back in the chair. As he smokes, he begins to think. The sound of a train in the distance is heard as the lights come up on the living room. The door opens, and the* MOTHER *and* FATHER *enter.*

MOTHER: Where are you going, dear?

FATHER: He's here. (*He goes into the living room and looks all around.*)

MOTHER: Who are you looking for?

FATHER: A baby.

MOTHER: Oh, come on; go back to your postcards.

FATHER: I have to look for my baby!

MOTHER: Sit down . . .

FATHER: I'll complain to the authorities! I'll tell them you don't want him baptized.

MARIO: Don't want who baptized, father?

FATHER: My son, Vicente. (*He turns around suddenly, listening intently.* MARIO *leans against the wall and observes him. The sound of the train dies down.*) Hush! Now he's crying.

MOTHER: No one's crying!

FATHER: He must be in the kitchen. (*He goes toward the hall.*)

MARIO: He's probably on the train, father.

MOTHER: (*Irritated.*) Are you starting that, too?

FATHER: (*Turning around.*) Of course! (*He goes toward the invisible basement window.*) Let's get on the train before the boy grows up. Where do you get on?

MOTHER: (*She shrugs her shoulders and plays along.*) We're already on the train, silly!

FATHER: (*Disconcerted.*) No, we're not!

MOTHER: Yes, dear! Don't you hear the engine? Piiii . . . Piiii . . . (*She begins to shuffle her feet like a child playing.*) Chuga, chuga, chuga, chuga. (*Laughing, the* **FATHER** *gets behind her and imitates what she is doing. The two of them trot into the hallway, laughing and chanting "chuga, chuga." They go into the bedroom and the door closes behind them. Pause.*)

MARIO *goes to the basement window and looks out, thoughtfully.* **VICENTE** *comes out of his reverie in the office, stubs out his cigarette, and gets up with a long sigh. He looks at his watch and exits rapidly, closing the door behind him. Lights flash briefly and then go down on the office. The* **MOTHER** *opens the bedroom door cautiously. She comes out into the hallway, closing the door behind her as she represses laughter.*

MOTHER: This man will be the death of me yet. (*She arranges cups and saucers on a tray at the sideboard.*) When he went by the mirror in the bedroom just now, he stared at himself, and I said, "What are you doing?" Then he pointed to the mirror and whispered, "Look who I found." So I said, "Well, talk to him." He answered: "Why should I? He doesn't talk to me!" (*She laughs.*) He's so funny! Want something with your coffee?

MARIO: (*Without turning around.*) No, thank you. (*The* **MOTHER** *picks up the tray and is about to leave.*) What train is he talking about?

MOTHER: (*She stops.*) About one he must have seen in the magazines . . . (*She starts to leave.*)

MARIO: Or a real one.

MOTHER: (*She looks at him curiously.*) Maybe. We've taken so many in our lives . . .

MARIO: (*Turning toward her.*) We've also missed a few.

MOTHER: That's right, too.

MARIO: But not really. People don't miss trains every day. We only missed one that I know of.

MOTHER: (*Motionless, with the tray in her hands.*) I didn't think you remembered.

MARIO: Do you suppose he's referring to that one?

MOTHER: He doesn't remember anything . . .

MARIO: But you remember.

MOTHER: Of course I do. Not so much because of the train, but because of those awful days . . . (*She puts the tray on the table.*) The train is the least of it. It took Vinny away, because he was able to climb in through a window, and then he couldn't get off. But it all worked out. I yelled at him to go to my cousin's house . . . and that we'd come later. The poor thing waited for us there without knowing that meanwhile . . . his baby sister had died.

MARIO: When I brought that friend of mine home, father called her Elvira.

MOTHER: What?

MARIO: You didn't hear it because you were in the kitchen.

MOTHER: (*Thinking it over.*) Words suddenly pop into his head . . . But he doesn't remember anything.

MARIO: Do you think about Elvira a lot, mother?

MOTHER: (*Lowering her voice.*) Every single day.

MARIO: Babies shouldn't die.

MOTHER: (*Sighing.*) But they do.

MARIO: And they die two ways.

MOTHER: Two ways?

MARIO: Some die when they grow up. We're all a little dead. (*The* MOTHER *looks at him sadly and picks up the tray.*)

FATHER: (*Leaving the bedroom and returning to the living room.*) Good afternoon, madam. Who are you?

MOTHER: (*Seriously.*) I'm your wife.

FATHER: (*Very seriously.*) How funny, funny, funny, Miss Sunny, Sunny, Sunny!

MOTHER: Be quiet, Mr. Silly Willy, Willy! (*The* **FATHER** *shuffles through papers and magazines on the table. He selects a postcard, sits down, and prepares to cut something out. The* **MOTHER** *puts the tray down again and goes over to* **MARIO**.) That friend of yours seems very nice. Is she someone special?

MARIO: No . . .

MOTHER: But you like her.

MARIO: Yes.

MOTHER: She's very down to earth and real. I liked her, and she liked us, too. If I were you, I'd think about marrying her.

MARIO: And what if she doesn't want to marry me?

MOTHER: Oh, sometimes you're not too smart.

MARIO: (*Smiling.*) Maybe I've already asked her, and she can't make up her mind.

MOTHER: Probably playing hard to get.

MARIO: You think so?

MOTHER: (*Sweetly.*) Of course.

FATHER: (*To* **MARIO**, *referring to someone in a postcard.*) Who is this person?

MARIO: (*He hugs his mother suddenly.*) I'd like her to live here with us.

MOTHER: She'll come . . . And she'll bring joy and children . . .

MARIO: Don't say anything to Vicente about her; not yet.

MOTHER: But he'd be happy, too . . .

MARIO: Try to understand. I want it to be a surprise.

MOTHER: Whatever you say. (*She lowers her voice.*) But don't you talk to your father about any train. We don't need to complicate things. . . . Life must go on! (*They look at each other intensely. The doorbell rings.*) Who can that be?

MOTHER: Did you invite her over?

MARIO: No . . .

MOTHER: But since she's already been here once and knows she's welcome . . .

MARIO: (*Happily.*) That's right! I hope it's Encarna! (*He goes toward the hall.*)

FATHER: Who is this person? (**MARIO** *looks at him briefly, and then goes to open the door.*)

MOTHER: (*To her husband.*) That's just a man wearing a jacket! (*She goes toward the hall to listen as* MARIO *opens the door to* VICENTE.) Vicente, dear! (MARIO *closes the door without saying anything as* VICENTE *enters. The* MOTHER *hugs him.*) Is something wrong?

VICENTE: (*Smiling.*) I promised you I'd come more often.

MOTHER: Today I'm not letting you go for the whole afternoon!

VICENTE: I really can't stay long.

MOTHER: I can't hear a word you're saying. (*They come into the living room. The* MOTHER *hurries to the cabinet and takes a coin purse out of the drawer.*) Just do me a favor and wait here nice and quiet until I get back! (*She rushes down the hallway.*) I won't be long! (*She opens the front door and leaves hurriedly, closing the door behind her.*)

MARIO: (*Who has also entered the living room and is leaning against the doorway.*) Think she'll bring sweet rolls?

VICENTE: (*Laughing.*) I bet she does. Hello, father. How's everything? (*The* FATHER *looks at him briefly and returns to his postcards.*)

MARIO: Same as ever. I think you can see that. I suppose you came to talk to me.

VICENTE: Yes.

MARIO: I'm listening. (*He crosses the room and sits at his desk.*)

VICENTE: (*Affectionately.*) Why don't you want to work at the publishing house?

MARIO: (*He looks at him, surprised.*) Is that what you wanted to talk about?

VICENTE: Of course! What else would I want to talk to you about? (*Irritated,* MARIO *hits the palm of his hand with his fist. He gets up and begins to pace.* VICENTE *comes close to him.*) You already work for the publishing house, Mario, correcting proofs. So what's the difference?

MARIO: (*Harshly.*) Sit down.

VICENTE: I'll be glad to if you'll start making some sense. (*He sits down.*)

MARIO: But maybe I won't. (*He smiles.*) I live here with our father. Not a very rational atmosphere, you know. (*He points to the* FATHER.) Look at him. This poor madman used to be simply a decent man. Do you remember? He taught us to be honest. That's a dangerous lesson in these times. (*In an accusatory tone.*) People don't live as honestly as they used to. They live by

193

lies, deceit, favors, and dirty deals. One person takes advantage of another; the big fish eats the little fish. What should you—or I—do about it? There are two options: you play that game and climb out of this pit . . . , or you stay in the pit.

VICENTE: (*Coldly.*) And why don't you climb out?

MARIO: I just explained it to you . . . What I'd have to do turns my stomach. The only possibilities are to destroy others or let them destroy me. It's like everyone says, "Get them before they get you!" They even give you soothing theories for your peace of mind: "Life is a struggle" or "Evil is inevitable to accomplish good" or "Charity begins at home." But I've made my choice: I just stay in my little space, trying to survive without being devoured . . . but without devouring others, either.

VICENTE: You come out sometimes, I suppose.

MARIO: Yes, I climb out every once in a while to take care of some unimportant little things . . .

VICENTE: You must take advantage of someone occasionally, wouldn't you say?

MARIO: Very little . . . I just defend myself. I even let people take advantage of me sometimes to avoid arguments. . . . But as you can see, I don't make a lot of money.

VICENTE: That sounds like an accusation. Am I right?

FATHER: Who is this person? (**MARIO** *goes over to his father.*)

MARIO: You told us you knew.

FATHER: And I do know. (*He looks at them slyly.*)

MARIO: (*To his brother.*) That's strange. Opera Square in Paris, the man with the derby. And he makes the same statement.

VICENTE: You yourself admitted he was a senile old fool.

MARIO: But someone capable of asking what he asks . . . must be more than just a senile old fool.

VICENTE: What does he ask?

MARIO: "Who is this person? And what about the one over there?" Don't you think those are important questions?

VICENTE: Why?

MARIO: Well, if you don't understand . . . (*He shrugs his shoulders and begins to pace up and down.*)

FATHER: Do you have children, young man?

VICENTE: What?

MARIO: He's talking to you.

VICENTE: You know I don't have any.

FATHER: (*Smiling.*) Then I have a surprise for you, young man. (*He begins to cut something out of a magazine as* **MARIO** *pauses to observe.*)

VICENTE: I suppose you were referring to me when you talked about people taking advantage of others to make money . . .

MARIO: I only meant that perhaps I wouldn't be able to play the game without getting caught up in it.

VICENTE: (*Getting up.*) But life in this place is impossible!

MARIO: Somebody had to stay here!

VICENTE: (*Confronting him angrily.*) If I hadn't left, I wouldn't be able to help all of you now!

MARIO: But during those years, someone had to take care of our parents . . . and I did it. Oh, I didn't do it very well, I'll admit.

VICENTE: But you were here, taking care of them. Congratulations! Now you can join me, and we'll take care of them together!

MARIO: (*Sincerely.*) I really can't do that!

VICENTE: (*Trying to control himself.*) Mario, all action is tainted in some way. But you'll never accomplish anything useful if you don't do something! You won't ever know what people are like unless you deal with them. You won't even know yourself if you don't get involved with others.

MARIO: I'd rather just watch from the sidelines.

VICENTE: But that's absurd! It's crazy! You're throwing your life away here watching a madman and peeping at nobodies through the basement window. You're dreaming! Wake up!

MARIO: Who should wake up? I see a lot of busy people on the go all around me, but they really aren't awake! The more corrupt they get, the more arrogant they are and the less accountable they feel!

VICENTE: I didn't come here to be insulted!

MARIO: But you keep coming. You come back to this pit more and more often. And that's what I like most about you.

FATHER: (*He stops cutting and points to a postcard.*) Who is this person, young man? I'll bet you don't know.

MARIO: There's that tremendous question again.

VICENTE: Tremendous?

MARIO: Of course. It's not enough to identify somebody by name. It's not even enough to know what he or she did, or what happened. When you found all that out, you'd have to ask other things . . . It's an endless . . . and infinite process of . . . questioning, learning.

VICENTE: What are you talking about?

FATHER: (*Without taking his eyes off of them and pointing again to the postcard.*) He's talking about this. (*He begins to cut again.*)

MARIO: Didn't you ever ask yourself that question looking at an old postcard? Didn't you ever wonder who that person was? Yes, it was someone who passed by at that precise instant . . . But who? Active people like you are always in a hurry. You don't care. But I see him as a person, frozen in the postcard, immobile . . .

VICENTE: You mean, dead.

MARIO: No; only immobile. It's like a hyper-real painting, or a very sharp photograph of some living being. That picture was taken, and the person didn't even realize it. And I wonder . . . But now you're going to laugh.

VICENTE: (*Wryly.*) That's very possible.

MARIO: I wonder if that person wasn't photographed for a purpose, so that years later I'd ask who he or she was. (**VICENTE** *looks at him in amazement.*) Yes, yes. And I wonder if we couldn't . . . (*He stops talking.*)

VICENTE: Couldn't what?

MARIO: Perhaps we could undertake some research . . .

VICENTE: I don't understand.

MARIO: Find out who that person was. We could go to Paris, put an ad in the paper, follow all the leads . . . Would we find any trace of that life? Would we even find that person at the end of the line, already old? And it might be that way with everybody who ever lived.

VICENTE: (*Dumbfounded.*) You want to go through that with everybody?

MARIO: It's crazy, I know. But imagine. It's like wanting to understand the individual function of each electron in a distant galaxy.

VICENTE: (*Laughing.*) You'd like to see what God sees! (*The* **FATHER** *gives them a penetrating glance.*)

MARIO: A vision we can never have, but one we all long for.

VICENTE: (*He sits down, bored.*) You're nuts.

MARIO: I know what I want is impossible. That's why I settle for watching things (*Looking at him.*) and people from unusual angles . . .

VICENTE: (*Contemptuous and irritated.*) And you even imagine things, just like we did as kids looking through the basement window.

MARIO: Won't those things that we imagine tell us something very real that the people we observe don't even know?

VICENTE: What do you mean?

MARIO: It's hard to explain . . . And besides, you don't play those games anymore. . . . People on the fast track, like you, rarely take time to observe, think, contemplate. You see and believe the same old things. I try to avoid those clichés, because if I dealt with people like that, I might fall into the same habits. Right now I see a bunch of poor devils and hypocrites; they're despicable enemies . . . criminals and idiots. But I keep looking at the people who pass by the window. And I understand that they represent other things . . . and can be unexpectedly beautiful . . . or surprising.

VICENTE: (*Mockingly.*) Give me an example.

MARIO: (*Hesitantly.*) It's not easy to give examples. A gesture, a lost word . . . I don't know. And occasionally, some important revelation.

FATHER: (*Looking at his hands.*) I have too many fingers!

VICENTE: (*To* **MARIO**.) What did he say?

FATHER: (*Holding up his hand.*) Too many fingers. I don't need these two. (*Taking the scissors to the small finger on his left hand.*)

VICENTE: (*Leaping up immediately.*) Be careful! (**MARIO**, *who has gone over to his father, makes a rapid gesture for* **VICENTE** *not to interfere.*) He's going to hurt himself! (**MARIO** *shakes his head and watches very attentively, prepared to intervene. The* **FATHER** *starts to cut himself but stops when he feels the pain.*)

FATHER: (*Laughing.*) That hurts, by golly! (*He goes back to cutting things out of his magazines.* **MARIO** *smiles.*)

VICENTE: He could have hurt himself.

MARIO: We would have stopped him in time. Now we know that his protective reflexes are working. (*Smiling.*) So one must observe, dear brother. One must observe more and act less. Shall we open the window?

VICENTE: (*Sarcastic.*) You want to offer me one of your great revelations?

MARIO: I'm only trying to go back to another time; back to when we were children.

VICENTE: (*He shrugs his shoulders and leans on the edge of the table.*) Do whatever you want.

> **MARIO** *approaches the invisible basement window and mimes the action of opening it. The sound of a pulley is heard, and the light in the room changes slightly. Against the back wall an enlarged rectangular reflection of the barred basement window appears. Interested, the* **FATHER** *puts down his scissors. Soon there are shadows of passersby.*

FATHER: Sit down!

VICENTE: (*Laughing.*) Just like in the movies! (*He takes a chair.*)

MARIO: Just like it used to be at home. (*He sits down. All three watch the basement window. Some feminine legs pass hurriedly. A short while later, the legs of two men cross slowly in different directions. Perhaps we hear the muffled sound of their conversation.*)

VICENTE: (*Ironically.*) All that's so commonplace, so trivial . . .

MARIO: Is that what you think?

> *As a couple passes the window, reflected on the back wall are the man's legs close to those of a woman; they are laughing. Then the shadow of another man appears. He stops a moment and turns around when he hears someone say: "Don't be in such a hurry!" The legs of the speaker cast their shadow as he reaches the one who was hurrying. Both walk off together, and their shadows disappear.*

MARIO: That's what I say: don't be in such a hurry. (*The shadows of three children pass amid laughter and shouts of "Last one's a rotten egg!"*) Neighborhood kids. Maybe they're going to the corner to buy their first cigarettes; that's why they're imitating the language of the grown-ups. Sometimes they stop and tap on the window, then run off . . .

VICENTE: You must have known who they were.

MARIO: (*Smiling and nodding.*) Yes. (*As the legs of a young man appear.*) And what about that one?

VICENTE: I couldn't see anything!

MARIO: He had a small piece of paper in his hand and was in a hurry. Was it a prescription? The pharmacy is close by. Maybe someone at home is sick. Perhaps his father . . . (VICENTE *shakes his head energetically in disbelief. The shadow of a woman's legs crosses slowly. She carries a suitcase.*) And what about this one?

VICENTE: What about her? She's gone!

MARIO: And you didn't notice anything.

VICENTE: Well, I saw a suitcase.

MARIO: A cardboard suitcase, a faded skirt, a hesitant walk . . . Maybe another small-town girl coming to the city. Her legs were sturdy, like a country girl's.

VICENTE: (*Scornfully.*) You're making things up!

MARIO: (*With a sudden and disconcerting laugh.*) Of course! Of course! Everything can be make-believe!

VICENTE: So?

MARIO: It's a game. We can see the obvious things about them, but the more important questions remain . . .

VICENTE: (*Scornfully.*) Mysterious, right?

MARIO: Exactly.

VICENTE: If it can't be explained, it's nothing.

MARIO: "Nothing" isn't the same as "unknown" or "mysterious." (*Three more shadows cross.*)

VICENTE: This is crazy!

MARIO: (*Ignoring him, he comments innocently on another shadow that crosses.*) Now a young mother with a baby carriage. The baby could die at any moment, but for now she doesn't think about that . . . (**VICENTE** *makes a gesture of irritation.*) Of course, it can just be my imagination. (*Seeing the shadow of another person who pauses.*) And what about this one? He doesn't have much to do. He's just out for a walk. (*Suddenly the shadow bends down and peers into the basement window. Silence.*)

FATHER: Who is that? (*The shadow straightens up and disappears.*)

VICENTE: (*Uncomfortable.*) Someone who's curious about us.

MARIO: (*Controlling his emotions with difficulty.*) Like we are about him. But who is he? He also wonders who we are. His look really got to me. It's as though I were a part of him . . .

VICENTE: Is this the miracle you were looking for?

MARIO: (*Looking at him enigmatically.*) It means nothing to you; I can see that. We'll have to experiment some other way.

VICENTE: Experiment?

The children pass again, this time going in the opposite direction. Their voices are heard: "They can see us here. Let's go to the park and do it there." "Yes, the park!" "Last one there's a rotten egg!" They run off, and their shadows disappear.

MARIO: The same kids as before. They were talking about smoking. You see; I was right.

VICENTE: Just a coincidence.

MARIO: Of course this wasn't the miracle either. Nevertheless, I would say that today . . .

VICENTE: What?

MARIO: (*He looks at him steadily.*) Oh, nothing. (*Two or three shadows pass by.* **VICENTE** *is about to speak.*) Hush. (*They look through the basement window. No one passes by.*)

VICENTE: (*Pensively.*) Nobody's out there.

MARIO: No.

VICENTE: Here comes someone else.

The Basement Window (Madrid, 1967), Part I, Mario (José María Rodero), the Father (Francisco Pierrá), and Vicente (Jesús Puente).

The reflection of a man's legs. They belong to a man who walks unhurriedly. He stops just in front of the basement window and turns around very slowly with his hands behind his back as though observing the street. He takes a few more steps and pauses again.

MARIO: (*Observing* VICENTE *out of the corner of his eye.*) It can't be.

VICENTE: What can't be?

MARIO: Do you think that's . . . ?

VICENTE: Who? (*Silence.*) Someone from the neighborhood?

MARIO: If that's who I think it is, I wonder what brings him around here. Perhaps he comes to observe . . .

VICENTE: What are you talking about?

MARIO: I could swear that's who it was. What do you think? Give him a closer look. Notice the dark trousers, the tweed jacket . . . That way of clasping his hands behind his back . . . And that calm, deliberate way of his . . .

VICENTE: (*Amazed.*) Eugenio Beltran? (*He gets up and hurries over to the basement window. The shadow disappears.* MARIO's *eyes are glued to his brother.* VICENTE *searches the street in vain from another angle of the window.*) I didn't see his face. (*He turns around.*) How ridiculous! (MARIO *says nothing.*) That's not who it was, Mario! (MARIO *makes no reply.*) Or were you referring to someone else? (MARIO *gets up without answering.* VICENTE's *voice becomes harsh.*) Don't you see that your imagination is running wild? (MARIO *approaches the window.*) If these are the revelations and miracles you see from here, you make me laugh! If this is your way of getting to know people, you're out of your mind! (*As he speaks, another shadow passes by.* MARIO *cranks the invisible pulley to close the window, and the patch of light with the bars disappears.*) Do you really believe that was Eugenio Beltran out there? It wasn't.

MARIO: (*Turning to* VICENTE.) Maybe not. And perhaps that's the miracle. (*He returns to his table, picks up a cigarette and lights it.*)

VICENTE *has become very quiet but does not take his eyes off* MARIO. *He is about to speak but changes his mind. The lights flash and come up brightly downstage.* ENCARNA *enters stage left, looks to the right, consults her watch, and sits down at the table. The* FATHER *gets up with a paper figure he has just cut out.*

FATHER: This is for you, young man. (VICENTE *looks at the paper figure, disconcerted.*) We must have children, and we must take care of them. This one's for you. (**VICENTE** *accepts the figure. The* **FATHER** *is about to return to his chair but pauses.*) Don't you hear someone crying again? (**VICENTE** *looks at him, shocked.*) I hear it in the hallway. (*He goes toward the hall. The door opens, and the* **MOTHER** *enters with a small package.*)

MOTHER: (*Closing the door.*) It took me longer than I expected, but we'll have coffee right away.

FATHER: The crying has stopped. (*He sits down again to look at the magazines.*)

MOTHER: I brought you some sweet rolls. (*She holds up the little package and puts it on top of the sideboard.*) I'll heat milk for coffee! (*She hurries to the hall and stops when she hears her son.*)

VICENTE: (*Coldly.*) I'm sorry, mother. I have to go.

MOTHER: But Vinny . . .

VICENTE: I didn't realize how late it was. (*He goes over to the* **FATHER** *to return the paper figure. The* **FATHER** *looks at it. He hesitates but finally puts it in his pocket.*) Good-bye, mama.

MOTHER: (*Rapidly opening the package.*) At least have a sweet roll . . .

VICENTE: No, thanks. I'm in a hurry. (*He kisses her and says good-bye to his brother without looking at him.*) Good-bye, Mario. (*He walks to the hallway.*)

MARIO: Good-bye.

MOTHER: Come back soon.

VICENTE: When I can, mama. Bye.

MOTHER: (*Kissing him again.*) Good-bye . . . (**VICENTE** *leaves, and* **MARIO** *puts out his cigarette brusquely. In a strangely euphoric gesture, he grabs a sweet roll and begins to devour it. The* **MOTHER** *watches him, intrigued.*) I'll heat some milk.

MARIO: All I want is this pastry. (*He picks up his cigarettes and puts them in his pocket.*) I'm leaving, too. (*He looks at his watch.*) See you later. (*His voice, from the hallway, has a happy ring.*) This roll is delicious! (*He leaves.*)

MOTHER: (*Turning to her husband, thoughtfully.*) If we could talk like we did years ago, maybe you could explain . . . (*She sighs and goes into the kitchen, closing the door behind her.*)

A pause. The brakes of a car squeal close by. **ENCARNA,** *agitated, looks to the right. To hide her face, she turns slightly.* **VICENTE** *appears stage right and approaches her.*

VICENTE: What are you doing here?

ENCARNA: Hello! What a surprise!

VICENTE: That's what I say.

ENCARNA: I was waiting for my girlfriend. (*She looks at her watch.*) I guess she's not coming after all.

VICENTE: How do you know?

ENCARNA: I've been here a long time . . .

VICENTE: (*Pointing to the table.*) Without ordering anything?

ENCARNA: (*Becoming agitated.*) I had a beer . . . They've already taken the glass away. (*She looks nervously toward the invisible entrance. Silence.*)

VICENTE: (*He looks suspiciously toward the right.*) My parents and brother live close by. Did you know that?

ENCARNA: What a coincidence . . .

VICENTE: (*Jokingly.*) I don't suppose it was a male friend you were waiting for?

ENCARNA: (*Flustered.*) I don't appreciate jokes like that.

VICENTE: Why don't you ask me to sit down? We can wait for your friend together.

ENCARNA: I'm sure she's not coming. (*She lowers her head, nervously.*) But . . . sit down if you like.

VICENTE: (*Looking at her steadily.*) Let's go. Now you can spend the evening with me . . .

ENCARNA: Of course! (*She gets up anxiously.*) Where are we going?

VICENTE: To my place, of course. (*He takes her by the arm, and they exit stage right.*)

The car starts. After a pause, the sound of tapping on the glass is heard. The FATHER *looks up from his magazines and stares intensely at the basement window.* MARIO *enters downstage right and frowns when he sees that there is no one at the sidewalk café. He looks at his watch. He makes a gesture of disappointment and approaches the table in front of the café. He hesitates but with a gloomy expression sits down. Pause. The tapping on the window is repeated. The* FATHER, *who was waiting to hear the sound again, gets up and looks toward the rear to make sure no one is watching as he hurries to open the window. The downstage lights dim noticeably, and* MARIO *becomes a motionless shadow. Against the living room wall, we see again the reflection of the bars from the basement window along with the shadows of three children, two boys and a girl. Their voices are heard as they crouch to peek in the window.*

FIRST BOY: (*Amidst the laughter of the other two.*) How's it going, gramps?

FATHER: (*He laughs along with them.*) Hello there!

SECOND BOY: Will you give us a postcard, grandpa?

FIRST BOY: We'd rather have a cigarette.

FATHER: (*Happily.*) You shouldn't smoke, you little rascals!

GIRL: Want to come to the park with us, grampy?

FATHER: You be careful in the park, Elvira, baby! You're so little! (*The children laugh.*) Mario! Vicente! Take good care of your baby sister!

SECOND BOY: (*As the others laugh.*) Come out and play with us!

FATHER: (*Laughing.*) Yes! Yes! Let's play.

FIRST BOY: Bye, grandpa! (*The shadow stands up.*)

FATHER: Vicente! Mario! Elvira! (*The shadows start to move away as the children laugh.*) Wait for me!

VOICE OF THE GIRL: Bye . . . (*The shadows disappear.*)

FATHER: (*Speaking over the fading laughter.*) My little Elvira! (*He sobs uncontrollably in silence.*)

The lights dim to almost total darkness as two spotlights illuminate the researchers, one on either side of the stage.

SHE: (*Smiling.*) Return to your own century, now . . . The first part of the experiment is over. (*The curtain begins to descend.*)

HE: Thank you for your attention.

CURTAIN

PART TWO

As the curtain goes up slowly, lights begin to flash. The researchers, one on each side of the semi-dark stage, stand in bright spotlights as the stage lights come up slightly on the office and living room. ENCARNA *sits motionless at the office table. The* MOTHER *and* VICENTE, *likewise motionless, stand in an embrace in the dimly lit hallway.*

SHE: The second part of our experiment begins.

HE: The first scenes take place a week after those you have already witnessed. (*Pointing to the stage.*) The projectors are just warming up, so you see only motionless images right now.

SHE: The fragments gathered from the previous week are not absolutely essential to our research. They just showed Encarna and Vicente working in the office, barely speaking . . .

HE: We also saw them in a bedroom, probably Vicente's, making love in a perfunctory kind of way.

SHE: And we retrieved some fragments of Mario with his parents and of other things like paper figures, corrected proofs, bland conversations . . . Empty moments, really.

HE: But we saw no new encounter between Encarna and Mario.

SHE: Probably there was none.

HE: The experiment begins again with some very clear images of Vicente's unexpected visit to the family home.

The light increases to normal intensity in the office area as well as in the living room. ENCARNA *begins to move slowly.*

SHE: You will recall that Mario remarked to his brother, "You're coming back here more and more."

HE: (*Pointing to the stage.*) This part of the case history tells us why.

HE *and* SHE *exit on opposite sides as lights come up on the* MOTHER *and* VICENTE. ENCARNA *listlessly goes over some papers and puts letters in order for filing. The* MOTHER *and* VICENTE *come out of the embrace. As they speak,* ENCARNA *walks to the file cabinet and puts some folders away. She pauses, lost in thought, before returning to the table to continue her work.*

MOTHER: (*Sweetly.*) You're like a new man! You come so often now. (**VICENTE** *smiles.*) Come with me. Wouldn't you like something to drink? We're out of milk, but I have other things. (*They enter the living room.*)

VICENTE: No, mama, thank you.

MOTHER: How about a little glass of wine?

VICENTE: No, mama; nothing, really.

ENCARNA *gloomily looks off into space.*

MOTHER: Oh, darn!

VICENTE: Hey! Don't get upset just because I don't want anything!

MOTHER: Oh, no; it's not that! I forgot to go up to Miss Gabriela's. She wants me to show her how to do eggs in that special sauce of mine. She's a little slow, you know . . .

VICENTE: Well, go up to see her.

MOTHER: She can wait! Your father went out for a walk with Mr. Anselmo. They won't be long, but when they get back, they go up to his place first.

VICENTE: (*Sitting down wearily.*) Is Mario around?

MOTHER: No.

ENCARNA *puts the papers down and holds her face in her hands.*

VICENTE: How's father doing? (*He lights a cigarette.*)

MOTHER: All right, for him. (*She goes to the small table to get an ashtray.*)

VICENTE: Has he had any more of those . . . outbursts?

MOTHER: (*A little ashamed.*) Are you asking because of . . . the incident with the TV?

VICENTE: No. Forget that.

MOTHER: He's always been irritable . . . He was that way before he got sick.

VICENTE: And he got sick a long time ago . . .

MOTHER: I remember back then, before . . . (*She places the ashtray beside him.*)

VICENTE: Thank you.

MOTHER: Your father and Mr. Anselmo are probably back by now. I'll check. (*She walks stage rear.*)

VICENTE: And about the train. Do you remember that?

The MOTHER *turns around slowly and looks at* VICENTE *just as the telephone rings in the office.* ENCARNA, *startled, looks at it without daring to answer.*

MOTHER: What train?

VICENTE: (*Forcing a laugh.*) What a short memory you have! (*The telephone continues to ring in the office.* ENCARNA *gets up and stares at it as she twists her hands nervously.*) We missed only one train that I know of . . . (*The* MOTHER *comes close to* VICENTE *and sits down beside him.* ENCARNA *is about to answer the telephone but changes her mind.*) Or did you forget about that?

MOTHER: And why do you remember it? Because your father has a silly idea that the window is a train? I'm sure it has nothing to do with . . .

The telephone stops ringing. ENCARNA *sits down as though exhausted.*

VICENTE: Of course it has nothing to do with that. But how could I forget what happened?

MOTHER: What a shame you couldn't get off. Those bullies held on to you. It was all their fault . . .

VICENTE: Maybe I shouldn't have been in such a hurry.

MOTHER: But your father told you to get on! Remember? We all tried to get on any way we could. You were agile and able to climb in through the lavatory window. The rest of us couldn't even get on the steps . . .

MARIO *enters downstage left with a book under his arm. He frowns as he fingers a coin for the telephone. The lights already shine on the sidewalk café and the little round table where* MARIO *takes a seat.* ENCARNA *raises eyes red from crying and looks off into space. Perhaps she is imagining that* MARIO *is precisely where he is. For a few moments,* MARIO *thoughtfully taps the coin on the table.*

VICENTE: Our poor baby sister . . .

MOTHER: Yes, dear. That was awful. (*She becomes thoughtful.* ENCARNA *gets up again, looks at her watch with a nervous, anguished gesture as she leans against the desk, apparently struggling with herself. The* MOTHER *comes out of her sad reverie.*) Only awful people start wars! (*The doorbell rings.*) Maybe that's your brother. (*She walks stage rear to open the door. Her husband enters and, without saying anything, goes into the living room. Meanwhile, the* MOTHER *goes into the hall and speaks to someone we do not see.*) Oh, thank you, Mr. Anselmo! Tell

Gabriela I'll be right up. (*She closes the door and returns to the living room. The* FATHER *is looking at* VICENTE *from the doorway.*) Look! Vinny's here.

FATHER: Of course Vinny's here! *I'm* Vinny.

MOTHER: I'm talking about your son, silly! (*She laughs.*)

FATHER: Good afternoon, young man. I think I've seen you around somewhere before . . . (*He goes to the table and searches among the postcards.*)

MOTHER: Would you mind staying with him a little while? Since I promised to . . .

FATHER: Maybe you're in the waiting room. (*He goes to the cabinet, opens a drawer, and rummages among some paper cutouts.*)

VICENTE: Go on upstairs, mama. I'll take care of him.

FATHER: Well, I don't find you here.

MOTHER: If Mario comes and you have to leave . . .

VICENTE: Don't worry. I'll stay till you come back.

MOTHER: (*Smiling at him.*) I won't be long, dear. (*She hurries to the door, muttering.*) That old lady always wants something . . . (*As she leaves, she closes the door.*)

VICENTE *looks at his father.* ENCARNA *and* MARIO *look off into space.* ENCARNA *moistens her lips as though preparing for a difficult task. With almost neurotic haste, she covers the typewriter, picks up her purse, and, with her hand on the doorknob, breathes as though frightened. Finally, she opens the door, exits, and closes the door behind her. Discouraged by the apparently futile wait,* MARIO *gets up and crosses to exit stage right.*

FATHER: (*Closing the drawer and turning around.*) No, you're not here either. (*Laughing.*) You're not anywhere. (*He sits down at the table and opens a magazine.*)

VICENTE: (*Taking a postcard out of his pocket and placing it in front of his father.*) Is this where I am, father?

FATHER: (*Examining the postcard closely and then looking at him.*) Thank you, young man. I always need trains. They're all so full . . . you can't ever get on one. (*He looks again at the card and then pushes it away as he returns to his magazine.*)

VICENTE: You really don't remember me?

FATHER: Are you talking to me?

VICENTE: Father, I'm your son.

FATHER: Ha! For some time now, I'm everybody's father. Now if you'll excuse me, I'm going to cut out this gentleman. I think I know who he is.

VICENTE: What about me? Who am I?

FATHER: I told you: you're not in my file.

VICENTE: (*Placing the postcard in front of him again.*) I'm not here either?

FATHER: No. (*He prepares to cut out a figure.*)

VICENTE: And what about Mario? Do you know who he is?

FATHER: I have a son named Mario; haven't seen him for years.

VICENTE: He lives right here, with you.

FATHER: (*Laughing.*) Maybe he's in the waiting room.

VICENTE: Do you know who Elvira is? (*The* **FATHER** *stops laughing and looks at him; then he suddenly gets up, goes to the window, opens it, and looks out. Partial shadows of passersby reflect against the wall.*) No. And those people out there didn't get on the train either.

FATHER: (*Turning around, irritated.*) They all got on. All of them or none of them!

VICENTE: (*Getting up.*) They couldn't all get on! You shouldn't hold a grudge against the one who could!

Two friends pass by, talking. The shadows of their legs cross slowly. Their words are barely audible.

FATHER: S-h-h-h! Don't you hear them?

VICENTE: Just passersby. (*Other shadows pass.*) You see? Some poor devils we've never met. (*Energetically.*) Come back and sit down, father! (*Perplexed, the* **FATHER** *slowly returns to his chair.* **VICENTE** *takes his arm and seats him gently.*) Don't keep asking who those people are out there. And stop asking about the ones in those postcards. . . . They have nothing to do with you, and lots of them are already dead. But two of your own children are still here. You've got to remember who they are. (*Two shadows cross quickly, and voices are heard saying:* "Run, or we won't make it!" "Oh, sure we will! We have plenty of time!") You can tell they're just ordinary people rushing home after work.

FATHER: They don't want to miss the train.

VICENTE: (*Angrily.*) That's a street, father! They're running so they won't miss the bus, or maybe because they're late for the movies. (*From the opposite direction, the shadows of women's legs pass. We hear their voices: "Luisa didn't want to, but Vicente made such a scene that . . ." Their voices drift off.* VICENTE *looks at the basement window in surprise and comments nervously.*) That's nothing; just girl talk.

FATHER: They said something about Vicente.

VICENTE: (*Nervously.*) That was another Vicente!

FATHER: (*Agitated, he tries to stand up.*) They were talking about my son!

VICENTE: (*Holding him in the chair.*) I'm your son! Do you have something to say to your son? Is there something you're holding against him?

FATHER: Where is he?

VICENTE: Right here in front of you!

FATHER: (*After staring at him sharply, he goes back to cutting the postcard, muttering contemptuously.*) Get out, sir. (*More shadows cross.*)

VICENTE: (*Sighing and going to the window.*) Why don't you simply say "get out" without the "sir"? I'm your son.

FATHER: (*Looking at him coldly.*) Well, get out then.

VICENTE: (*Wheeling around.*) Ah! At last you admit I'm your son! (*He goes close to his father.*) So let me tell you something: you're judging me unfairly. I was hardly more than a child.

FATHER: (*Listening to the sounds from the window.*) Hush! They're talking.

VICENTE: Nobody's talking! (*As he speaks, shadows of a man's legs reflect against the wall, followed by those of a woman moving at a slower pace. The couple stops to speak, and their voices are heard.*)

FEMININE VOICE: (*After* VICENTE *stops speaking.*) Would you at least help me with the baby?

VICENTE: (*As soon as she has spoken.*) Nothing out there has anything to do with us! (*He had hardly spoken when he turns, frightened, to the window. The man's shadow, which had almost disappeared, now reappears.*)

MASCULINE VOICE: Let's go!

FEMININE VOICE: Answer me first!

MASCULINE VOICE: I'm in no mood for such foolishness. (*The shadows indicate that the man is urging the woman along and that she resists him.*)

FEMININE VOICE: But if I get pregnant, what will you do?

MASCULINE VOICE: Come on, I said! (*The man continues tugging at the woman.*)

FEMININE VOICE: (*Anguished.*) Tell me! Would you help us? (*The shadows disappear.*)

VICENTE: (*Losing his composure.*) It can't be . . . Must be another coincidence . . . (*To his father.*) Did someone just go by?

FATHER: A couple . . . Lovers . . .

VICENTE: Were they talking? Or maybe they didn't say anything?

FATHER: (*After a moment.*) I don't know.

> Shaken, **VICENTE** looks first at him and then at the window, which he suddenly closes with a bang.

VICENTE: (*His voice trembles as he mutters to himself.*) I'm not coming back here anymore. I can't. No. (*The* **FATHER** *laughs softly for some time without looking at him.* **VICENTE**, *livid, turns and looks at his father.*) No. (*He backs up to the cabinet as he speaks.*) No. (*A key sounds in the latch.* **MARIO** *enters, closes the door, and enters the living room.*)

MARIO: (*Surprised.*) Hello.

VICENTE: Hello.

MARIO: Is something wrong?

VICENTE: No. Nothing.

MARIO: (*Looking from one to the other.*) Where's mama?

VICENTE: She went upstairs to help Miss Gabriela with something. (**MARIO** *crosses the stage and leaves the book he was carrying on the table.*)

FATHER: (*Singing in a low voice.*) Rosita's a beauty, Maria's a cutie . . .

MARIO: (*Turning around to look at his brother.*) Something's wrong.

VICENTE: You'd better get out of this place, Mario.

MARIO: (*Smiling as he paces.*) To play the game?

FATHER: Come here, young man. I'll bet you don't know who this person is.

MARIO: Which one?

FATHER: This one. (*Handing him the magnifying glass.*) Take a good look.

ENCARNA *enters downstage left and pauses hesitantly beside the café table. She looks at her watch, not knowing whether to sit down and wait or leave.*

MARIO: (*To his brother.*) It's a busy street in Vienna.

FATHER: Who is that?

MARIO: You can hardly make her out. She's standing at a sidewalk café. Who do you suppose she was?

FATHER: That's the question!

MARIO: What did she do?

FATHER: That's just it! What did she do?

MARIO: (*To* VICENTE.) And what did others do to her?

FATHER: I know some of what they did. Let me have that, young man. She'll tell me the rest of the story. (*He grabs the card and gets up.*) But not here. She won't talk in front of strangers. (*He starts down the hall, examining the card with his magnifying glass as he goes into the bedroom and closes the door.*)

VICENTE: Join us at the publishing house, Mario. You can sleep at my place for a while. (**MARIO** *looks at him in amazement and sits down in his father's chair.*) You're in danger. You act like the prophet of some weird god . . . and a cult whose rituals include postcards, a basement window, paper dolls . . . Come to your senses!

Having reached some decision, ENCARNA *walks slowly stage right and exits.*

MARIO: I am perfectly aware of how strange we must seem to you. But I choose to be this way.

VICENTE: You choose it?

MARIO: Lots of people don't have choices, or they don't dare make them. (*He straightens up slightly and speaks very seriously.*) Fortunately, you and I had choices. I'm glad I decided to live modestly.

VICENTE: (*He stops pacing and confronts him.*) People can have their worldly ambitions without sacrificing their ideals.

MARIO: (*Coldly.*) Spare me your clichés. People who devote themselves to some ideal—or some cause—don't think about money; consequently they don't have any. Sometimes they even lose their lives . . . So don't talk to me about your ideals, not even the literary ones.

VICENTE: I'm not going to argue with you. Go ahead and think whatever you want, but can't you still think that way at . . . the publishing house?

MARIO: The publishing house? (*Laughing.*) What game are you playing there? Because I don't know anymore . . .

VICENTE: You know I have progressive ideas. And not just about literature.

MARIO: (*He gets up and begins to pace.*) And what about the group financing you right now? Are they progressive too?

VICENTE: What difference does that make? We just use their money; that's all.

MARIO: And what about them? Do they use you, too?

VICENTE: You don't understand! It's a little game we play.

MARIO: Of course; I understand the game! You talk out of both sides of your mouth; liberal for a while, then conservative; nothing wrong with that! You show off your progressive ideas. The new group uses you. And that's all right, since you use them. And to hell with everybody else! Who knows what game anybody is playing for sure these days? Only the poor know that they're poor.

VICENTE: You're accusing me again, and I don't like it.

MARIO: I don't like your publishing business either.

VICENTE: (*Coming close and taking* **MARIO** *by the shoulder.*) And I don't like your insinuations!

MARIO: I'm speaking very clearly. What kind of dirty tricks are you up to with Beltran?

VICENTE: (*Flushed and angry.*) What do you mean?

MARIO: You think nobody sees what's going on? The Beltran novel you people were going to publish suddenly isn't being published. In the proofs for the next issue of your magazine, I find three negative references to Beltran, one in your own column. Another article even attacks him openly. Why?

VICENTE: (*Turning his back on his brother and pacing.*) Our contributors are free to express themselves as they see fit.

MARIO: And you're free to accept or reject their articles. (*Ironically.*) Or are you?

VICENTE: There are reasons for all that!

MARIO: There are "reasons" behind every dirty deal.

VICENTE: But who is Beltran, after all? Did he choose obscurity and poverty?

MARIO: Maybe. He still doesn't own a car, but you have one.

VICENTE: He can buy a car whenever he wants to!

MARIO: That's the point: he chooses not to. (*Going over to* **VICENTE**.) The things that interest him are very different from the things that interest you. He's not one of those poor devils who have to have "things": a new TV, new appliances. And he's not one of those idiots behind the wheel, proud of creating even more congestion in this insane city of ours. He has chosen . . . indifference to all that materialism.

VICENTE: You're insulting me!

MARIO: Beltran represents hope! He shows us that people can succeed the way he does, even though it's not easy. (*Seriously.*) And you people are doing your best to destroy that decent, honest man. That's what your publishing house is about. (*They look at each other intently. The doorbell rings.*) I don't mean to offend you, Vicente. What I'm trying to do is wake you up; save you. (*He goes to the hall, opens the door and finds* **ENCARNA** *standing there with downcast eyes.*) What are you doing here? (*He turns instinctively toward the living room and lowers his voice.*) Go to the café. I'll be there soon.

VICENTE: (*Looking into the hallway and recognizing* **ENCARNA**.) No, no! Have her come in! I doubt this is her first visit here. Come on in, Encarna! (**ENCARNA** *enters hesitantly.* **MARIO** *closes the door.*) You know, I suspected this all along. (*Raising his voice.*) What are you standing there for? (**ENCARNA**, *eyes downcast, enters.* **MARIO** *follows her.*) You didn't fool me. You're both pretty naïve. But now the mysteries are all cleared up! (*Laughing.*) Including the ones about the window and the old man! There are no mysteries. There are only human beings, each with needs and agendas. Maybe we're all hypocrites, but that "all" includes you, too. So she was the informant, huh? Except she didn't tell you everything, of course. She's also hypocritical with you, little brother. What else could she be? And I'm sure she sweetened it with a bit of romance. Are you in love? Has she promised to marry you? (*He sits down laughing.*) I'll bet she hasn't.

MARIO: You're right. I couldn't get her to.

VICENTE: (*Laughing.*) I'm not surprised.

MARIO: (*To* ENCARNA.) Did you talk to him about the letter? (*She shakes her head.*)

VICENTE: Sit down, Encarna! Make yourself at home! (*She sits down.*) Let's see! What letter did you want to talk to me about? (*Silence.*)

MARIO: I'm here, and will back you up. (*Silence.*)

VICENTE: This is getting interesting!

MARIO: Now or never, Encarna!

ENCARNA: (*Dejected.*) I . . . had come to say something to you, Mario; just you. I would have talked to him later. But now . . . (*She shrugs her shoulders in a gesture of hopelessness.*)

MARIO: (*Putting his hand on her shoulder.*) It's all right, I promise you. (*Gently.*) Do you want me to tell him? (*She looks away.*)

VICENTE: Come on! You tell me! Let's see what the mystery is all about. What letter?

MARIO: (*After looking at* ENCARNA, *who avoids his eyes.*) One from a publisher in Paris requesting the rights to one of Beltran's works.

VICENTE: (*He thinks about it and stands up.*) Yes . . . A letter came and was misplaced. (*In an incredulous tone.*) You have it?

MARIO: (*Going toward him.*) It was in your wastebasket, torn up.

VICENTE: (*Coldly.*) Have you taken to going through the trash, Encarna?

MARIO: It was a coincidence. When she threw something else away, the letter-head caught her attention.

VICENTE: Why didn't you say something to me? We would have responded immediately to the interested party. Don't forget to bring that letter tomorrow. (ENCARNA *looks at him, perplexed.*) I must have tossed it away by mistake when I was getting rid of other papers . . .

MARIO: (*Calmly.*) Liar.

VICENTE: I'm not putting up with your insults!

MARIO: And what about that campaign in your magazine against Beltran? Is that unintentional, too? He's lying, Encarna! Don't let him get away with it! You can tell him lots of other things!

VICENTE: She won't say anything! Isn't that right, Encarna? You don't have any complaints, do you? That's for the dreamers who gaze through basement windows and see giants where there are really windmills. (*Smiling.*) No, Mario, she won't say anything . . . (*He and* ENCARNA *look at each other.*) And I won't either. (*She lowers her head.*) And now, Encarna, listen carefully. Do you want to go on working for me? (*Silence. Upset,* ENCARNA *gets up and walks away.*)

MARIO: Answer him!

ENCARNA: (*Very tired, and in a voice barely audible.*) Yes.

MARIO: No. (*She looks at him.*)

VICENTE: What?

MARIO: Encarna, tomorrow you're getting out of that office.

VICENTE: (*Laughing.*) She can't do that! That's something I know for sure. Has the window driven you so crazy that you don't even know what kind of girl you're going out with? Don't you listen to her? Haven't you seen her face? Or did you only look at her legs, like you look at the ones that pass by the window? Don't you know she spells explain with an "s" and doesn't know the difference between Brussels and Belgrade? Since she didn't learn to cook or sew, it looks like she's destined for poverty . . . unless she stays with me, that is. And she'll stick with me, because . . . in spite of every-thing, she knows I'm fond of her . . . And I like to help people when I can. You know that, too.

MARIO: In your condescending, subtle way, you're trying to insult us. But aren't you the naïve one? You've showed us just how you intimidate her.

VICENTE: Intimidate?

MARIO: You're just a two-bit CEO; a small-time tyrant with your little empire of employees that have to smile at you as you pay them as little as possible to have more money for yourself! You're a petty dictator, spouting the same old false propaganda all dictators spout!

VICENTE: Shut up!

MARIO: He's the one who should be ashamed, Encarna, not you! I'm sorry I didn't understand it before. I don't want you to be afraid or ashamed ever again. From now on, you have someone here who wants to protect you and take care of you.

VICENTE: Are you proposing marriage?

MARIO: I am proposing to her again.

VICENTE: But she still hasn't accepted. (*Slowly.*) And I don't think she will. (*Silence.*) You see? She's not saying anything.

MARIO: Will you marry me, Encarna?

ENCARNA: (*After a moment and with great difficulty.*) No. (**VICENTE** *breathes a sigh of relief and smiles, satisfied. Stunned,* **MARIO** *looks at* **ENCARNA** *and slowly sits down in his father's chair.*)

VICENTE: Well! Let's forget what happened here; just one of those sentimental disappointments and totally inconsequential. Encarna remains loyal to the publishing house, and I bet she'll be even more faithful from now on. Don't bother about coming in for the proofs. I'll mail them to you. Coming to the office could be uncomfortable. And I'll take the proofs you've finished. It'll be a while before I come back here. Let's go, Encarna. (*He heads for the hall and turns around. Extremely nervous,* **ENCARNA** *looks at both brothers.* **MARIO** *fingers the postcards gloomily.*)

ENCARNA: All right, but not like this . . .

VICENTE: (*Dryly.*) I don't understand you.

ENCARNA: Not like this, Vicente . . . (**MARIO** *looks at her.*) Not like this!

VICENTE: (*Taking a step forward.*) Let's go!

ENCARNA: No! No!

VICENTE: Would you prefer to stay?

ENCARNA: (*With a cry that sounds like a plea.*) Mario!

VICENTE: That's enough! Let's go!

ENCARNA: Mario, I came to tell you everything! I swear! And I'm going to tell you the only thing left to say . . .

VICENTE: Are you out of your mind?

ENCARNA: . . . that I was your brother's lover. (*Losing his composure,* **MARIO** *jumps up. There is a short pause.*)

VICENTE: (*Stepping forward and suppressing his rage.*) Actually, she's wrong about one thing. It's not just that she *was* my lover. She *is* my lover. Until yesterday, that is.

MARIO: You low-down . . . !

VICENTE: (*Raising his voice.*) Because now, of course, that's over. And she's not my secretary anymore either.

MARIO: (*Grabbing his brother and spinning him around.*) You parasite!

ENCARNA: (*Crying out and trying to separate them.*) Stop!

MARIO: Bastard! (*Hitting him.*)

ENCARNA: No, please!

VICENTE: Stop it, you fool! (*He successfully contains* MARIO. *The brothers confront each other, panting. Standing between them,* ENCARNA *looks from one to the other in anguish.*) She's free to do whatever she wants!

MARIO: She has no choice!

VICENTE: You're saying that to console yourself. She loved me . . . a little. (ENCARNA *backs up to the cabinet, nervous.*) And she's not a bad girl, Mario. Marry her, if you want to. I don't care about her anymore. She's not bad, but she's a liar, like lots of women. Besides, if you don't come to her rescue, she's out on the street . . . with a month's salary and no place to go. So you have that time to think it over. Come on, Sir Galahad: offer her your hand in marriage again. What's the matter? Don't tell me you have reservations now? That's so old-fashioned.

MARIO: Her past is unimportant!

VICENTE: (*With a slight and partially suppressed laugh.*) I understand . . . Suddenly, she just stopped being of interest to you. That happened to me, too. Drop by the cashier's office tomorrow, Encarna. Your check will be ready. Bye. (*He is about to leave, but* MARIO's *words stop him.*)

MARIO: Her severance pay. Sure, I get it: you pay; then you can forget about it . . . But you won't be able to forget this time, even if you don't come back here! When you do your next dirty trick, remember I'll be watching and judging. (*He stares at him intently and speaks with a strange tone.*) Because I know.

VICENTE: (*After a moment.*) What are you talking about?

MARIO: (*He turns his back.*) Get out.

VICENTE: (*Coming close to him.*) I've had it with your insinuations! What are you talking about now?

MARIO: You destroyed other people, even before Encarna came along . . . I'm
sure you've thought about that.

VICENTE: About what?

MARIO: That you might be to blame for our father's mental problems.

VICENTE: Because I left home? Don't make me laugh!

MARIO: But you're not laughing! (*He goes to the table and picks up a postcard.*)
Take this. You missed your chance to bring it yourself. (VICENTE *gets quiet.*
ENCARNA *tries to see the postcard.*) Yes, Encarna, the same one he refused to
bring home a few days ago. He knows why.

VICENTE: (*Snatching the postcard.*) You have no right to think what you're thinking!

MARIO: Get out! And don't send any more checks!

VICENTE: (*Exploding.*) You haven't heard the last of this!

MARIO: (*Forcing a laugh.*) That's up to you!

VICENTE: (*Fingering the card nervously.*) This isn't over yet! (*Frowning, he turns
around, disappears into the hallway, and leaves, slamming the door behind him.*)

MARIO *gives* ENCARNA *a long, sad look, which she returns with enormous anxiety.*
He goes to the window where, lost in thought, he looks at the brightness outside.

ENCARNA: Mario . . . (*He does not respond. She takes a few steps toward him.*)
He tried to keep me from saying anything, but I wanted to tell you . . .
(*Silence.*) At first I thought I loved him . . . And more than anything, I was
scared . . . I was scared, Mario . . . (*Lowering her voice after a pause.*) like I'm
scared right now. (*Long silence.*) At least try to understand. Please pity my
fear, Mario.

MARIO: (*With a catch in his voice.*) But you're not . . . the Encarna I thought you
were.

ENCARNA *blinks tremulously, finally understanding what he means. He whispers
the words to himself again as he shakes his head. With her head bowed,* ENCARNA
walks toward the hall where she turns to look at him, eyes brimming with tears.
Then she goes down the hall quickly and leaves as the lights go down. HE *and* SHE
reappear from either side, illuminated by separate spotlights. HE *points to* MARIO,
who is now motionless.

HE: Perhaps Mario thought it would be better not to ask about anything or
anyone.

SHE: That it would be better not to know.

HE: Nevertheless, it's always better to know, even when the truth hurts.

SHE: Even though knowledge brings new questions and leads us to other mysteries.

HE: So we ask, who is that person? This is *the question* we constantly ask ourselves.

SHE: *The question* reached our planet in the twenty-second century.

HE: Children taught us why we needed it so much. The lies and disasters of the two previous centuries made it absolutely necessary . . .

SHE: But perhaps there were lots of people during those terrible years who *did* ask *the question* and kept it alive in their hearts . . . Did they use that expression then?

HE: Just as we do now: in their hearts.

SHE: So maybe there were people who kept *the great question* alive in their hearts. But they were probably obscure individuals, inhabitants of basement dwellings and other modest places.

The light goes out on MARIO, *and his shadow moves away slowly.*

HE: As we attempt to bring back the story of these shadows, we ask who those people were. We'll also try to bring back the stories of all the others, even those who never felt *the question* in their hearts.

SHE: We know now that we are solidly linked not only to those now living, but to everyone who has ever lived. We stand innocent with the innocent and guilty with the guilty.

HE: For centuries, we thought we had to forget, so that the past wouldn't paralyze us. Now we know to remember constantly in order to keep the past from poisoning the present.

SHE: To carry the past with us makes our progress slower, but surer.

HE: To identify, one by one, all the people who ever lived may be an impossible, insane dream. But that insanity constitutes our pride.

SHE: We are forced to be selective, for we will never be able to recover completely everything that was ever said, thought, or done. But in this effort lies the answer to *the great question*, if there is one.

221

HE: Perhaps there's a separate answer for every period in time, or perhaps there is none at all. In the nineteenth century, a certain philosopher ventured a kind of provisional response. For the crude logic of even the next hundred years, it seemed absurd. Today we have adopted this solution as our own, but we do not know if it is the optimum or final answer to *the question*, who is that person?

SHE: That person is you, and you and you; I am you, and you are me. We have all lived—and will live—all lives.

HE: If all of us had thought, when we hurt someone or took advantage of someone or tortured someone, that we ourselves would feel the pain, we wouldn't have done it . . . Let's hold that thought, anyway, as we await the definitive answer to *the question*.

SHE: Let's think that, in case the answer never comes . . . (*Silence.*)

HE: Twenty-six hours after the scene you have just witnessed, this obscure story concludes in that basement dwelling with the window.

> **HE** *points toward the rear, where the oscillating lights begin. The researchers disappear on separate sides, and the light becomes normal on the living room.* **MARIO** *and the* **FATHER** *are walking down the hall. The* **FATHER** *stops and listens.* **MARIO** *goes to his table, sits down, and absentmindedly thumbs through a book.*

FATHER: Who's talking out there?

MARIO: Probably the neighbors.

FATHER: I've been hearing voices for days . . . people crying, laughing . . . Now they're crying. (*He goes to the window.*) It's not here either. (*He goes toward the hall.*)

MARIO: Nobody's crying.

FATHER: It's out there. Can't you hear it? It's a little girl and an older woman.

MARIO: (*Sure of what he says.*) The older woman's voice is mama's.

FATHER: Hee, hee! Are you talking about the woman who lives here?

MARIO: Yes.

FATHER: I don't know who she is. But I do know who the little girl is. (*Irritated.*) And I don't want her to cry!

MARIO: She's not crying, father.

The Basement Window (Madrid, 1997), Part II, the Mother (Victoria Rodríguez) and Mario (Juan Ribó)

FATHER: (*Listening.*) No. Not now. (*Irritated again.*) And who called her before? It was the same voice. You talked to her at the door.

MARIO: That was a mistake. She didn't mean to come here.

FATHER: She's out there. I can hear her.

MARIO: No! You're wrong!

FATHER: (*Slowly.*) She has to come in.

> They look at each other. The **FATHER** sits down and becomes absorbed in a magazine. After a moment, a key in the latch sounds. The **MOTHER** enters, closes the door and comes into the living room.

MOTHER: (*Looking furtively at her son.*) Go out for a while if you like, dear.

MARIO: I don't feel like it.

MOTHER: (*Anxiously.*) But you haven't been out all day . . .

MARIO: I don't want to go out.

MOTHER: (*Approaching* **MARIO** *hesitantly and speaking softly.*) There is someone waiting for you just outside the door.

MARIO: I know.

MOTHER: She's sitting on the steps . . .

MARIO: I've already asked her to leave.

MOTHER: Let her come in!

MARIO: No.

MOTHER: That way, you can straighten things out.

MARIO: (*He gets up and begins to pace.*) Please, mama! This isn't just a lovers' quarrel. You can't possibly understand. (*Silence.*)

MOTHER: An hour ago, I found that girl sitting on the steps, and I took her for a walk. She told me everything. I told her to come with me; that I'd ask you to let her in. (*Silence.*) It's embarrassing, Mario! The neighbors are going to talk. . . . Don't listen to her if you don't want to, but let her in. (**MARIO** *looks at her angrily and moves quickly toward his room to be alone. The* **MOTHER***'s voice stops him.*) You don't want to do what I ask, because you don't think she told me everything. But she did tell me about being involved with your brother. (*Astounded,* **MARIO** *slams the door he had just opened.*)

MARIO: And now that you know that, what do you want me to do? Marry her?

MOTHER: (*Weakly.*) She's a good girl.

MARIO: Shouldn't you be saying that to my brother?

MOTHER: He . . . Well, you know how he is . . .

MARIO: I know; but do you, mama? Do you know what your favorite son, your pet, is really like?

MOTHER: He's not my favorite or my pet!

MARIO: You'll make excuses for what he did with Encarna: just one of those things all men do, right? Let's forget it, like we've forgotten a lot of other things! He's so good! He's going to buy us a refrigerator! And at heart, he's just a child! He still loves his sweet rolls!

MOTHER: Don't talk like that!

MARIO: Oh, no, Encarna isn't a bad girl. And besides, what she did is under-standable! (*Sarcastic.*) That devilish Vinny is irresistible! But she's really not the right girl for him. He deserves something better. But she's fine for Mario. He can have her!

MOTHER: I want both of you to be as happy as possible . . .

MARIO: And for that, you're suggesting Encarna for me?

MOTHER: I'm suggesting what's best for you.

MARIO: Because he doesn't want her?

MOTHER: (*Energetically.*) Because she loves you! (*Coming close to him.*) Your brother is the loser; not you . . . I don't want to judge him . . . He has other qualities . . . He's my son. (*Taking him by the arm.*) That girl is very special, dear. I know it. That's why she confessed about Vicente yesterday.

MARIO: That doesn't make her so special, mama. She just lost her nerve. And that's all I have to say about it! (*He breaks away from his mother. The doorbell rings. They look at each other. The* **MOTHER** *goes to open the door.*) Don't let her in!

MOTHER: It might be Mr. Anselmo or his wife . . .

FATHER: (*Getting up and bowing.*) My respects, madam.

MOTHER: (*She bows, sighing.*) Good afternoon, sir.

FATHER: Please, let the little girl in. (**MOTHER** *and son look at each other. The doorbell rings again. The* **MOTHER** *goes to the door. The* **FATHER** *looks toward the hallway.*)

MARIO: What little girl, father?

FATHER: (*The reply seems obvious to him.*) The little girl! Our baby! (*The* **MOTHER** *opens the door and* **VICENTE** *enters.*)

VICENTE: Hello, mama. (*He kisses her.*) Ask Mario if Encarna can come in.

MARIO: (*Turning around when he hears his brother's voice.*) What are you doing here?

VICENTE: Let's talk about Encarna first. I hope you're not going to make her sit out there all night.

MARIO: Are you also afraid of what the neighbors will think?

VICENTE: (*Calmly.*) Just let her in.

MARIO: Close the door, mama. (*The* **MOTHER** *hesitates but closes the door.* **VICENTE** *comes in followed by the* **MOTHER**.)

FATHER: (*Sitting down and going back to his magazine.*) I guess she's not the little girl I thought . . .

VICENTE: (*Smiling and calm.*) What you do about her is up to you. Anyway, I'm going to tell you something. I admit I didn't treat her as I should have . . . (*To the* **MOTHER**.) You don't know what we're talking about, mama. I'll explain later.

MARIO: She already knows.

VICENTE: You told her? I guess it's better that way. Yes, mama. It was a mistake, and I'll try to make up for it. I wanted to tell you, Mario, I was wrong to fire her, and that I have hired her back.

MARIO: What?

VICENTE: (*Smiling, he sits down on the sofa.*) I told her this morning when she came to pick up her check.

MARIO: And . . . did she stay?

VICENTE: She didn't want to at first, but I kept talking to her and insisting . . . I needed to get a letter out to Beltran, and I especially wanted her to take it to the post office. And that's what we did. (**MARIO** *gives him a hard look and goes brusquely to the table to get a cigarette.*) I'll be honest. I don't know if she'll come back tomorrow. She said she'd think it over . . . Why don't you talk to her? There is no reason to make a big deal out of these things . . .

MOTHER: That's right, dear . . .

VICENTE: (*He laughs and gets up.*) I forgot! (*Taking some postcards out of his pocket.*) More postcards for you, father. Look how pretty they are.

FATHER: (*Accepting them.*) Oh! Good . . . Fine.

MARIO: Fine! Vicente does what he can. He adores his family. Mama smiles at him. Father thanks him, and with a little luck, Encarna will fall in line, too . . . Isn't life beautiful . . .

VICENTE: (*Gently.*) Please . . .

MARIO: (*Coldly.*) Why are you here?

VICENTE: (*Seriously.*) To set things straight.

MARIO: What things?

VICENTE: Yesterday you said something I can't let you get away with. And I don't want you to repeat it.

MARIO: I don't plan to. (*Calmly lighting a cigarette.*)

VICENTE: But you think it! I'm here to convince you you're wrong. (*Nervously and without taking her eyes off them, the* MOTHER *sits down in a corner.*)

MARIO: Coming down here is dangerous for you . . . Or don't you realize that?

VICENTE: I'm not afraid of anything. We have to talk, and we're going to talk.

MOTHER: Not today, please. . . . Talk another day, when things are calmer.

VICENTE: Do you know what he said?

MOTHER: Another day . . .

VICENTE: He had the nerve to say that a certain person . . . present in this room . . . lost his mind because of me. (*Pause.*)

MOTHER: That's just old age, Mario.

VICENTE: Of course, mama! That's what you, or anyone else in their right mind, would think. But he thinks differently.

MARIO: And you've come to forbid me to think that way?

VICENTE: I've come so we can discuss it!

MOTHER: But not today . . . You're both upset.

VICENTE: Today.

MARIO: You heard him. Leave us alone, mama, please.

VICENTE: No! (*To* **MARIO**.) Her word is as good as yours. You want her to leave so she can't correct you!

MARIO: And you want her to stay to support you.

VICENTE: No! I don't want her left with that crazy story you made up.

MARIO: Crazy story? (*He goes over to the* **FATHER**.) What do you say, father? (*The* **FATHER** *looks at him with a blank expression. Then he begins to cut out a paper figure.*)

VICENTE: He can't say anything! You speak! Explain to us, if you can, that madness of yours!

MARIO: (*Turning around and giving him a very serious look.*) Mama, if that girl is still out there, tell her to come in.

MOTHER: (*Standing up, surprised.*) Right now?

MARIO: Yes. Right now.

MOTHER: Perhaps your brother is right! Maybe you are crazy!

VICENTE: It's all right, mama. Let her come in.

MOTHER: No!

MARIO: Have her come in! She's another witness!

MOTHER: To what? (**VICENTE** *goes brusquely to the hall and opens the door. The* **MOTHER** *presses her hands together in anguish.*)

VICENTE: Come on in, Encarna. Mario wants to see you. (*He stands aside and closes the door after she enters. They both come into the living room. The* **FATHER** *looks at* **ENCARNA** *with keen interest.*)

ENCARNA: (*Eyes downcast.*) Thank you, Mario.

MARIO: You're not here to talk, but to hear what we have got to say. Please sit down and listen. (*Alarmed by the harshness of his tone,* **ENCARNA** *is about to sit down in a corner when the* **FATHER**'s *voice makes her pause.*)

FATHER: Come over here and sit with me . . . I'm cutting out something for you . . .

MOTHER: (*Sobbing.*) Oh, my God. (**ENCARNA** *hesitates.*)

MARIO: Since you don't want to leave, mama, sit down. (*Leading her to a chair.*)

MOTHER: Why are you doing this, son?

MARIO: (*Gesturing toward his brother.*) Because that's what he wants.

FATHER: (*To* **ENCARNA.**) Look how pretty . . . (**ENCARNA** *sits beside the* **FATHER,** *who continues cutting.* **VICENTE** *sits down in the chair beside the coffee table.*)

MOTHER: (*Restless.*) Shouldn't we take your father to his room?

MARIO: Would you like to go to your room, father? Shall I take your magazines and paper people for you?

FATHER: I can't leave.

MARIO: You'd be more comfortable there . . .

FATHER: (*Angrily.*) I'm working here! (*He smiles at* **ENCARNA** *and pats her hand.*) You'll see.

VICENTE: (*Sarcastically.*) What solemnity!

MARIO: (*Looking at him and caressing his mother's head.*) Mama, forgive us the pain we're about to cause you.

MOTHER: (*Lowering her head.*) You're acting like some sort of judge.

MARIO: I am a judge . . . because the real judge is unable to perform his duties. But, who knows? Can you judge, father? (*The* **FATHER** *gives him a strange look; then he begins to cut again.*)

VICENTE: Mama will do it for him and for you. You were only a kid.

MARIO: We'll get around to that. But first, take a look at your most recent victims. They're all around you.

VICENTE: The way you talk! Don't make me laugh.

MARIO: (*Unperturbed.*) You can also look behind you. There we have the image of another victim of yours. They photographed him writing, and he too seems to be looking directly at you. (**VICENTE** *turns to look at the clippings and photographs tacked to the wall.*)

MARIO: Yes; Eugenio Beltran.

VICENTE: I didn't come here to talk about him!

FATHER: (*Handing* **ENCARNA** *one of the paper figures.*) Take this pretty one.

ENCARNA: Thank you. (*She takes the figure and clutches it nervously as the* **FATHER** *searches for another picture in the magazine.*)

VICENTE: You know very well what I've come to talk about!

FATHER: (*To* **ENCARNA**, *who has nervously rumpled the paper figure.*) Be careful! You might hurt him! (**ENCARNA** *has, in fact, compulsively torn the figure.*) You see?

ENCARNA: (*With difficulty.*) There's no reason to keep this to myself any longer . . . I don't want to hide it anymore . . . I'm going to have a baby. (*The* **MOTHER** *moans and hides her face in her hands.* **VICENTE** *stands up slowly.*)

FATHER: Did I hear correctly? You're going to be a mother? Of course. You're grown up now! (**ENCARNA** *bursts out crying.*) Don't cry, little girl! To have a child is the most wonderful thing in the world! (*He searches feverishly in the magazine.*) It will be like this beautiful baby here. You'll see. (*He turns the pages.*)

MARIO: (*Softly, to his brother.*) Don't you have anything to say? (*Disconcerted,* **VICENTE** *rubs his hand over his face.*)

FATHER: (*Finding the picture.*) See how beautiful! Do you like this one?

ENCARNA: (*Crying.*) All right, I'll be careful.

FATHER: (*Picking up the scissors.*) Be careful now, will you? Take care of this one; don't let it get hurt. (*He begins cutting.*)

ENCARNA: (*Crying.*) No, I won't!

VICENTE: We'll have to think about what's best, Encarna. I won't deny the baby is mine . . . and I'll help you.

MARIO: (*Softly.*) With money?

VICENTE: (*Shouting.*) This is none of your business!

MOTHER: You have to marry her, Vicente.

ENCARNA: I don't want to marry him.

MOTHER: But you ought to get married!

ENCARNA: No! I won't. I will never marry him!

MARIO: (*To* **VICENTE**.) Well, that's out as a solution. But don't worry. Maybe she'll go crazy, too, and be happy . . . like the person beside you.

VICENTE: She and I will come to some agreement about what to do! But not now. I came to talk about our father. I have to settle that first. (*The* FATHER *pauses and looks at him.*)

MARIO: Careful . . . He's watching you, too.

VICENTE: His eyes are vacant. Why haven't you paid more attention to our mother rather than concentrate on him? Look at her! She's always been a lively, outgoing woman. Her head's not in a fog like yours.

MARIO: Poor mama! How could she ever have put up with everything without a sense of humor and that happy front?

VICENTE: (*Laughing.*) You hear that, mama? He accuses you of pretending.

MARIO: She's not pretending. She really believes it.

VICENTE: And you believe nothing! Our father is the way he is because he's old, that's all. (*He sits down and lights a cigarette.*)

MARIO: The doctor said otherwise.

VICENTE: Oh, yes; the famous "precipitating factor"; the moral outrage and all that!

MARIO: Mama heard it, too.

VICENTE: And I suppose she also heard your explanation about how he got up one night, years ago, muttering strange things in the hall . . . And by some coincidence, that was shortly after I left home.

MARIO: You have a pretty good memory.

VICENTE: But no one heard it except you.

MARIO: Are you accusing me of making it up?

VICENTE: Or of dreaming it. An imagination like yours can't be trusted. But even if it were true, it wouldn't prove anything. Maybe it was selfish of me to leave home, but I've tried to make up for it. And anyway, nobody goes crazy because a son moves out, unless there's a tendency to break down over the slightest little thing. And that releases me of any blame.

MARIO: Unless you yourself, on a previous occasion, had created that tendency.

FATHER: (*Giving the paper figure to* ENCARNA.) Here; it's a picture of your baby.

ENCARNA: (*Accepting it.*) Thank you.

VICENTE: (*Very deliberately.*) Are you referring to the train? (*The* MOTHER *is startled.*)

MARIO: (*Watching his father.*) Be quiet.

FATHER: You like it?

ENCARNA: Yes, sir.

FATHER: Sir? Around here, everybody calls me father . . . (*He presses her hand affectionately.*) Take good care of the baby, and this one will live. (*He picks up another magazine and becomes absorbed looking at it.*)

VICENTE: (*In a low voice.*) You referred to the train. That's what I came to talk about. (*The* FATHER *looks at him a moment and goes back to his magazine.*)

MOTHER: No, please!

VICENTE: Why not?

MOTHER: We have to forget about that.

VICENTE: I understand it's a painful memory for you . . . because of the baby. But I'm your son, too, and I'm being accused! You tell him what happened, mama! (*To* MARIO, *pointing toward the* FATHER.) He told us to get on that train any way we could. And I did. Then, when it started to move away, and I saw all of you were still on the platform, I tried to get off but couldn't; they wouldn't let me. Isn't that what happened?

MOTHER: Yes, dear. (*She avoids his eyes.*)

VICENTE: (*To* MARIO.) You hear that? I got on because he told me to!

MARIO: (*Remembering.*) He didn't say a word all the rest of the day. Do you remember, mama? And then, that night . . . (*To* VICENTE.) You don't know this yet, but she will remember it, because that night she did wake up . . . That night, he got up suddenly and began beating on the walls with his cane . . . until he broke it; that thin little cane he used. Our mother was so frightened, and the baby was crying, and I heard him repeat again and again just one word as he banged on the walls of the waiting room where we had gone to spend the night. (*The* FATHER *listens attentively.*)

MARIO: He said just one word, and he shouted it over and over. "Traitor! Traitor! Traitor!"

MOTHER: (*Shouting.*) Hush!

VICENTE: What makes you think he was referring to me?

MARIO: Who else, if not you?

VICENTE: Those could have been the first symptoms of his dementia.

MARIO: Of course. Because he wasn't just an average man. He was the kind who never gets over another person's disloyalty.

VICENTE: Are you deaf? I'm telling you he told me to get on!

MOTHER: He told us all to get on the train, Mario!

MARIO: And he told you to get off. "Get off! Get off!" That's what he shouted at you from the train platform . . . And he was angry. But the train started up . . . and it took you away forever; because you never ever got off that train . . .

VICENTE: I tried to and couldn't! I climbed on through the little window in the lavatory. Five others were already in there. We couldn't even move.

MARIO: They held you there.

VICENTE: We were packed in so tight . . . It was harder to get off than to get on. They held me in place to protect me. I couldn't even move.

MARIO: (*After a moment.*) And what did you have with you?

VICENTE: (*After a moment's hesitation.*) What?

MARIO: Have you forgotten what you were carrying?

VICENTE: (*Disturbed.*) What I was carrying?

MARIO: Hanging around your neck. Or don't you remember? (*A moment's silence, because VICENTE is now speechless.*) A bag with our meager provisions and some milk for the baby. Father trusted you with our food because you were the strongest . . . The baby died a few days later . . . of starvation. (*The MOTHER cries silently.*) Our father never spoke of that incident again. Never. He preferred to lose his mind. (*Silence.*)

VICENTE: (*Weakly.*) It was . . . a terrible thing . . . At that moment, I didn't even think about that bag of food . . .

MOTHER: (*Very weakly.*) And he couldn't get off, Mario. They held him . . . (*Long silence.*)

MARIO: (*Speaking finally in a very calm, deliberate manner.*) They weren't holding him. They were trying to push him out!

VICENTE: (*He gets up, red in the face.*) They were holding me!

MARIO: They were pushing you!

VICENTE: You remember it wrong! You were only ten years old!

MARIO: If you weren't able to get off, why didn't you just toss us the bag?

VICENTE: I tell you I didn't think about it! I was struggling with them!

MARIO: (*Firmly.*) Yes; you were fighting to stay on! For years now, I've tried to convince myself that I remembered it wrong. I tried to believe in the family's version. But I couldn't; I always saw you, framed in that window of the train, pulling away right in front of my astonished young eyes. You pretended that you were trying to get off as you resisted the soldiers who shoved you and laughed. What do you mean, you couldn't get off? That's just what your friends in the lavatory wanted! You were in their way! (*Brief silence.*) Just as we were in your way. The war had been awful for everyone. The future was uncertain, and suddenly you realized that the bag of food was your ticket out of there. I'm not blaming you completely. You were scared and hungry. It was our lot to grow up in hard times. But now that you're a man, you're responsible for your actions! You've only sacrificed a few victims, of course. Others have sacrificed thousands, millions. But you're like them! In time, your numbers will grow . . . as will your booty. (**VICENTE**, *showing from time to time a timid desire to respond, has gradually lost his aggressiveness. Now he looks from one to the other with the eyes of a sad, trapped animal. The* **MOTHER** *looks away.* **MARIO** *comes close and speaks to him very quietly.*) That child who saw you in the window of the train is also one of your victims. The older brother taught that sensitive young boy what the world was really like.

FATHER: (*To* ENCARNA *with a postcard in his hand.*) Who is this person, girlie?

ENCARNA: (*Very quietly.*) I don't know.

FATHER: Hee hee! I do! I know who he is! (*He takes out his magnifying glass and examines the postcard with a great deal of interest.*)

VICENTE: (*Looking at no one in particular.*) Leave me alone with him.

MARIO: (*Very quietly.*) All right, but what for?

VICENTE: Please! (*He looks at him with vacant eyes.*)

MARIO: (*Watching* **VICENTE** *for a moment.*) Let's go to your room, Mother. Come, Encarna. (*He helps his mother get up.* **ENCARNA** *gets up and goes toward the hall.*)

MOTHER: (*Turning toward* **VICENTE** *before leaving.*) Son!

MARIO *leads his mother, and* **ENCARNA** *follows. The three go into the bedroom and close the door. There is a pause. The* **FATHER** *continues to examine his postcard.* **VICENTE** *looks at him, gets up, and slowly goes over to him. He sits down at the table, facing slightly away from his father so as not to look at him directly.*

VICENTE: It's true, father. They were pushing me. And I refused to get off. I abandoned all of you, and it's my fault the baby died. I was so young, and human life wasn't worth anything then. . . . Half a million people died in the war . . . Even little children died . . . of starvation or the bombs . . . When I found out about the baby's death, I thought, just another child. A child that hadn't even begun to live . . . (*Slowly he takes from his pocket the paper figure his father had given him days before.*) She was hardly more than this doll you gave me . . . (*He shows it to him with a sad smile.*) Yes. I thought that awful thing to ease my conscience. I wish you understood me, but I know you don't. I'm talking to you now as someone who prays to God without believing, just because he wants God to be there . . . (*The* **FATHER** *slowly stops looking at the postcard and begins to look at* **VICENTE** *very intently.*) But there is no God, and no one is ever punished, and life goes on. Look at me. I'm crying. In another moment, I'll go away with the illusion that you've heard me, and I'll keep on taking advantage of people, making victims . . . From time to time I'll think I did all I could by confessing to you and that I had no other alternative since you don't understand . . . That other madman, my brother, will tell me that there are other ways. But who can put an end to corruption and evil in a corrupt, evil world? (*He fidgets with the rumpled paper figure.*)

FATHER: I can.

VICENTE: (*Looking at him.*) What are you saying? (*They look at each other.* **VICENTE** *looks away.*) Nothing. What can you say? And yet, I wish you understood me and that you would punish me, like when I was a little boy, and then forgive me . . . But who can forgive now or punish? I don't believe in anything, and you're insane. (*Sighing.*) I assure you that I am tired of living. This frightening, senseless life sometimes is more than I can bear. But I can't go back and start over.

FATHER: No. (*A little tapping sound is heard on the window. The* FATHER, *suddenly anxious, looks at the window.* VICENTE, *disturbed, looks also.*)

VICENTE: Who knocked? (*Brief silence.*) Children. Some child is always knocking. (*Sighing.*) Now I have to go back out there . . . and continue taking advantage of people. Here. You can have this back. (*Handing him the paper figure.*)

FATHER: No. (*Energetically.*) No!

VICENTE: What?

FATHER: Don't get on the train.

VICENTE: I already did, father.

FATHER: You're not getting on the train. (*In the distance, the sound of the train is heard.*)

VICENTE: (*Looking at him.*) Why are you looking at me like that, father? Don't you know who I am? (*The* FATHER, *with a terrible and distant gaze, does not take his eyes off* VICENTE.) No. And you don't understand either . . . (*He looks away, anguished.*) It was my fault that Elvira died, father! I killed her! But you don't even know who Elvira is anymore. (*The sound of the train has been gaining in intensity and is now very loud.* VICENTE *shakes his head sadly.*) Elvira . . . got off. And I got on . . . And now, I must get back on that train that never stops . . .

These last words, almost drowned out by the frightful noise of the train, are barely audible. Although his words are not distinguishable, he continues speaking as the almost unbearable noise of the train continues.

FATHER: (*Getting up.*) No! No!

The FATHER's *compulsive cries of "No! No!" are likewise drowned out. Standing behind his son who continues to say words we do not hear, he picks up the scissors. His lips and his face express angry denials when, with enormous fury, he unleashes a first blow, then a second and a third . . . The scream of the son with the first blow is barely audible, but his eyes and his mouth open grotesquely. Over the tremendous sound, his final cry is heard with the fourth blow.*

VICENTE: Father!

Two or three more blows, obsessively struck by the old man between his pitiful cries of "No! No!" fall on the son's now inanimate body that first leans forward in the chair, and then slumps to the floor. The FATHER *looks at* VICENTE *with expressionless eyes. He puts the scissors down, goes to the window, opens it, and looks out.*

No one passes by. The sound of the train diminishes but prevents our hearing the cry clearly formed by his lips.

FATHER: Elvira!

The lights go down gradually. The sound of the train drifts off and fades away with the lights. Total darkness and absolute silence on stage. A spotlight comes up on the researchers.

SHE: The world was full of injustice, wars, and fear. The active people had forgotten how to observe, and those who observed and saw didn't know how to act.

HE: We don't make those mistakes today. A relentless all-seeing eye watches us, and it's our own eye. The present keeps watch over us, and the future will know us, just as we have known those who preceded us.

SHE: We must, then, continue this impossible task: to rescue from obscurity, tree by tree and branch by branch, the endless forest of our brothers and sisters. It is an endless and melancholy effort. We know nothing, for example, about that writer these phantoms mentioned so often. But our next experiment will not seek him out. First, we must study the case history of that woman who has crossed in front of you several times without speaking.

HE: The council promotes this research to help us deal with life's ultimate enigmas.

SHE: About time . . . and *the question* . . .

HE: If, at some moment, you have not felt like beings of the twentieth century, observed and judged by a kind of future conscience; and if at some time you have not felt like beings of a future made present who pass judgment with rigor tempered by mercy on peoples of a distant past, perhaps very much like you, this experiment has failed.

SHE: But wait until the end of the story. Only one scene remains. It took place eleven days later. Here it is. (**SHE** *points stage left, where flashing lights begin. Then she exits with her partner.*)

Lights come up stage right. **ENCARNA** *and* **MARIO**, *seated at the outdoor café, look off into the distance.*

ENCARNA: Have you seen your father?

MARIO: He's quiet now. I took him magazines, but they don't let him have any scissors. He tried to cut out a figure . . . with his fingers. (**ENCARNA** *sighs.*) Who is my father, Encarna?

ENCARNA: I don't know what you mean.

MARIO: Is he real?

ENCARNA: Don't talk like that.

MARIO: And what about us? Who are we?

ENCARNA: Maybe we're nothing. (*Silence.*)

MARIO: I killed him!

ENCARNA: (*Startled.*) Who?

MARIO: I killed my brother.

ENCARNA: No, Mario.

MARIO: I kept tugging at him . . . until he fell into the chasm.

ENCARNA: What chasm?

MARIO: Remember that dream I told you about when we were here before?

ENCARNA: It was just a dream, Mario . . . You're a good person.

MARIO: I'm not so good; and my brother wasn't so bad. That's why he came back again and again. In his own way, he wanted to make up for what he did.

ENCARNA: So you're not to blame.

MARIO: Yes, I am. I kept pulling him back. I thought I was passive, but I was being enormously active!

ENCARNA: He wanted to go on playing games. Remember that. You just wanted to wake him up; save him.

MARIO: He wanted to go on deceiving himself . . . but he also wanted to know the truth. I wanted to save him . . . but I killed him. What is it we all really want? What did I want? What am I really like? Who am I? Who is the victim here? Now I'll never know . . . Never.

ENCARNA: Don't think about it.

MARIO: (*Looking at her and speaking in a low voice.*) And what did we both do to you?

ENCARNA: Hush!

MARIO: Didn't we both use you to hurt each other even more? (*Silence.*)

ENCARNA: (*With eyes down.*) Why did you call me?

MARIO: (*Coldly.*) I wanted to know how you were. Are you still at the publishing house?

ENCARNA: They fired me.

MARIO: What do you plan to do now?

ENCARNA: I don't know. (*The PROSTITUTE enters stage right. With a slightly bored but practiced swaying of the hips, she leans against the wall. ENCARNA sees her and gets very quiet. She rises brusquely and picks up her purse.*) Good-bye, Mario. (*She walks to the right.*)

MARIO: Wait.

ENCARNA *stops. MARIO gets up and goes to her side. The PROSTITUTE looks at them curiously out of the corner of her eye. Seeing that they are silent, she crosses in front of them and exits slowly stage left as the lights come up on the living room. Dressed in black, the MOTHER enters and caresses her husband's empty armchair with enormous sadness.*

ENCARNA: (*Without looking at MARIO.*) Don't play games with me.

MARIO: I won't. If I can help it, I won't create any more victims. If you still love me a little, accept me.

ENCARNA: (*Taking a few steps away from him, trembling.*) I am going to have a baby.

MARIO: That baby will be our baby. (*She trembles, not daring to look at him. He shakes his head sadly as he goes closer to her.*) I'm not doing this out of pity. You're the one who should pity me.

ENCARNA: (*Turning to look at him.*) Pity you?

MARIO: Yes, pity me, and for the rest of my life.

ENCARNA: (*She hesitates but finally says with great tenderness.*) The rest of our lives!

The MOTHER approaches the invisible basement window. Full of memories, she opens the window and stands watching the people pass by. The bars reflect against the back wall along with shadows of men and women as they pass by. Vague street sounds are heard. ENCARNA's hand timidly seeks MARIO's. Both look straight ahead.

MARIO: Perhaps someday, Encarna, they will . . . Yes, someday . . . They . . .

Against the wall of the living room, the shadows pass by more and more slowly, and finally the **MOTHER, MARIO,** *and* **ENCARNA** *stand motionless as the lights gradually fade. Only the rectangular reflection of the barred basement window remains. When this image, too, begins to fade,* **HE** *and* **SHE** *reappear from opposite sides.*

HE: That concludes our experiment.

SHE: Thank you for coming.

CURTAIN

MISSION TO THE DESERTED VILLAGE

(*Misión al pueblo desierto*)

A Fiction in Three Acts

By Antonio Buero-Vallejo

Translated by Patricia W. O'Connor

This play opened in Madrid's Español Theater on March 8, 1999.

Characters

Officers of a discussion club

PRESIDENT

SECRETARY

ADJUNCT

At the Commission to Preserve and Protect Artistic Treasures

BERT, president

SANDRO, advisor

LOLA, specialist

DAMIAN, specialist

In the war zone

COMMANDING OFFICER

CAPTAIN

SOLDIER

In the village

AARON

Much of the action takes place during
the now-distant Spanish Civil War.

Stage directions (left, right, etc.) are
from the audience's perspective.

THE SETTING

At a present-day meeting of a large discussion club, a narrated memory of the
Spanish Civil War will be read. Visualized will be Madrid streets under siege,
an unidentified war zone, the Commission to Preserve and Protect Artistic
Treasures, and the village of Brushfire. The last location features large coat-of-
arms-emblazoned portals with vistas of the surrounding terrain. All these scenes
represent spectators' thoughts as they hear the story.

The club's meeting hall resembles the inside of a theater. On both sides of
what looks like a stage are facsimile box seats for the club's executive committee.
Facsimiles are preferable because they allow visibility from all angles, but if nothing more suitable is available, tables on each side of the stage can be substituted.
The table on the right has two chairs and the table on the left only one. Other
props, few and imprecise, represent the mental images of the audience. Appearing
in scenes as called for in the dramatic action, these items will be positioned close to
the wings on either side. Appropriately located toward center stage and barely visible in the half-light are rustic but magnificent stone portals bearing a coat of arms
over which, in better light, one might distinguish this motto: RUBUS ARDENS
DOCUIT ME VINCERE.[1]

PART ONE

ACT ONE

The total darkness on stage is mitigated presently by illumination of the lateral
areas. Stage right, the **PRESIDENT** and **SECRETARY** of the discussion club occupy facsimile box seats. The **PRESIDENT**, about seventy, has a robust, lively, and appealing
appearance. The club's **SECRETARY**, young and attractive, has papers, a ballpoint
pen, and a recorder in front of her. With a finger on the recorder's starter switch,
she awaits the call to order. Illuminated stage left is the **ADJUNCT** member of the
executive committee, a young man of very determined demeanor who will listen
intently to the speakers. All three sit motionless for a few seconds as the **PRESIDENT**
and **SECRETARY** smile at the audience.

PRESIDENT: As president of this discussion club, I call the meeting to order.
Today's topic marks our twentieth discussion in two years and concerns a
complex issue related to a specific event in our now-distant civil war.

---

1. The burning bush leads me to victory.

ADJUNCT: I'd like to say something. (*The* SECRETARY *makes a note on one of her papers.*)

PRESIDENT: (*Icily.*) In a minute. (*To those present.*) This afternoon, we have not distributed copies of what will be read, but you can pick those up when we approve the subject. It has to do, I think, with a highly unusual situation described by one who lived it.

ADJUNCT: I'd like the floor.

PRESIDENT: (*With a slight gesture of impatience.*) Not yet. Beforehand (*Addressing the audience.*), I want to inform those present that our secretary has provided the text. She will, I hope, explain how she happens to have it. (*The* ADJUNCT *shows both impatience and displeasure.*)

SECRETARY: Thank you, Mr. President. Ladies and gentlemen, today's text was written by a relative of mine. As many of you know (*With modest hesitation.*), she had quite a reputation as an art historian and never published the piece I came across quite by chance in going through some old papers. Our executive committee found it of interest and approved its reading for today. (*Pause as she looks at the* PRESIDENT.)

PRESIDENT: But before we begin, a certain adjunct member of that committee has asked to speak.

ADJUNCT: Thank you, Mr. President. Ladies and gentlemen, with all due respect to the memory of the prestigious author of this story and her distinguished descendant (*Smiling and indicating the* SECRETARY.), I don't think what that document contains should be brought up here. (*In apparent response to gestures noted among those present.*) I'll explain! I'll explain! The situation described there pertains to a range of issues relating to our civil war, and they simply lack relevance today. Wouldn't it be preferable to discuss one of the other topics on file that await our attention that concern current problems? You do have some of those, don't you, Madam Secretary?

SECRETARY: (*Smiling sarcastically.*) Yes, as a matter of fact, I do, and two of those, by some curious coincidence, you yourself submitted. (*Directing her comment to a section of audience from which she may have heard amused laughter.*) The committee decided, however, that certain aspects of our war are still very relevant, even though it's fashionable in some quarters to say otherwise. . . .

ADJUNCT: I beg your pardon. I'm not complaining that one of my suggestions wasn't selected, and I wouldn't have challenged today's choice if we didn't have topics, other than the ones I submitted, that are simply timelier.

SECRETARY: I respect your opinion, but you know that selections are made by majority vote. I might also add that I abstained for this particular session because of a possible conflict of interest; I wanted to avoid any appearance of impropriety.

ADJUNCT: (*Smiling.*) Obviously, I didn't vote for it either.

SECRETARY: Mr. President, in order to leave the decision up to the members present, may I be excused? (*Starting to get up.*)

PRESIDENT: (*Stopping her.*) That won't be necessary. You are just doing your job, and you are in charge of the reading.

ADJUNCT: I, too, Mr. President, urge the secretary to stay; if she leaves, she won't hear me express suspicions that, if proved correct—and quite aside from my respect for her relative's recollections—will make the case for postponing, at least, this reading. What I have to say about the anecdote contained in that document is that . . . (*Emphatically.*) it never took place! (*Startled, the* SECRETARY *once more attempts to get up but is detained by the* PRESIDENT.)

SECRETARY: What are you saying?

ADJUNCT: Having read that story as an adjunct member of the executive committee, I am aware that it is incomplete, perhaps intentionally so in order to stimulate interest in the subsequent discussion . . .

SECRETARY: I found it incomplete!

ADJUNCT: Fine. But let me ask you this: among those papers attributed to your relative, weren't there examples of her creative writing? Didn't she write short stories and novels she preferred not to publish because she was known as a historian? Might not this text be one of those attempts? Perhaps some unfinished piece of fiction?

PRESIDENT: That wouldn't lessen in the least the human interest of what she says. (*The* SECRETARY *glares at the* ADJUNCT *as she faces him.*)

SECRETARY: Those literary attempts did exist, but today's text is not an example of her creative writing; it is a memory in literary form.

ADJUNCT: (*Very softly.*) How are we supposed to know the difference?

SECRETARY: It's common knowledge that she worked in the Commission to Preserve and Protect Artistic Treasures. Her text is written in the first person, and she uses her own name.

ADJUNCT: In my opinion, other names used there are not authentic.

SECRETARY: That doesn't prove anything. . . .

ADJUNCT: (*Leafing through his copy.*) What was the name of your relative's husband?

SECRETARY: He wasn't well known.

ADJUNCT: Does his name figure, perhaps, as one of the protagonists of this story?

SECRETARY: (*Stammering slightly.*) I . . . don't know for sure . . . In the case of distant relatives, people frequently don't know their names . . .

ADJUNCT: (*With an exaggerated show of surprise.*) And of course you wouldn't know if the given name of that distant relative matches one of the characters in this tale.

SECRETARY: That would be an indication of the incident's authenticity.

ADJUNCT: It might also suggest a frustrated desire to live the events described. . . . Something like poetic license on the part of the narrator. Was there an Aaron among your relatives? Or maybe a Damian? Could one of them have been a painter, even though he wasn't well-known?

SECRETARY: I'm not aware he was a painter or had either of those names.

ADJUNCT: (*Sighing.*) What a shame the author left her story unfinished, as you assure us it was.

SECRETARY: Are you accusing me of altering it?

ADJUNCT: Not at all.

SECRETARY: (*Hesitantly.*) Mr. President . . .

PRESIDENT: (*Interrupting her and addressing the* **ADJUNCT.**) My response to your request remains negative.

ADJUNCT: (*Irritated.*) Perhaps our president believes the event actually took place . . .

PRESIDENT: The incident for debate is important even if it never happened as described; that's what the committee decided. You may begin reading the selected paper, Madam Secretary. (*Grateful and smiling, the* SECRETARY *stands up with the text in her hand. Sulking, the* ADJUNCT *looks away, and the* SECRETARY *glances at the* PRESIDENT.) You're hesitant? (*Smiling.*) But you read very well. . . . (*To the audience.*) You'll see. As she reads, you may imagine scenes very much like actors might portray them in real theaters. . . . The text deserves that. Go ahead. (*She begins to read. Her words fade away as a manly voice in the distance gains in volume. Lights go down on the three club members as they come up center stage and dimly illuminate the large stone portals. Projected on that broad expanse are images of war-torn Madrid streets with stone barricades made of transported cobblestone. These scenes were common on many city streets at that time.*)

SECRETARY: (*Her voice.*) The document goes like this: "During the war, I worked for the Commission to Preserve and Protect Artistic Treasures. My job was to classify paintings of uncertain origin gathered by our forces. That particular specialty was something my father, who died early in the war, taught me so much about. I also studied art at the university, where I expanded my knowledge with eminent professors subsequently assigned to the commission. . . . So when the boss there consulted me one day about a potential mission of great interest . . ." (*Her voice trails off as the sound of distant singing gains in intensity. Heard is a song popular when Madrid was under siege and is sung to the melody of "The Four Mule Drivers." The voice of the anonymous singer gradually fades into the distance as the song ends.*)

ANONYMOUS SINGER: On the Bridge of the French,
The French, the French, the French,
Oh, mother of mine,
You walk safe, safe, safe.
Because our militia, militia, militia,
Oh, mother of mine,
Protect you well, well, well.

The street scene center stage fades and is replaced by a sharp image of the Lope de Vega statue and a long flight of stone steps at the entrance to Madrid's National Library.[2] The statue, now headless, has fallen prey to a fascist projectile. Meanwhile, downstage left, lights come up on BERT *and* SANDRO *standing close to a*

---

2. Felix Lope de Vega (1562–1635) is Spain's great dramatist of the Golden Age and comparable in many ways to Shakespeare. There will be other references to this statue at the entrance of the National Library.

small table surrounded by old chairs. In his fifties, BERT, slender with a deeply receding hairline, has lively mannerisms. At one time he had been a famous painter. BERT's attire, including a tie, is ordinary but proper. Standing motionless, he listens expectantly to the song now barely audible. SANDRO, wearing a high-necked sweater and tweed jacket, is an older man with slightly bulging eyes and heavy lids. At one time he had been a famous sculptor. He listens seated behind the table as the song fades into the background.)

SANDRO: I don't think they'll attack. The resistance seems to be holding.

BERT: (*Doubtfully.*) I hope you're right. (*He takes a few steps.*) So what do you think of that letter?

SANDRO: What it wants us to do isn't easy.

BERT: Why do you suppose it took that guy so long to tell us about it?

SANDRO: And why didn't our soldiers get the painting and send it to us before leaving the village? They've always done a good job with those rescues before.

BERT: They probably didn't even know who El Greco was. These improvised field promotions often go to rural types who don't know much about art.

SANDRO: (*Thinking about it.*) Do you suppose some enemy patrol took off with the painting?

BERT: (*Shaking his head.*) Whoever signed that letter said it was there and to come as soon as possible.

SANDRO: But what about that guy? Do you suppose he's still in the village?

BERT: You think he'd stick around? Fat chance! I'm sure he took off right away for safer ground.

SANDRO: (*Nervously.*) The letter was written several days ago . . . , which means somebody could have taken the painting by now. (*Changing his tone.*) And what's the matter with Lola? Why doesn't she show up?

BERT: She's still classifying the art from yesterday. (*He begins to pace.*)

SANDRO: She hasn't given us her first impressions of that painting yet. What are yours?

BERT: (*Pausing to consider the question.*) She says the picture of it is of very poor quality. (*He continues to pace.*)

SANDRO: The person who signed the letter says he's a painter, like you. Do you know him?

BERT: Only slightly . . . I'm a better painter than he is, but in a fall exhibit years ago he did win a prize with a huge, very conventional landscape. That's all I know about him.

SANDRO: Maybe he has a good eye for artistic treasures. . . . But that reconnaissance mission is extremely risky.

BERT: You're right about that. But the village is quiet and deserted, and we have to go.

SANDRO: I don't know . . . I don't know

BERT: (*Sitting down beside him.*) Headquarters ordered this mission and sent instructions about what route to take. If it's over in one day, there's no big danger.

SANDRO: You've already been to headquarters?

BERT: Yes.

SANDRO: I thought they'd kick you out as soon as they heard the plan.

BERT: (*Smiling.*) Actually, the order came from higher up . . . from the president's office.

SANDRO: (*Getting up.*) The president of the government?

BERT: Yes. The general discussed it with President Azaña.

SANDRO: (*Stammering.*) With President Azaña himself? . . .

BERT: Yes, and he got all excited. Seems he's heard about that lost painting. He even went so far as to baptize the rescue mission: "Operation Burning Bush" he called it.

SANDRO: Called it what?

BERT: Brushfire is the name of that village and the local nobles, the Duke and Duchess of Brushfire.

SANDRO: Wow! Is there anything that guy doesn't know? (*Stopping short.*) But how come the general couldn't talk him out of it?

BERT: I don't know. Oh, well, we've done harder things. Headquarters authorized crossing enemy lines. Imagine! An El Greco!

SANDRO: I wonder what Lola will tell us . . . Who do you plan to send?

BERT: (*Smiling as he gestures toward some distant place.*) Who do you think? . . . The guy that was in that battle on that Bridge of the French.

SANDRO: (*Stepping back with a gesture of astonishment.*) "The Jackal."

BERT: He's got balls . . .

SANDRO: Yeah, big ones. I heard he beat up those fascists in that campus skirmish, and he sure lost no time in getting well connected around here.

BERT: It has nothing to do with connections. We asked for someone from the Federation of University Students and got him because of his specialty in old editions and dead languages. How's that for irony?

SANDRO: Maybe someone a little less daring would be better . . .

BERT: But there's nobody like that around! And the commission is hardly a safe haven. . . . Any day now we could get our heads blown off, like Lope out there. (*Looking at his watch.*) Damian ought to be along any minute now.

SANDRO: Does he know what he's in for?

BERT: Since he knows Lola will give us her impressions, he'll be punctual. (*They chuckle as they look at each other knowingly.*)

SANDRO: We'd better get the supplies ready. . . . They'll need the small pick-up truck, a supply of gas . . .

BERT: And provisions for three or four days. (*At a soft knocking at the door, they look at each other.* BERT, *serious-faced, shakes his head.*) That's not our guy.

SANDRO: How do you know?

BERT: We would have heard his motorcycle. (*More knocks on the door.*) You keep your mouth shut with both of them! (SANDRO *bows slightly in submission.* BERT *steps to the right.*) Come in! (*Carrying some papers,* LOLA *enters stage right. Attractive and about thirty, she wears a gray lab jacket over a simple outfit. On the portals center stage, the image of the decapitated statue of Lope de Vega shifts gradually to a large but blurred projection in black and white of a possible El Greco Annunciation similar to other well-known paintings by this artist.*)

LOLA: (*Crossing the stage.*) The letter and the photograph: here they are. (*She places both on the table. The three bend over them as the projected image brightens.*) The picture isn't very good, but some elements there suggest authenticity. Notice the paint on the fingers, for example.

BERT: (*Picking up the picture.*) That's what it looks like . . .

LOLA: We'll have to see the painting, examine the canvas, and check the mounting . . . There's very little solid information to go on right now. The duke and duchess didn't talk about the painting, not even with their friends.

SANDRO: (*Picking up the photograph* **BERT** *leaves on the table.*) Maybe they knew it was a fake; some old imitation.

BERT: (*Laughing.*) I don't believe that's what our president thinks.

LOLA: (*Sitting down very deliberately.*) What did you say? (**BERT** *likewise sits down.* **SANDRO** *returns the photograph to the table as the lights go down, and the image of the painting center stage dims.*)

BERT: Do you hear a motorcycle? (*Heard, in effect, is the sound of a motorcycle coming to a stop.* **LOLA**'*s jaw drops in surprise. The lights go down on these three as they come up downstage on the* **SECRETARY** *as she reads.*)

SECRETARY: I could never have imagined what was in store for me, but I was the one who got me involved. . . . To study and authenticate an important and undocumented El Greco was beyond the wildest dreams of the ambitious young specialist my father's efforts, my university studies, and some practical experience had turned me into. On the other hand, I understood the opportunity immediately and lost no time in doing what seemed most advantageous. (*The lights dim on the* **SECRETARY** *as* **BERT**'*s voice sounds. The lights once more come up on the group of three around the table at the commission office.*)

BERT: Looks like the mission is authorized.

LOLA: To go behind enemy lines?

BERT: Of course there is some danger, but not a whole lot. The enemy hasn't seen fit, for some unknown reason, to advance into that zone, and the village is totally deserted. (*Short pause.*) Someone's got to do it.

LOLA: But who?

BERT: (*Smiling, he points in the direction of the motorcycle sounds.*) Didn't you hear that?

LOLA: Yes, that's Damian's motorcycle. (**BERT** *nods slightly.*) Damian's going to be in charge?

BERT: The papers are already signed. (*He stands up and walks right. Knocking on an invisible door is heard.*) Come in. (*Taking off his gloves,* **DAMIAN,** *a young man about twenty with a very determined countenance, enters from the left wearing a leather jacket, a pistol at his belt and on his head the red and black hat popularized by Durruti.*[3])

DAMIAN: Greetings, comrades.

BERT: Greetings.

DAMIAN: Lola, sorry I got here late for your decision.

BERT: She hasn't said anything yet, but the mission is decided.

SANDRO: And from very high up.

BERT: Have a seat. (*Intrigued,* **DAMIAN** *sits down.*) Lola, give us your take on that letter.

LOLA: It's a mystery to me. I don't know who wrote it.

SANDRO: Bert knows. According to him, it was some mediocre painter.

LOLA: But we really can't be sure about anything without seeing the painting. The photograph is awful, and that particular work doesn't figure in any catalog. There are only vague references that suggest it might have existed and could have been lost. The author of the letter gives us exact dimensions and assures us that many villagers thought the duke and duchess kept an El Greco in their private chapel.

BERT: Our president seems to think so, too.

DAMIAN: Wow!

BERT: And he authorizes the rescue mission.

SANDRO: Against the better judgment of the military commanders, I suppose.

LOLA: In that region, there were other El Greco paintings in convents and palaces . . . and maybe the Duke and Duchess of Brushfire owned one of those. It's taken a war to discover some of those carefully hidden treasures. This could be one of them. (*Picking up the picture and looking at it.*) I'm

---

3. Anarchist leader Buenaventura Durruti (1896–1936) was among the most radical of the Republicans. Electing to wear something associated with Durruti suggests Damian's political inclinations.

inclined to think so, anyway. On the other hand, why do you suppose the guy who wrote that letter waited so long to tell us about it?

BERT: Maybe the idea came to him just as he was leaving the village . . .

DAMIAN: Before deciding which side he'd favor?

BERT: (*Laughing.*) Looks like he chose ours.

SANDRO: After that, he must have taken off for safer ground.

DAMIAN: Is Brushfire still deserted?

BERT: Completely. It's out there in no-man's-land. Neither side has claimed it.

DAMIAN: How come?

BERT: We have no idea. Secret military plans, I guess.

DAMIAN: So . . .

BERT: So we have to rescue that painting. The Ministry of War authorizes the mission because President Azaña wants it. Apparently that battle zone is stable right now. But even though our troops have left the village—as well as another one close by—the enemy forces still aren't entering. . . . Again, the mysteries of strategy . . . Therefore, we need to get all the necessary packing materials together in a hurry. Troop movements could start up any minute, even though back at headquarters they think it's unlikely.

DAMIAN: Why do they think that?

SANDRO: (*Insinuating.*) Maybe they're just naturally clever.

DAMIAN: (*Thinking it over.*) Our troops retreat and the enemy does nothing. I don't get it.

BERT: Those crafty devils must be up to something.

DAMIAN: The village is deserted, and the enemy deserts us, too. What's going on?

BERT: Maybe they're scared. That region is a Republican stronghold, and the people who move in could be afraid of death squads.

SANDRO: But there's nobody there now right now. So we thought . . . May I tell him, Bert? . . . (**BERT** *smiles and nods permission.*)

DAMIAN: (*Smiling.*) I get it: that I should be the one to rescue the painting. When do I leave?

BERT: Within a day or two; that's time enough to get everything ready. You'll go in the small pick-up.

DAMIAN: And I'll take an assistant. I want a guy who can drive a truck.

LOLA: (*Who until now had been biting her lip.*) Not a guy! A woman! (*The men look at her in astonishment.*)

BERT: Absolutely not!

LOLA: I can also hammer nails and take them out!

BERT: You don't belong in a battle zone!

LOLA: Madrid's a battle zone!

BERT: But not as dangerous!

LOLA: Oh, no? Ask Lope out there, headless in front of our building!

BERT: You're part of the military effort now and, as such, subject to my command. I say you're not going. (*Short silence after which* **DAMIAN** *rises and, without saying anything, takes a few steps away.*)

LOLA: (*Softly.*) If that's an order, I'll obey, of course. But why don't you let me be the first to authenticate that painting, in case it really is an El Greco? There seems to be no danger in the village right now. (*Insinuating.*) Even the most contemporary specialist in El Greco can't resist the temptation of rushing to see it . . . So it's a bad imitation? We'll get right out of there; we won't even bring it back. In any case, that mission shouldn't take more than twenty-four hours!

BERT: Whether you authenticate the painting here or there doesn't matter; you'd still be the first.

LOLA: It's not the same!

BERT: Of course not! It's better to do it here!

SANDRO: What do you think, Damian?

BERT: (*Irritated, he stands up.*) Stay out of this, Sandro! (*He steps downstage.*)

SANDRO: (*To* **LOLA**.) Well, I'll say you've got guts anyway!

LOLA: We're at war.

DAMIAN: (*Turning his back on everyone.*) If Lola wants to come along, I say it's her right as specialist and as soldier. I'm sure she'd be a big help. (*Slight gesture of assent from* **BERT**.)

LOLA: Please, Bert; prepare me a safe-passage permit, too.

BERT: Don't you have to catalog yesterday's paintings?

LOLA: They're done. They can go into storage whenever you give the word.

BERT: Let's take a look at them, Sandro. (*As an accomplice might,* SANDRO *winks at the couple and approaches* BERT, *who, without turning around, speaks in a hushed voice.*) This is a dangerous mission, Lola.

LOLA: (*Also in a hushed tone.*) What I'm doing here is dangerous, too.

BERT: (*Without turning around.*) All right, you two: make a list of everything you'll need for the trip.

LOLA: (*Euphoric.*) Oh, thank you, President Azaña!

BERT: (*To* SANDRO.) Let's go. (*As they exit, stage right, he deforms his voice for a barely audible comment.*) You pimp! (*They exit.* LOLA *and* DAMIAN *look at each other as the light softens and focuses on them.*)

DAMIAN: So you want to come with me.

LOLA: Yes.

DAMIAN: Nothing could please me more, and you know why. (*She looks away.*) But the trip's risky; maybe you shouldn't . . .

LOLA: Because I'm a woman?

DAMIAN: Lola, a real El Greco is extremely valuable (*Approaching her.*), but someone like you is even more valuable. War takes lives but war needs lives, especially valuable ones, for the postwar effort.

LOLA: Do you consider a single life more valuable than an El Greco painting?

DAMIAN: Absolutely! No question!

LOLA: But you're risking your own life for an El Greco.

DAMIAN: It's not the same. You know my nickname: "The Jackal." I do things to keep others from dying. (*He smiles and seems amused.*) And in the process, I have fun. (*Turning serious.*) But an El Greco can wait when it involves risking a life like yours . . . Just anybody who's a little handy can come along to help.

LOLA: If that El Greco is authentic, we have to get it out of there right away.

DAMIAN: Nobody's going to destroy it . . .

LOLA: Except a raid or some bombs. And I can save that painting in time. That's why Bert authorized the mission with me along. (*Silence.* DAMIAN *approaches her.*)

DAMIAN: I'm not trying to avoid your company. Quite the contrary. (*Speaking confidentially.*) Around here, they think that you and I . . . could have something going . . . that maybe we're attracted . . .

LOLA: I know. (*He takes her by the shoulders. She resists, but without being brusque.*)

DAMIAN: (*Sitting down beside her and taking her hand.*) For a minute, I dared to believe that you wanted to go along not just because you're interested in the painting . . . Why not? War is a time of personal liberation; of finding out who we are . . . Would I be totally off base to think you might have some interest in me? (*After withdrawing her hand gently,* LOLA *gets up and moves a few steps away.*)

LOLA: Last year, a bomb . . . one of many in my neighborhood, destroyed the home I shared with my father . . . and it killed him. That bomb killed the person who taught me everything and who had passed along certain aptitudes . . . including a kind of sixth sense about things. The Commission to Preserve and Protect Artistic Treasures took me on because of my training and my publications and, thanks to this job, life is still worthwhile. (*Turning to look at him.*) Like all loners, I need security and affection. But I'm older than you . . .

DAMIAN: That's not it. (*Gently.*) If you'll allow me . . . You loved your father a lot, and with good reason. Now, it's hard to give in to an even stronger feeling. But I'd give you that love; I could become something of a father rather than the boy you still see in me.

LOLA: (*Shaking her head sadly.*) No one could love me the way my father did.

DAMIAN: Yes, someone could; because a more complete love is born when there is a physical bond as well.

LOLA: (*Smiling.*) I don't believe you. I'd be just another one of your adventures. I like you and find you attractive, but I'm not out for fun and games. . . . Let's concentrate on saving that El Greco.

DAMIAN: I'm not giving up.

LOLA: About saving the painting? Neither am I.

DAMIAN: All right; joke about it if you want to . . .

LOLA: (*Laughing.*) That's always a healthy thing to do.

DAMIAN: On this trip, I'll show you I'm more mature than you think.

LOLA: If you're so mature, make that list of supplies! We'll need food for at least three days, a little kerosene stove, and blankets and bedrolls in case we have to camp out. (*Sounds of distant shellfire and explosions; they both look up and listen.*)

DAMIAN: Now it starts again.

LOLA: Just like every day. (*After a few seconds, the sounds die down and the scene darkens. On one side, lights come up on the* **SECRETARY** *as she continues reading.*)

SECRETARY: Neither one of us knew what was in store . . . I must admit, however, that deep inside me, the possibility of the love that Damian offered intrigued the woman I was then. I wasn't your typical feminine type and hadn't had much experience with love. I think what really made me beg to go along was the adventure; of being the one to discover and authenticate a wonderful El Greco! In those days, what made my heart—the heart of a young researcher—pound was ambition. . . . Yes, I was that vain, proud specialist my beloved father, always so encouraging, had turned me into. (*Lights go down on the* **SECRETARY,** *and her voice fades away as lights of a different kind come up on the left corner of the stage previously occupied by the Commission to Preserve and Protect Artistic Treasures. The same furniture is now part of a different place. Framed in the huge portals now are sketchy images of trenches and barbed-wire fences that suggest closer proximity to the battle zone. At this point,* **LOLA***'s voice picks up the story begun by the* **SECRETARY.**)

LOLA: (*Her voice.*) With our relationship unclear, Damian and I went to the brigade commander. He would give us permission to enter no-man's-land. (*On the table: maps, a field telephone, and an unlit piston lamp. The* **COMMAND-ING OFFICER,** *wearing combat boots, a uniform shirt with rows of medals, and a field beret bearing the metallic symbol of his rank, stands as he speaks on the telephone. With the insignia of his rank on jacket sleeve, the* **CAPTAIN** *wears the round officer's hat with the encircled red star indicative of his rank. Both are young adults, typical officers forged in war.*)

COMMANDING OFFICER: (*On the telephone.*) Yes, General, sir. They just arrived and are bringing them. . . . But with all due respect, I can't understand how you agreed to something that can compromise our operation here. . . . Don't worry, sir; of course we'll take the necessary precautions. . . . No, they

257

won't have a field telephone. . . . Yes, they've brought a supply of food. Tonight we'll feed them here. . . . Yes. . . . Yes sir; of course, General. Don't worry. As you say, sir. (*He hangs up the telephone.*) What a lot of bother for a painting.

CAPTAIN: We're fighting for those things, too.

COMMANDING OFFICER: But not to the point, I hope, of jeopardizing war plans. (*Irritated, he pounds one fist into the palm of his other hand.*) I certainly wouldn't have authorized that crazy mission! (*Pacing.*) That's no way to win a war.

CAPTAIN: Well, it doesn't look like the enemy is mobilizing. Either they don't know what's going on, or they want more troops in place before starting anything. (*He pauses.*)

COMMANDING OFFICER: What if up at headquarters they suddenly change their minds and order us to attack?

CAPTAIN: Even if someone alters the plan, I don't think it will be before they retrieve the painting; they'll get that right away. (*Short pause.*) I'm worried about something else.

COMMANDING OFFICER: Something else?

CAPTAIN: Why is a woman going along? Remember those gals in the militia?

COMMANDING OFFICER: Yes, but what's your point?

CAPTAIN: They did a great job, of course, but some were . . . let's say . . . extremely . . . accommodating.

COMMANDING OFFICER: This one isn't in the militia. Anyway, what business is that of ours?

CAPTAIN: (*Approaching and speaking confidentially.*) But this could be a couple. What if they have cooked up this mission just to be together?

COMMANDING OFFICER: They're doing it for the painting, I say.

CAPTAIN: (*Lowering his tone.*) Or maybe also to desert to the other side. They'd have that pick-up truck and the painting, in addition to all the fun they'd have on the trip; in case they're in cahoots, that is.

COMMANDING OFFICER: Oh, come on!

CAPTAIN: Look, I don't trust anybody or anything these days. There are gullible people all over, unknowing accomplices of a possible pair of lovebirds who might just want safe passage to the enemy. I don't trust upper-crusty city types anyway, but we'll see.

COMMANDING OFFICER: Too bad somebody got to our president about this stupid mission. (*Contemptuously.*) Intellectuals! . . .

CAPTAIN: Yep; that's our president: an intellectual. These people could be doing this on the whim of an egghead and because of some nutty painter in that village. And our soldiers pay the price! (*A* **SOLDIER** *enters from the right and salutes.*)

SOLDIER: They're here, sir.

COMMANDING OFFICER: Show them in. (*The* **SOLDIER** *salutes again and exits.*)

CAPTAIN: Act nice. After all, this is a cultural mission. (*The* **COMMANDING OFFICER** *gives him a chilly look.* **LOLA** *and* **DAMIAN** *enter from the right.* **LOLA** *now wears camouflage fatigues.*)

DAMIAN: (*Raising a fist.*) Greetings, comrades. This is Lola, one of our specialists in old paintings.

COMMANDING OFFICER: She's going to cross enemy lines, too?

LOLA: (*Serious-faced.*) I'm the one who decides if we bring the painting back and who prepares the documents for whoever's in charge of the palace. This is a cultural mission. (*The* **COMMANDING OFFICER** *and* **CAPTAIN** *look at each other and chuckle.*) You find that amusing, sir?

CAPTAIN: No, comrade. It's just that a minute ago we were talking about the mission, respectfully . . . and used those same words. But in that village, there's nobody left.

LOLA: But I have to make a report.

COMMANDING OFFICER: I'll take care of that.

DAMIAN: (*Taking a step forward and extending some papers.*) Our safe-conduct papers.

COMMANDING OFFICER: (*Taking the papers and glancing at them.*) Fine. (*He returns them.*) Headquarters already informed us . . .

DAMIAN: May we leave right away, then?

COMMANDING OFFICER: No; not until nightfall.

DAMIAN: Why is that?

COMMANDING OFFICER: You've got to leave in total darkness with no headlights and making the least possible sound.

CAPTAIN: Getting to the turnoff toward the village is no problem, but the road is bad, and the enemy is vigilant.

DAMIAN: We thought that zone was deserted.

COMMANDING OFFICER: It is, but the enemy keeps an eye on things from a distance, and it's better not to alert them. . . . We can't provide you with an escort, either. None of our soldiers can leave here without special orders.

DAMIAN: (*Badly masking his displeasure.*) We'll have to manage, then. How far is that village?

COMMANDING OFFICER: From the turnoff, it's four or five miles, but from enemy lines, only about two.

DAMIAN: We'll hurry and be back tomorrow.

COMMANDING OFFICER: I hope so. It doesn't look like the enemy is mobilizing for the moment. (*Looking at* **LOLA**.) Good thing for our comrade here. (*Brief pause as the men look at one another.*)

DAMIAN: I'll watch out for her, but I don't expect any trouble.

CAPTAIN: (*Who hasn't taken his eyes off* **DAMIAN**.) But . . . I know you from somewhere . . .

DAMIAN: Well, I remember you from the campus battle. (*Beginning to sing very softly.*) "The Bridge of the French . . ."

CAPTAIN: (*Singing contentedly.*) On the Bridge of the French, the French, the French, Oh mother of mine . . ."

DAMIAN: "You walk safe, safe, safe."

CAPTAIN: (*Singing along with* **DAMIAN**.) "You walk safe, safe, safe." (*Smiling.*) I didn't remember your name . . . So what are you doing in that Commission on Artistic Treasures?

DAMIAN: I'm there because of an unpardonable sin in an adventurer like me. I'm a paleographer.

COMMANDING OFFICER: How did a guy like you get into something like that?

DAMIAN: In the university, I wanted to outdo a fellow student who bragged he knew more about those things than anybody . . . So little by little I got really good at it, and here I am, a top specialist. How did you get to be a captain in the army?

CAPTAIN: I guess we fall into jobs based on our talents. Just like you! And since the militia does such a good job of defending the entrance to Madrid[4] . . .

DAMIAN: Yes, the militias are soldiers now, and they mean it when they say, "They shall not pass!"[5]

COMMANDING OFFICER: And that motto will prove right.

CAPTAIN: (*Smiling at* LOLA.) Don't you agree, comrade . . . militiawoman?

LOLA: That's what we're all working toward, each of us in our own way.

COMMANDING OFFICER: Is that painting really so important?

LOLA: It could be.

COMMANDING OFFICER: (*Looking outside.*) Well, then go for it, I say! It's getting dark . . . You'll eat here with us, and then be off, eh?

DAMIAN: All right. Will the guy who wrote that letter still be in the village?

COMMANDING OFFICER: There's nobody left there! He brought us the letter to send to you people. After that, he probably took off for safety on the motorcycle that got him there.

DAMIAN: So he has a motorcycle, too! I thought of bringing mine, but we need a truck.

LOLA: And why isn't there anyone left in the village?

COMMANDING OFFICER: (*Shrugging his shoulders.*) Between the fascists being so close and our troops having left the place, the villagers lost no time in getting out of there . . .

CAPTAIN: The palace is just a hamlet, and people were scared. At the very beginning of the war, they executed two or three rightist types . . .

LOLA: The duke and duchess?

---

4. The militias were volunteer guerrilla fighters from various labor unions and political parties at the beginning of the war.

5. The motto "They shall not pass" was an exhortation to Spaniards to resist the rebels in their march on Madrid and was made famous by communist parliament member Dolores Ibárruru (1985–1989), who first used the expression in a 1936 speech.

CAPTAIN: You think they'd get those two? No a chance! But there were deaths; the solders who occupied the village killed right and left; they even shot the dogs.

COMMANDING OFFICER: (*Serious-faced.*) On a much smaller scale, sounds like what happened in Madrid when the insurgents began their offensive and the government took off.

LOLA: But the government ordered a halt to our atrocities.

COMMANDING OFFICER: They couldn't stop all of them, though, and when the fascists take over a village, they really go on a rampage. People have no idea how many deserted villages there are when those people advance.

LOLA: You mean even the rightists take off?

COMMANDING OFFICER: And how do you know which ones are rightists? There's no way to tell. There's a lot of hatred in war, and too many people enjoy the freedom to kill.

CAPTAIN: That's right. And the other side's been mowing 'em down from day one. (*Sighing.*) We'd better not lose this war, 'cause if we do, things will get a lot worse.

COMMANDING OFFICER: Who's talking about losing? We're going to win!

DAMIAN: Just like in that campus battle! But . . . why didn't our forces stay on in Brushfire? (*The* COMMANDING OFFICER *and the* CAPTAIN *look at each other.*)

COMMANDING OFFICER: (*Dryly.*) Orders from higher up.

CAPTAIN: Come on; I'll draw you a map of how to get there. But your operation will have to be carried out very quietly! It's much better if the enemy doesn't notice any movement.

DAMIAN: We'll only be there a day . . . And we could certainly use a couple of soldiers as protective escort . . . Even the Republic has guerilla fighters who sabotage enemy encampments.

COMMANDING OFFICER: (*Coldly.*) Those daredevils are active in another zone. This place is not in enemy territory; it's in no-man's-land. Sorry I can't accommodate you.

DAMIAN: Whatever you say.

CAPTAIN: And it might be a good idea to park your truck in the palace garage. It's left of the entrance and out of the line of fire.

COMMANDING OFFICER: (*Getting up.*) That's it, then. Go right through there. (*Motioning* LOLA *and* DAMIAN *to the right.*) I'll join you in a minute . . . , in case you like rabbit stew, that is!

LOLA: (*Pausing to chuckle.*) For something like that, I'd walk twenty miles!

COMMANDING OFFICER: That won't be necessary; right this way! (LOLA *and* DAMIAN *exit.*) At least it's clear they don't plan to desert. You were with him at the Bridge of the French.

CAPTAIN: What bothers me is that the enemy might get wind of what they're up to.

COMMANDING OFFICER: They do just routine vigilance . . . If only the president hadn't recommended this mission! And even at that, headquarters should have vetoed it!

CAPTAIN: We'll just have to hope they're lucky.

COMMANDING OFFICER: Let's go. (*He exits, and the* CAPTAIN *follows him. Darkness envelops the stage as string and wind instruments softly play the melody of "The Four Mule Drivers."*)

ACT TWO

*The curtain goes up on Act Two a few seconds after coming down on Act One.
There is daylight, and the portals of the duke's palace are now clearly illuminated.
The table and chairs remain on the left, but have a different look. Standing in
the palace doorway, AARON, about forty and dressed in old clothes, peers intently
inside and hears vague sounds of talking. As the voices approach, he grabs a rock
and runs to the table to place it on a paper he leaves before rushing off. Surrounding the duke's coat of arms carved over the palace door is the worn but now legible
motto: ARDENS DOCUIT ME VINCERE. As LOLA and DAMIAN emerge, they
seem disconcerted as they look at each other.*

LOLA: I don't like the looks of this.

DAMIAN: Me neither.

LOLA: What should we do?

DAMIAN: I think it's pretty clear: we get out of here.

LOLA: You mean without the painting?

DAMIAN: Well, it's not in the palace, and it's not in the village. Either that
painter who sent the message—or someone else—took it.

LOLA: Do you suppose we didn't search carefully enough? The palace is huge. (*A
little tired, she sits down close to the table.*)

DAMIAN: We looked everywhere. And we waited until daylight to start. It wasn't
in the chapel either. Maybe that crazy artist had second thoughts and took
the painting to the enemy camp with him. We need to get out of here, but
without letting our nerves get the better of us. Let's eat something first
and . . .

LOLA: Outside? Shouldn't we eat inside?

DAMIAN: Out here we have a better chance of avoiding enemy fire, and it looks
like we have a table all set up for us. I'll get the bread and a can or two
of something to eat from the truck. (*Taking a few steps.*) Did you get any
sleep?

LOLA: No; didn't even close my eyes. And bring the thermos, too, will you?

DAMIAN: I'm on my way.

LOLA: Why do you suppose this furniture is out here?

264

DAMIAN: (*Stopping.*) Maybe our soldiers had a little victory celebration before taking off.

LOLA: (*Swiping a finger across the table.*) But there's no dust. Someone used this table very recently. (*They look at each other in silence.*)

DAMIAN: (*In a low voice.*) Could the enemy have been here? There's nothing else for us to do here, Lola; we'd better eat on the road. (*He walks stage left.*)

LOLA: (*Getting up and looking at the palace door.*) What's that writing up there? It's so worn, I can hardly make it out. Can you read it?

DAMIAN: (*Reading with some difficulty but with correct pronunciation.*) "Rubens árdens dócuit me víncere." . . . Well, there's the burning bush! Like I say, our president knows everything! (*Translating.*) "The burning bush leads me to victory."

LOLA: That's from the Bible.

DAMIAN: Right. God was speaking to Moses from the burning bush, urging him to save his people enslaved by Pharaoh.

LOLA: And this village underbrush must have had something to do with the original duke's victory . . . but who could the enemy have been?

DAMIAN: (*Chuckling.*) Probably the Moors.

LOLA: Or maybe his victory was economic. They could have used the bushes for some medication.

DAMIAN: (*Laughing.*) Yeah, probably tonic water! Or a cola! (*They chuckle, but then look at one another in alarm.*) All right, let's get out of here.

LOLA: (*Looking around as though bidding farewell to the adventure, she notices the paper that AARON left under the rock.*) Wait a minute. (*Pointing.*) What's that?

DAMIAN: Well, it sure isn't the painting. Shall we get out of here?

LOLA: (*Removing the rock to pick up the paper.*) Did you see this last night?

DAMIAN: No.

LOLA: I didn't either. (*Reading.*) "Welcome." Do you suppose someone left it here during the night?

DAMIAN: That's all it says? Just "welcome"?

LOLA: (*She shakes her head and continues reading.*) "Don't be alarmed," it goes on.

DAMIAN: Let me see that! (*Grabbing the paper and reading.*) "I'm the one who wrote the letter so you'd come for the painting. I've been waiting for you." (*Immediately suspicious,* **DAMIAN** *looks around.*)

LOLA: Go on.

DAMIAN: "I'm leaving this note so you won't shoot me when I come out of hiding. Please sit down. You will see me shortly." (*Wary,* **DAMIAN** *reaches for his revolver.*)

LOLA: Hold it, Damian. Let's try sitting down like he says. (*She sits down.*)

DAMIAN: But let's not get careless. (*Very deliberately, he too takes a seat, his hand firmly on the revolver. Several tense moments pass before* **AARON**'s *voice sounds.*)

AARON: (*His voice.*) Friends . . . (*He reappears, smiling, from the right.*) Here's to the Republic, and El Greco, too! (*Advancing.*) I know you're from the Commission on Artistic Treasures. It's a good thing you're here. I couldn't wait much longer.

DAMIAN: Why not?

AARON: (*Laughing.*) No more potatoes. (*Serious.*) And the enemy might decide to come any minute and occupy the village.

DAMIAN: They could have done that before now . . .

AARON: (*Smiling.*) But they didn't. They still don't understand why our troops left.

DAMIAN: You do?

AARON: I'm not sure, but I think our side wants to surround them in this area to lessen the pressure on Madrid and other cities. Since the fascists don't understand what we're up to, they're mulling it over. But they keep advancing. All armies want to occupy abandoned territory, and when they're confident our troops have left for good, they'll do just that.

DAMIAN: Then we need to get out of here right away.

AARON: Without the painting?

DAMIAN: (*In a low voice to* **LOLA**.) This guy talks like you.

LOLA: The painting isn't in the palace.

AARON: (*Laughing.*) It was in the chapel, like I told you in the letter, but I took it away.

DAMIAN: Why is that?

AARON: May I come a little closer?

LOLA: Come ahead.

AARON: But get your hand off that gun, man! Can't you see I'm unarmed? Until they call up my unit, and I expect it any day now, I'm a civilian!

DAMIAN: Don't try to fool me! You're fighting for one side or the other, or will be very soon.

LOLA: Unless we win the war beforehand.

AARON: Or lose it . . .

DAMIAN: (*Irate.*) What?

AARON: (*Looking at them.*) You're charming but naïve . . . (*The word irritates* DAMIAN, *and he is on the verge of responding when* LOLA, *noticing his attitude, steps forward.*)

LOLA: (*Very serious.*) Where's the painting?

AARON: Just a minute. (*He sits down.*) It's here in the village; in my house.

DAMIAN: In your house?

AARON: (*Sighing at what he considers ridiculous incomprehension.*) Comrades, the enemy forces are watching this village from the distance, even though they don't come here. It's like I say: they don't trust the situation either. Oh, well, actually they did come once, and not because they had decided to advance; no, that wasn't it. A patrol came to the palace. They went through it, and got out fast. I hid and watched everything. . . . So why did they come? I don't know, but maybe to get the painting, or to see if we were using the palace to store supplies, or to see if we'd come back. . . . How do I know?

DAMIAN: (*Trying to trick him.*) And they took the painting.

AARON: You forget everything! I just told you I have the painting at my house! If they were looking for it, they must have thought our soldiers took it, but then I'm not sure they were looking for it. All I know is they left and haven't come back.

DAMIAN: You already had the painting.

Mission to the Deserted Village (Madrid, 1999), Act II, Damian (Juan Carlos Naya) and Aaron (Manuel Galiana)

AARON: I took out the nails and very carefully lowered it off the wall. As a painter, I know how to do those things.

DAMIAN: And why didn't you get out of here then, like that patrol?

AARON: Another stupid question! You people don't seem to understand anything. You think I wanted to leave without showing you where I hid the painting? I had to wait it out till you got here. (*He smiles.*) Yes, I was scared; really, really scared. Can't you tell by looking at me?

LOLA: (*Serious.*) No, it doesn't show.

AARON: Since I left that note on the table . . .

LOLA: But you speak very calmly, and your voice is firm. Could some enemy patrol be spying on us?

AARON: Oh, please! They'll be back only when ordered to. Meanwhile, I'm sure this territory is off limits for them, just like it is for us. They probably know why, and I think I do, too. But this quiet won't last more than a day or two. They have their reasons and are surely up to something.

DAMIAN: Why didn't you leave the village with the other people? You could have given us the exact location where you hid the painting.

AARON: (*His emotions increase; he is now really alarmed.*) It's just like I said! You guys don't understand a thing! And we're supposed to win the war with people like you?

DAMIAN: (*Irritated, he is about to get up.*) Listen here, you! . . .

AARON: Slow down! Don't get all worked up. I had to take care of the painting. I wasn't going to abandon it. I couldn't take it on my motorcycle, and the mayor didn't want anything to do with it. He had things besides transporting paintings on his mind!

DAMIAN: You have a motorcycle?

AARON: That's the only transportation a poor painter like me can afford. But it's a Harley and even has a sidecar.

DAMIAN: Well, a poor soldier like me doesn't own a car either. I have a motorcycle back in Madrid, too, but not as fancy as yours and no sidecar.

LOLA: (*Distrustful.*) Didn't you consider some other way to transport the painting?

AARON: Like what? There weren't even any carts left in this village.

LOLA: And you never thought of asking our soldiers to pick it up?

AARON: Without proper packing? I might do that with some little painting of mine, but with a large El Greco? . . . It's really a magnificent work of art; you'll see. That's why I wanted people from the commission here, so you'd transport it properly; that's why I gave you exact dimensions.

DAMIAN: And that's the only reason you stayed behind?

AARON: Well, that among others.

LOLA: What others? (**AARON** *hesitates to respond.*)

DAMIAN: Maybe I can clear that up for you, Lola.

AARON: (*Spontaneously.*) Lola, what a pretty name!

DAMIAN: (*To* **LOLA**.) You see he's not answering. Serves you right, Miss "pretty name"! (*Ironically.*) So let's suppose, Miss "pretty name," that our friend here says to you: when you come here and pack up the painting properly in an appropriate vehicle that runs, I can get away (*Looking fixedly at* **AARON**.) safely . . . to the enemy camp?

AARON: (*Thinking it over a minute.*) Comrade, you're hopeless.

DAMIAN: (*Irritated.*) What?

AARON: What's your name?

DAMIAN: Damian!

AARON: Well, this is how it is, Damian. If I had wanted to give that painting to the fascists along with your truck, the two of you, and even toss me into the bargain, nothing would have been simpler. I just wouldn't have written to the Republican Commission. I would have taken a very comfortable stroll a couple of miles to the glorious insurgent encampment and told them I was giving them a wonderful painting to return to the owners. I think they've already tried to get it back for them. Then neither you nor I would've had to cross paths.

LOLA: He's right about that, Damian.

DAMIAN: Let me handle this my way, Lolita.

AARON: (*Chuckling.*) Lolita! Check that endearing little diminutive! (*To* **LOLA**.) This guy must be your boyfriend.

DAMIAN: (*Furious, he gets up.*) That's enough out of you! (*They all glare at each other. Feigning calm,* AARON *sits down.*) Where's the painting?

LOLA: Please. Let's calm down. (*Getting up very deliberately.*) The painting is the important thing here. Are you going to show it to us? We need to pack it up immediately.

AARON: (*Getting up.*) All right.

DAMIAN: Let's pack it up and get back. Come on! Let's go!

AARON: Very soon. When we finish, I'll follow you on my motorcycle, not to the enemy zone, but to ours: yours and mine. Maybe the fascists will hear some noise, but they'll notice it's fading into the distance, and we'll be way ahead of them by then. First, I want to clear up a couple of things.

DAMIAN: We're in a hurry!

AARON: Yes, we're in a hurry, but by the time we get to my house, pack up the painting, and bring it back to your truck—and I've seen it's in the palace garage—we'll need to wait until nightfall to leave.

DAMIAN: (*Trying to control himself as he smiles.*) Even though we're in a hurry, right? (*Sitting down in front of him.*)

AARON: The painting is in the basement of my house, hidden under a lot of ropes I got just in case you came in a car and needed to secure the painting to the roof.

LOLA: Aren't we going?

DAMIAN: I have something to clear up, too. What if, for example, you wanted to get over to the enemy camp and had told them about our coming. . . . (**LOLA** *watches with increasing disapproval reflected in her body language.*) Just a hypothetical question, Lola! (*To* AARON.) And if that's the case, remember I'm armed.

AARON: (*Ironically.*) Yeah, I know. If you think my letter was a trick to let Franco catch a pair of crazy art lovers and a truck, well, go ahead. That would explain why you didn't find the El Greco in the palace . . . or in the village.

DAMIAN: You got that one right.

AARON: No; that's what you said. Now let me tell you something. (*Speaking to both of them.*) If we go on with these stupid suspicions, things could go wrong. We'll all be safer if you trust me. Let's pack up the painting and leave tonight.

DAMIAN: Trust you? (*Intrigued,* **LOLA** *sits down again.*) Convince us; go ahead.

AARON: I already told you I'm no hero. If I had wanted to cross over with some vehicle of yours, the painting and I would already be there. If I waited, it wasn't to surrender to Franco; I waited partly so the Republic, not the rebels, would have the painting, but more importantly so it wouldn't be destroyed.

LOLA: That sounds reasonable, Damian.

DAMIAN: Only if the painting is really here in the village. That's what we have to find out. (*To* **AARON**.) Are you really such a good Republican? (**AARON** *laughs.*) What's funny?

AARON: That *I* suspected the two of *you* might be trying to desert to the enemy! (*With a chuckle.*) But I heard what you had to say and understood immediately that I'm smarter than you are. (**DAMIAN** *is about to get up when* **LOLA** *stops him with a gesture.* **AARON** *speaks very calmly.*) Yes, I'm against the fascists. (*Lowering his voice.*) I'm also an artist; just a run-of-the-mill painter. And from what I know, our side tries to protect artistic treasures. We don't bomb the Prado or Guadalajara's Art Museum, like the fascists. And it's the Republic that will save the El Greco, just like it saved the Prado from the insurgents. . . . and from some of our own people, too.

DAMIAN: (*Aggressive.*) Who?

AARON: People on our side.

DAMIAN: What are you talking about?

AARON: About the senseless destruction our people cause. Want an example?

DAMIAN: (*Dismissive.*) Those things happen in war.

AARON: Oh, you just want to forget all about that. (**DAMIAN** *shakes his head.*) I get it. You don't want to discredit our cause. But we really aren't any better than they are if we don't recognize . . .

DAMIAN: What are you talking about?

AARON: So you don't know, huh? . . . I'm talking about a certain important city. (**LOLA** *represses a gesture of concern.*) And in the main church there, our troops destroyed . . .

DAMIAN: It's not the same! What they did is understandable! The Church has done some awful things . . . !

AARON: (*Agreeing.*) And I know it wasn't an official order. It was an explosion of anger; of mob violence. But if our side doesn't repudiate these atrocities . . .

DAMIAN: You don't understand anything. If the enemy does terrible things and we don't retaliate, they'll just keep doing them!

AARON: But if we don't learn how to avoid those things, or if we don't condemn the murders, even though the person "taken for a walk" is a real fascist, how are we going to build a better Spain, even if we win the war?

DAMIAN: You're dreaming.

AARON: Like some of our leaders. I refer to the ones who, rather than bomb a museum, organize the "Commission to Preserve and Protect Artistic Treasures."

DAMIAN: Sometimes you have to bomb, sometimes you have to execute. War isn't a finishing school for young ladies, you know.

AARON: Oh, I've heard that one before. But if we can't be more humane than the people who want to take away our freedoms—I'm talking about the fascists—our cause will surely fail.

DAMIAN: (*Chuckling.*) See what I mean? You're a dreamer.

AARON: Maybe so. But those man-made treasures are worth dying for.

DAMIAN: We shouldn't be dying at all, and certainly not for an El Greco. We should be saving lives. Art is for the living, not the dead.

AARON: Oh, how philosophical. But here the two of you are risking your lives for an El Greco.

DAMIAN: Yes, we came to fight for art. And for a more just future for everyone, even though it's without an El Greco! Maybe you haven't gone over to the enemy yet, but you sure think like a reactionary.

LOLA: No, he doesn't; he's absolutely right.

DAMIAN: Don't talk crazy! We're alive, and El Greco is dead!

LOLA: If he weren't more alive than we are, we wouldn't be risking our lives this way.

AARON: (*With a pleased expression.*) Thank you, comrade.

LOLA: Can we go to your house now and pack up the painting? It shouldn't take long to get the crate and the tools there.

AARON: But we need to be careful. It's broad daylight now. I'll show you how to go so nobody will see us.

DAMIAN: (*Surly.*) Can't we take the truck to your house?

AARON: That's too dangerous. We'll carry the crate between the two of us and then bring it back with the painting all packed. We need to travel to our zone at night and starting from here. That's the safest way. (*Getting up.*) Ready?

LOLA: We have to get the materials and tools . . .

DAMIAN: Then let's get started. (*As they walk toward the left,* DAMIAN *pauses.*) And you're going to travel with us?

AARON: Yes.

DAMIAN: On your motorcycle?

AARON: Yes. I have plenty of gas; there'll be no problem.

DAMIAN: So we're leaving here tonight in the truck making noise and you'll follow making noise, too.

AARON: (*With a half smile.*) My house isn't far from here.

DAMIAN: And couldn't it be that . . . ?

LOLA: (*Fearful about his hostility toward* AARON.) Damian, please! Let's not waste any more time! If our people see we're not back in a couple of days, they could think we've been killed, and headquarters might order an attack . . .

DAMIAN: (*Raising his voice.*) Why don't we take the painting on the truck? (*To* AARON.) You stay behind, there'll be no noise, and you can leave later on your motorcycle (*Pointing.*) to join the fascists.

AARON: You mean after some patrol of theirs that I've alerted (*Smiling.*) has captured you and the painting? (*Brief silence.*) Lola, what kind of amateur did the commission send on this mission?

DAMIAN: (*Holding back his anger.*) I'm no fool! All right, rather than letting our tempers get out of hand, shall we get the painting?

LOLA: Absolutely!

DAMIAN: Let's go! (*He starts walking again, and the three exit stage left. As lights go down on this scene, they come up on the* **SECRETARY**, *who continues reading.*)

SECRETARY: Things were very tense, because we were under pressure to finish the mission. From time to time, shots in the distance or planes on the horizon made us fear the fascists were approaching. But despite all the frightening moments, when things quieted down, I felt an unexpected calm. It was as though the silence of that abandoned village communicated a kind of serenity. I asked Damian if he noticed it, but he was too busy looking around, keeping his hand on his gun, and cursing the person who had hidden the El Greco in his own basement. . . . On the way there, Damian and Aaron carried the wooden crate between them. I tried to help, but they wouldn't let me. . . . I took the tools in a bag and just watched. Damian acted very nervous. Aaron, though, was quite calm. I had to admit I was attracted to that man. . . . He intrigued me. . . . When we got to Aaron's house and saw the painting . . . (*Brief silence.*) Damian, less easily impressed, admitted it was a wonderful canvas, but I was absolutely speechless. . . . We wrapped the painting very carefully and brought it up to the main floor to take to the truck. (*The* **ADJUNCT** *is suddenly illuminated. A blurred but suggestive image of the Annunciation is projected on the palace doors but disappears as lights come up on the left.*)

ADJUNCT: (*Standing.*) So now come the explosion and the part I find . . . so fictitious.

SECRETARY: But others may not have the same reaction. (*The* **ADJUNCT** *shrugs and begins to retreat as the light goes down on him. The* **SECRETARY** *addresses the audience.*) The story doesn't talk about that yet. The focus is on the sudden interest my relative showed for other artworks she sees there. (*Reading.*) Aaron—Lola is talking now—showed us some of his own paintings, and I asked him to explain them . . . (*The* **SECRETARY** *continues, visible as silvery moonlight invades the central area. The position of the table and chairs has shifted; they are now on the right.* **LOLA** *and* **AARON** *sit at the table downstage on the ground floor of his house. Undecided,* **DAMIAN** *paces back and forth as he munches a sandwich and the other two finish a light meal.*)

LOLA: To pass the time, Aaron insisted on making sandwiches with herbs, tomatoes, and some hard bread he humidified, he told us, to keep it edible. I thought eating something might lessen the tension between those two.

DAMIAN: (*Stopping.*) Shouldn't we take the painting to the truck? After all the hurry . . .

AARON: (*Shaking his head as he pours water into an old jug.*) When it gets completely dark . . . The enemy is probably watching us from a safe distance. It's smarter to take the painting out at the very last minute.

LOLA: This is good spring water. (*Laughing.*) And something that won't run out! (*Drinking from another jug.*)

DAMIAN: (*Conceding.*) It tastes like bottled water.

LOLA: What do you think of our friend's paintings, Damian?

DAMIAN: (*Smiling.*) Well, they're not El Grecos; that's for sure.

AARON: (*Glancing at some paintings against the wall.*) I never intended them to be.

LOLA: I find two especially intriguing; the ones with duplicated or overlapping images.

DAMIAN: (*He pauses and adopts a superior attitude.*) That's just modern art, Lola. They wouldn't qualify as cubist. The figures are too blurred. (*To* AARON.) Wouldn't you agree?

AARON: Yes . . . But no . . .

LOLA: What would you say about them?

AARON: I don't want to bore you.

LOLA: You won't bore anybody. Please, what are they?

AARON: It's no particular style. But I don't want to defend those paintings; they're failed attempts at something. (*To* LOLA.) I'm sure your friend doesn't like them. (*He looks at* DAMIAN, *who disdainfully steps away from them.*) I don't either. They were mistakes.

LOLA: Mistakes?

AARON: You probably noticed the attempt at realism. . . .

LOLA: Only in the middle of the painting. The blurred figures are more peripheral. And the more peripheral they are, the more blurred they are.

DAMIAN: (*He approaches, speaking ironically.*) Well, aren't you the observant one!

LOLA: (*To* AARON.) I don't think I understand.

AARON: Sure, you do! That's the way we see each other without realizing it.

LOLA: What?

AARON: We see with both eyes, but we focus on single images. As we look here or there, we change focus, and that gives a hint of seeing in relief; in three dimensions.

DAMIAN: (*Vaguely uncomfortable at* **LOLA**'s *increasing interest.*) Excuse the interruption, but you have a Harley like I do, so I wonder if you've noticed . . .

LOLA: Forget that for now! (*To* **AARON**.) I know we see that way, but why paint that fleeting vision?

AARON: Silly reasons, I guess. I was trying to suggest a sensation of the void around the central figure that stands out as we focus on it, but the duplications and mixtures surrounding it are difficult to reproduce exactly, and if we gaze directly at the central image, lateral vision is hard to replicate, and we wouldn't notice it anyway. (**LOLA** *looks at him in amazement.* **DAMIAN**, *who continued pacing, pauses again.*)

DAMIAN: So it was a failed attempt. Well, I was wondering if you've noticed any problem with your Harley's carburetor.

AARON: The carburetor?

DAMIAN: You know, the cylinders, or maybe the pistons.

LOLA: Oh, wait a minute! (*To* **AARON**.) You mean, if you don't shift your gaze, you won't see things in relief . . .

AARON: That's right. And it's more noticeable in paintings without repeated figures.

LOLA: Like in *Las Meninas* . . .

AARON: Exactly. Velazquez knew all that intuitively, but he wanted to do paintings people understood, so he softened the effect. With the hand of a master, he showed some figures more clearly than others and simply accentuated the focal points.

LOLA: That's amazing

AARON: I really didn't want to show you those paintings. I'm glad I realized my mistake in time.

DAMIAN: (*Coldly.*) Very interesting. (*Sitting down close to them.*) An art lesson, of course. But out of place right now.

LOLA: On the contrary. The miracle of art and its power are important even at moments like these.

AARON: But only when the attempts are successful. (*To* **DAMIAN**.) You asked me about my Harley's carburetor in case yours was defective, I suppose. (*His voice is expressionless; his thoughts, as well as* **LOLA**'s, *remain on the previous subject. They pay little attention to* **DAMIAN**.)

LOLA: Those aren't silly reasons. You wanted to go a step beyond; to experiment. Maybe you didn't achieve exactly what you wanted, but perhaps your attempt will lead to important innovations in the future . . .

AARON: Maybe one day science will produce excellent photographs in relief unlike the three-dimensional images I attempted. Painting may not be able to do that, but painting can do a whole lot more.

LOLA: Like what El Greco attempted.

AARON: And others . . . (*He becomes quiet.* **DAMIAN**, *humiliated by the lack of attention, stands up.* **LOLA** *stops looking at* **AARON**. *Taking a few steps as he looks at them out of the corner of his eye,* **DAMIAN** *mutters unintelligible words and exits stage left as* **AARON** *observes him.*)

LOLA: (*Unaware of* **DAMIAN**'s *departure.*) Your attempts aren't failures, Aaron; they're important. (*Noticing* **DAMIAN**'s *absence, she gets up and walks hesitantly stage left.*)

AARON: (*Lost in thought.*) No. It was crazy . . . I was wrong.

LOLA: (*She turns toward* **AARON**, *approaches him, walks behind his back to the right, and finally speaks very softly.*) You didn't stay in this village just to tell us where you hid the El Greco, did you?

AARON: You think I'm with the enemy, too?

LOLA: No, but you said that you had stayed behind for other reasons. I don't know; maybe it was . . . to take refuge in the brush from the atrocities of war? Here, in an abandoned village with nobody around, it's like the war doesn't exist. (*Short pause.*) There's a strange kind of peace in all this silence . . . Is that it? Or am I talking crazy?

AARON: (*After a moment and hardly daring to look at her.*) My wife and I were so used to this village. We loved it . . .

LOLA: Your wife?

AARON: She died three years ago. She was high-spirited, but her health was fragile. The tranquility here inspired us both, but it didn't cure her lungs. Sometimes when I breathe in this fresh air, it's like she's still here. That's one of the reasons I didn't leave. (*Sighing.*) But now I'll have to go. . . .

LOLA: (*Walking toward him and putting a hand softly on his shoulder.*) When the war is over, I can visit you here, like a tourist who wants to make sure you survived. . . . And maybe I'll commission you to paint my portrait (*Smiling tenderly.*) . . . even though you might blur my image. (*Sitting beside him.*)

AARON: I wouldn't blur your image. You'd be the focal point of the painting . . . Perhaps my own image, palette in hand, would be blurry as I studied you intently . . . Another crazy idea. Sorry.

LOLA: (*Speechless, she smiles.*) That's not crazy. It'll be a wonderful memory of these hours.

AARON: (*Flustered.*) Lola . . . (*He becomes quiet.*)

LOLA: What?

AARON: If your . . . fiancé sees us . . .

LOLA: (*Coldly.*) He's not my fiancé.

AARON: (*Without looking at her.*) I'm over forty, and I have memories that will never go away.

LOLA: But they might be softened. (*Placing her hand on his as the lights go down and brighten on the* SECRETARY.)

SECRETARY: These sudden new feelings surprised me, but I doubted that he felt the same way about me. Like Aaron, I noticed the quiet, clean air of the village. But soon . . . (*The lights once again come up on the couple, and the* SECRETARY *is enveloped in darkness.* DAMIAN *reenters from the left, and* AARON *slowly withdraws his hand.* DAMIAN *notices immediately the situation between the two and pauses.*)

AARON: (*Aware of* DAMIAN's *presence but without looking at him.*) What we have to do is save the painting.

LOLA: That's our mission, and we'll accomplish it. (*Looking at* DAMIAN *as she gets up.*)

DAMIAN: (*Advancing as he speaks dryly.*) This very night.

AARON: (*He gets up and speaks softly.*) We could also take a couple of nineteenth-century paintings that are pretty good.

LOLA: I saw them; they're Palmarolis.

DAMIAN: So if we hurry, we can save the El Greco . . . and a few other paintings. (**LOLA** *and* **AARON** *look at each other in silence.*)

AARON: I'll bring them right up. They'll be fine between blankets. (*He stutters slightly.*) This . . . is something we can do together. (**LOLA** *sits down again.*)

DAMIAN: Whatever you say. (**AARON** *exits stage left.*) What did he mean? I didn't get it.

LOLA: I didn't either. (*After a pause,* **DAMIAN** *approaches the table.*)

DAMIAN: Interesting guy, huh?

LOLA: And a wonderful mind. To conceive of painting as stereoscopic vision makes you think.

DAMIAN: But he considers his attempts failures.

LOLA: That's not important. A mind like that will find other things to accomplish. (*Smiling.*) According to your standards, his life would be more valuable than any painting.

DAMIAN: But we came to rescue an El Greco, right?

LOLA: And as you say, it will happen tonight, if all goes well. (**DAMIAN** *sits down beside her with a kind of distant familiarity.*)

DAMIAN: (*Attempting to make light of the situation.*) We sure didn't take advantage of this little vacation. If he hadn't moved the painting, we'd be on our way to Madrid right now.

LOLA: You're forgetting that if we were on that road, an enemy patrol would get the painting. (*Silence as she looks at him, and he looks even more intently at her.*)

DAMIAN: That's not a sure thing. (*Uncomfortable, he looks away but takes her hands.*) Lola . . .

LOLA: (*Trying to withdraw her hands.*) Damian, please.

DAMIAN: (*Without letting go.*) I don't mean to pressure you. I just want to open your eyes!

LOLA: To what?

DAMIAN: (*Getting angry.*) To the fact that we're in love! Yes! You resist, but I'll convince you! That motto on the palace door is more ours than theirs.

LOLA: What motto?

DAMIAN: The burning bush leads to victory! Let yourself feel and be won!

LOLA: I'm not on fire.

DAMIAN: That's not necessary. In the Bible, the bush burned as God's miracle that would free an enslaved people. We don't need miracles anymore. We can free the people with our words, our logic; words can even win over people like you who resist seeing clearly within themselves.

LOLA: You're always thinking about winning, aren't you?

DAMIAN: I've already won you! You just won't admit it! (*He kisses her forcefully. Sounds in the distance commence, but the characters don't notice them immediately. Holding two small canvasses in antique frames,* AARON *reappears and observes them. The sound of an approaching plane becomes increasingly audible.*)

LOLA: (*Successfully separating from* DAMIAN.) Please!

DAMIAN: (*Noticing the painter's presence.*) Sorry, Aaron; I'm crazy about this woman, and she says she doesn't love me. What do you think? Nothing bad about me, I hope, since you went back to the palace to get two little paintings we could have picked up tonight when we take the El Greco to the truck.

LOLA: (*Getting up.*) I hear a plane. (*All three listen.*) It's getting closer.

DAMIAN: (*Walking left, he stops and points toward to the door.*) And I think there's more than one. Let's get down to the basement. (LOLA *crosses and exits first.* DAMIAN *indicates that* AARON *should precede him. Center stage is dark as lights come up on the two lateral areas, the ones on the left more slowly than the ones on the right. The* SECRETARY, *standing with the manuscript in her hands, is interrupted by a smiling* PRESIDENT.)

PRESIDENT: (*To the* SECRETARY.) Read just what they said as they were going down the stairs, please.

SECRETARY: Yes, Mr. President. (*As she begins to read, curtains hide the central area.*) We went down the steps quickly. Suddenly, I stopped and burst out crying. Aaron and Damian supported me so I wouldn't fall. My nerves had just given out. I tried to stop crying . . . (*Meanwhile, the* ADJUNCT *enters slowly from the left; without sitting, he observes the* SECRETARY.)

ADJUNCT: Excuse me. Did Lola cry before or after the bombing?

SECRETARY: Before.

ADJUNCT: That part isn't clear, and one might think she cried because of the bombing. If I remember correctly, that's when she cried.

PRESIDENT: But you're getting ahead of the story. Did you tell our secretary to omit that part? You must be well aware that without that (*Accentuating the next word.*) detail, the story makes no sense. I can't believe you meant to do that . . . , not even now, no matter how much you'd like to invalidate this whole reading.

ADJUNCT: (*Indignant.*) Mr. President! You're insulting me!

SECRETARY: My reading is faithful to the text. No one asked for omissions. (*To the* PRESIDENT.) Shall I continue?

PRESIDENT: Of course. (*Irritated, the* ADJUNCT *takes his seat.*)

SECRETARY: Lola is speaking: I asked my companions, "Is that plane going away from us?" Aaron commented: "Sounds like more than one to me. . . . Maybe they're just passing over." Damian was sure there were several planes, and the noise was getting louder and louder. Then suddenly . . .

ADJUNCT: (*In disbelief.*) A bomb hit the palace.

SECRETARY: (*Reading.*) The bomb exploded. A terrible noise . . . I screamed again, and we rushed down to the basement and . . .

PRESIDENT: (*Stopping the* SECRETARY *with a motion of his hand.*) Let's give our listeners a rest. We'll continue in ten minutes. (*Gestures of disapproval from the* ADJUNCT, *who gets up and leaves. The theater lights come up slowly. With a gesture, the* PRESIDENT *invites the* SECRETARY *to precede him. He then exits behind her as the music "On the Bridge of the French" plays before slowly fading away.*)

PART TWO

As soon as the audience is seated, the hall lights go down and stage lights come up on the two lateral areas occupied by the club's officers and the ADJUNCT *who had filed in as the audience was returning to their seats.*

PRESIDENT: Let's continue the reading. We now come to the most serious event of the story. Direct your attention to our secretary.

SECRETARY: Thank you, Mr. President. Our listeners can only imagine the sound of the explosion. (*Consulting her text.*) The narrator tells of hovering in the basement shelter and hearing the sound of the approaching planes getting louder and louder . . . until . . . at close range . . . (*Partly reading, partly summarizing.*) a bomb exploded, and then another bomb a few seconds later. Her fear is very apparent as she tells the story. They were all under tremendous pressure to make a decision but couldn't agree about it during the three days spent in that basement, engulfed in an eerie silence that settled once more over Brushfire . . . (*Her voice fades, as do the lights on the* SECRETARY, PRESIDENT, *and* ADJUNCT. *Meanwhile, lights come up center stage on the basement. All the places previously imagined and projected have disappeared, and we see only a section of the basement. There are paintings leaning against the wall, a couple of rickety cots, stools, and piles of big books. On the right, sparse light filters through a barred window, and on the left, there is a closed door.* LOLA *and* AARON *sit on stools as* DAMIAN *paces and eventually pauses at the window to peer out.*

DAMIAN: From here, you can't see or hear a thing.

AARON: That window is ground level. From there you should at least see some bushes.

LOLA: (*Looking up.*) Really?

AARON: The woods start a few hundred feet away, in that hollow.

DAMIAN: Upstairs you don't hear anything either. The village is still deserted. And those planes dropped their bombs an hour ago.

AARON: And very close to us; maybe on the palace. It's the most visible structure in the village; even more visible than the church.

DAMIAN: But we haven't heard any more explosions. And it doesn't sound like anyone's coming. I don't hear any tanks. It looks like we're alone again.

Mission to the Deserted Village (Madrid, 1999), Act II, Aaron (Manuel Galiana) and Lola (Paula Sebastián)

LOLA: (*Frightened.*) You think they'd bomb the palace and just leave it at that? They know who it belongs to. They'd have to show more respect. . . .

DAMIAN: But it doesn't look like they've initiated an offensive. Their troops apparently aren't advancing. (*Crossing to the closed door and starting to open it.*) We need to check things out. I'm going upstairs.

LOLA: Why don't we wait until we hear something? (*Getting up.*)

DAMIAN: We can't do that! While the enemy is quiet, we need to get out of here! (*He opens the door slightly, revealing a simple stairway.*)

LOLA: Be very careful!

DAMIAN: I won't be long. Keep your voices down and stay alert. (*He slips through the door and closes it.* **AARON** *goes to the window and listens attentively. When he returns to* **LOLA,** *they just look at each other.*)

LOLA: (*Barely above a whisper.*) There really aren't any cars out there?

AARON: None. Nobody's left in the village.

LOLA: And there's no sound. (*Silence.*) Why did they bomb this place?

AARON: Probably testing; wanted to make sure our soldiers hadn't come back to occupy the village.

LOLA: Or because they noticed movement?

AARON: Send planes for that? They'd just send some patrol.

LOLA: (*After a moment.*) I hope Damian gets back soon. (*Her voice trembles, and* **AARON** *takes a step toward her.*)

AARON: Are you crying? (*Nodding affirmatively.*) Of course. Come over here with me. (*She hesitates briefly but joins him, and they both look through the window. She begins to cry again, this time seeking the refuge of his shoulder. He puts an arm around her.*)

LOLA: I'm sorry. I'm so scared.

AARON: Maybe we'll come out of this alive yet. We can still get away. That silence isn't a bad sign. It reminds me of the old silence; her silence. It makes me feel calm. I'll come back to this place. Yes, I'll come back someday.

LOLA: After the war.

AARON: That's right. And you'll come, too.

LOLA: (*Smiling through her tears.*) For you to paint my portrait?

AARON: (*Smiling.*) You'll see . . . everything will be all right. Let's believe that. (*Silence as they peer through the window.*)

LOLA: The bushes aren't burning . . .

AARON: They didn't set them on fire. Good sign.

LOLA: Of what?

AARON: Everything isn't in books.

LOLA: (*Showing surprise.*) What do you mean by that?

AARON: Although God hasn't spoken to us from a burning bush, perhaps that quiet underbrush is telling us something.

LOLA: What could that be?

AARON: Oh, I don't know! Books teach us lots of things, but not everything. We have to keep thinking, reflecting . . . before deciding whether people who revolt and those who exploit them require military action or whether all wars just might be imposed. . . . (*The basement door opens slowly, and* DAMIAN *enters. The two separate.*)

LOLA: (*Rushing to meet him.*) Damian! Damian! (*They take each other's hands.* AARON *smiles in sad resignation. After a short pause, she steps away to look at him.* AARON *also looks inquiringly at* DAMIAN.)

DAMIAN: They hit the palace. But in the village, not a sound, and no sign of the enemy either. Maybe the bombs were just a warning. They don't trust us either.

AARON: But bombs for no reason?

DAMIAN: It's been over an hour. . . . What do we know about their decisions? For that matter, we don't even know what they are in our own central command. One group is about as smart, or as dumb, as the other. I give up trying to understand them. (*Serious.*) But there are other things we need to talk about. Come over here and sit down. (*Returning to his old seat as* LOLA *and* AARON *hasten to theirs.*) The palace is pretty much destroyed . . .

AARON: Maybe when they found out the El Greco wasn't here anymore, they allowed . . . Maybe even the noble owners allowed . . . the palace to be destroyed to show solidarity and warn our side not to be so bold. And if they win, the duke and duchess can demand reparation. . . .

DAMIAN: Maybe. It's just that the . . . a bomb fell on . . . the garage.

LOLA: (*Shocked.*) What?

DAMIAN: Yes. The truck was destroyed. There was no way to bring it here for the painting. The truck is gone, and without the truck, looks like our mission is impossible. (*Stunned silence.*) We've got to think, and fast! What are we going to do?

AARON: And they still aren't coming. They'll come eventually, though, but they'll keep taking their time, just like our people do. Let's see what options we have. One would be to walk at night very quietly to the crossroads. That's about six miles. Can you do that, Lola?

LOLA: Of course!

DAMIAN: (*With an insidious softness.*) And leave the painting behind?

AARON: We have to! (*Smiling.*) We'll leave a note on the crate . . .

DAMIAN: (*Ironic.*) How like you.

AARON: I suppose they'll take care of the painting since they made a trip just to get it a few days ago.

DAMIAN: (*Looking intensely at him.*) What about your motorcycle?

AARON: I hate to lose it, but we have to walk so as not to make any noise . . .

LOLA: Or the three of us could escape on the motorcycle during the day now that they're leaving us alone, temporarily at least. (*Sighing nervously.*) Even if they try to come after us, we'll have a good head start.

AARON: (*To* DAMIAN.) And since you know how to handle this motorcycle, you can get rid of those suspicions that I'd take off in the opposite direction.

DAMIAN: With my pistol aimed at you? You wouldn't be that crazy.

LOLA: Please, you two! Stop all that stupid bickering! I vote for the motorcycle. It's safer and faster than a long hike in the dark.

AARON: (*Undecided.*) All things considered . . . (*The three look at each other in silence as lights go down on them and come up on the* SECRETARY, *who looks out at the audience before reading.*)

SECRETARY: Despite the need to hurry, we just stood there, looking at each other. Damian was vague about what we ought to do; maybe he wanted to stall since we weren't following his plan. From time to time, we had a sandwich and saw that the enemy wasn't advancing in our direction, and even two days later, we were still discussing what to do. But in that awful confinement of the basement . . . , I kept remembering how we'd taken refuge there and how very different my companions were. (*Lights come up on the three as they go down on the* SECRETARY. *They continue looking at each other, and their expressions reflect strain and fatigue.*)

AARON: We've got to decide, and it seems more obvious than ever that we should get on the motorcycle right away and beat it out of here.

DAMIAN: Without accomplishing the mission?

AARON: You mean take the painting? We can't do that! (DAMIAN *walks downstage and squints through the small window.*)

DAMIAN: This window is street level. We can see from here.

AARON: That's why we've got to get out of here, and right now!

DAMIAN: And leave the painting behind?

AARON: Right!

DAMIAN: No.

AARON: What do you mean: "no"?

DAMIAN: I mean we have to try to take it.

AARON: (*Forcing a smile.*) You tell me how.

DAMIAN: (*After a moment's pause, he turns toward them.*) On the motorcycle.

AARON: The motorcycle can barely hold the three of us! Picture Lola in the sidecar, you in the driver's seat, and me behind you as Lola and I hold the crate up in the air, like this. (*He mimes comically the described action.*) Is that your crazy plan? The painting would fall off, and so would we . . .

DAMIAN: There's plenty of rope around here. You brought it yourself.

AARON: In case we were traveling in a car! The motorcycle has no roof or any other place to tie anything to, and that crate is huge.

LOLA: Damian, you're out of your mind.

DAMIAN: No, I'm not. It's difficult but not impossible. The crate would ride straight up and down and slightly bent. It would crowd Lola, but that way she'd help hold it in place. Her legs would have to be tight against a corner of the crate.

AARON: In the sidecar?

DAMIAN: Yes.

AARON: There's not enough room!

DAMIAN: There has to be!

AARON: And most of the packing up in the air? It would fall, of course, with all that motion. I thought you knew something about motorcycles. Mine's upstairs! Let's go up, and you'll see your plan is impossible! (*Starting to walk.*) Let's go! Come on, let's go!

DAMIAN: You have ropes! We'll put them under the sidecar, then over the crate, and tie everything to the motorcycle. We'll tie things down wherever we need to!

AARON: But there's no space! You could only tie things to the sidecar handles, and you know it! There aren't any other places!

DAMIAN: We'll find them!

AARON: He thinks we can do this, Lola. The ropes would certainly press against your legs and your body, but wouldn't steady anything. With you in the sidecar, whenever we hit a bump, you could put an elbow right through the canvas. . . . Let's try it out, if Damian insists! Maybe we still have time. But I know it's useless.

LOLA: So do I. (*With a resigned sigh.*)

DAMIAN: What are you saying, Lola? Help me! We have to accomplish the mission and get the painting out of here!

LOLA: We can't, and not just because tying it down won't work, but for an important reason related to the painting.

DAMIAN: An important reason? What story are you going to make up now?

LOLA: (*Taken aback.*) Me? Make up stories? That's an insult! Supposing for a minute that the crate could be supported, like you say, with one of us is in the sidecar and that it wouldn't fall off on the way. That road is awful, and the painting would bounce around way too much. (*Absolutely convinced.*) It already has too many cracks. (**LOLA** *looks firmly at both with her considerable professional experience and authority. As they look at her expectantly, she speaks more softly.*) Whole areas of paint could slough off! Held in place by those braces we have in the van, it would have been supported all the way, but it could never withstand all that jostling around on a motorcycle. And to rescue the painting means to preserve it, not destroy it. (*She sighs and pauses.*) Sorry, Damian. What you suggest is simply out of the question.

DAMIAN: (*After a pause, he speaks, but without conviction.*) I don't think it's in such bad shape! Even if it gets damaged on the road, it can be restored . . .

LOLA: (*Raising her voice, showing some anger.*) Which do you prefer? A ruined El Greco delivered to the Republic or an intact El Greco here with Aaron's instructions about transporting it safely?

DAMIAN: (*Repeating like an echo.*) Aaron . . . always Aaron. (*Looking at both of them.*)

AARON: I think we should write that note and get out of here right away.

DAMIAN: I know a little something about paintings, too, and that Annunciation isn't in such bad shape. Of course I don't want to destroy it! But carefully wrapped in blankets, the way it is in that crate, we won't lose many fragments!

AARON: On the motorcycle, it wouldn't last six miles, and we're not doing it.

DAMIAN: (*Getting excited again.*) But we'd have the painting! It can be restored! Old paintings can be restored!

LOLA: Stop insisting. You know we're not going to do it. I vote to protect that canvas and follow Aaron's—and my—plan. Let's go upstairs. (*Approaching the door.*)

DAMIAN: (*Muttering to himself.*) Always Aaron. (*To* **LOLA**.) Stop! (*Shocked by his tone, she pauses. He positions himself between her and the door.*) This isn't parliament. It's a mission, and I'm in command. Votes don't count; only my orders, and we're going to do it my way. That's an order.

AARON: I'm not in the army, so I'm not subject to your commands. I will not be part of your crazy scheme.

DAMIAN: You *will* help. I order it.

AARON: Lola's right! The painting will be seriously damaged!

DAMIAN: But it will be ours. Let's go.

LOLA: I'm not taking a single step until you calm down, and I know you're even more worked up than you look. (*A tense silence.*)

AARON: (*Speaking very softly.*) Will you go upstairs a minute, Lola? I'd like to talk to Damian alone. Wait for us up there, please. You can write down those instructions about the painting that we'll leave beside it.

DAMIAN: We're not leaving a note.

AARON: You and I need to talk alone. Is that all right, Lola? We won't be long. (**LOLA** *looks at him, disconcerted.*)

DAMIAN: Lola. (*Without looking at her, he stands aside.*)

AARON: Write in big print letters on one of my sketchpads.

LOLA: (*Nervous and hesitant, she looks inquiringly from one to the other but decides to leave.*) All right. (*She exits closing the door behind her. Pause.*)

DAMIAN: So what the hell do you want? You're not going to change my mind.

AARON: Since the fascists have favored us by considering this village as mysterious as we do and haven't invaded, I'm going to tell you a few things. Although you don't seem to understand it, our real mission is to preserve that El Greco from harm, and without the truck we can't move it.

DAMIAN: I repeat what I said to both of you before: the painting is in good shape and will suffer minimal damage in transport. By taking it with us, we accomplish the mission.

AARON: But it can't be secured as you suggest; it's impossible.

DAMIAN: We're going to do it my way.

AARON: (*Softly.*) You're forcing me?

DAMIAN: If I have to.

AARON: You're the only one armed here. Would you really go that far to make us help you? But we won't do it in any case. . . .

DAMIAN: We're at war. We have to keep this valuable painting out of enemy hands.

AARON: So you'd destroy it first, even this irreplaceable work of art?

DAMIAN: It won't be destroyed. Is that all? Let's go upstairs.

AARON: Just a minute. (**DAMIAN** *narrows his eyes.*) Since we're leveling with each other here, let me ask you this: do you still think I want to give the painting to the enemy to return to the owners?

DAMIAN: This is no time to talk about that. We're leaving right now, and with the painting. That's an order!

AARON: And if we lose the war . . .

DAMIAN: (*Decisively.*) No need to talk about that either. Action wins wars.

AARON: But if we lost the war, the painting would go back to the owners, wouldn't it?

DAMIAN: Their names are in our file. But we're going to win. (*Smiling.*) Look, Aaron. We didn't start this. Our actions need to be decisive; those guys asked for it.

AARON: You mean actions like setting fires, destroying property, murdering people? What about stealing? (*Lowering his voice.*) Maybe even torture?

DAMIAN: Yes, as much as they do, not more, even though they use other words for their actions. You want us to have principles and behaviors less reprehensible than theirs, but we can't afford that kind of idealism right now.

AARON: Why not?

DAMIAN: Because we're at war.

AARON: And for special assignments, those in charge select decisive people like you. I'll bet at the university, you were one of the major rabble-rousers. Am I right?

DAMIAN: Oh, shut up!

AARON: Our leaders haven't learned yet that to be successful in what our cause is all about, they should choose the most intelligent and thoughtful individuals for their missions . . . (*Lowering his voice.*) What I'm saying—even though you refuse to believe it—is that I consider myself, as a Republican, a soldier for our cause. That's why I wrote the letter. And deep down, I believe that a change in war tactics is necessary. But maybe I'm wrong . . . maybe for the time being, it's enough for the Republic just to win. . . . But don't you think that a hundred years from now, struggles for change will be more respectful of human rights? I'm talking about the values we, of the Republic, give lip service to. . . . Or are we hypocrites?

DAMIAN: No!

AARON: I'd like to agree. I'd like to think that we're progressing toward more humane treatment of the enemy, even though it's gradual. We don't have to stop being Republicans to do those things.

DAMIAN: Where do you get all those strange ideas? You can't have social change without force and some measure of violence. Since the fascists give up nothing voluntarily, we have to take things by force in order to provide social justice.

AARON: (*Very serious.*) The old class struggle . . .

DAMIAN: About time you remembered it!

AARON: . . . and those inevitable wars, whether fought as defense or aggression. But it's the people—the majority—who should impose change when it's their turn to govern and they're prepared and empowered to do so. At that point, they'll institute, by democratic force, new institutions and systems without recourse to crimes of violence. That's the only force for change I consider legitimate.

DAMIAN: What a naïve position. No real fighter can avoid some violence . . . or that other kind routinely practiced by politicians in power. If we have to explain all that at this stage of the game . . . Don't kid yourself. You don't care about the Republic.

AARON: If at this stage of the game, you still need your eyes opened . . . The acceptable Republican cause should be both effective and noble. Too bad that people like you give it a bad name.

DAMIAN: (*Exploding.*) That's enough out of you! You're some kind of reactionary.

AARON: I don't want to stifle our efforts but rather make them more just. If we don't try to do that, our cause—our vision—will never be a reality. (*Silence.*)

DAMIAN: (*Sighing with disdain.*) This discussion is a waste of time. All that was decided a long time ago. Just like I said the first day: you're a reactionary; even more reactionary than you realize. Not only are you soft on the enemy, but you side with them. If you could, you'd take that painting to the rebels, our attackers. But I won't allow it!

AARON: Because you're armed.

DAMIAN: If a gun is necessary, it's ready!

AARON: Who manufactures those weapons? And who sells them wherever they can? Because some so-called Republicans do sell to the enemy . . .

DAMIAN: That's enough out of you! Let's go up.

AARON: And tie the painting to the motorcycle?

DAMIAN: Exactly!

AARON: (*Smiling sadly as he shakes his head.*) My motorcycle can't hold the three of us with the painting. In the sidecar, there is barely room for one person; there's no space at all for even a corner of the packing. No matter who rides where, one of us has to stay behind, just like the painting. You and Lola go back and declare the mission incomplete. I can stay behind.

DAMIAN: (*His hand moving instinctively toward his gun.*) So you can inform the enemy?

AARON: Don't be naïve! I want my motorcycle back. I could start walking now those six miles to the fork; the enemy won't notice. You two—Lola in the sidecar or riding behind you—will pass me on the road. I'll wave, and you can wait for me on the highway or a little farther on, or wherever our forces are camped, and then you can return the motorcycle. Believe me: it's the only sensible plan.

DAMIAN: But Lola and I, alone on the motorcycle, could take the painting tied to the sidecar, and you could still get your motorcycle back when we're in our zone . . .

AARON: You know very well that Lola absolutely opposes all that bouncing around of the painting. (*Short pause.*) And I feel the same way. She won't have it, even with just two passengers on the motorcycle.

DAMIAN: (*Looking grim.*) And if we don't find you along the way?

AARON: (*With a smile that suggests both superiority and resignation.*) Since you can't get that idea out of your thick skull, I know you'll probably say I went to inform the enemy. (**DAMIAN** *looks at him stunned as* **AARON**, *pleased with himself, laughs.*) Are you daring enough to tell that lie? Just a minor vilification of a painter called Aaron. (*Laughing again.*) Or if you decide to eliminate me like some enemy, they'll shrug it off; you just got rid of another fascist. Lola will be waiting for us, so the shot should be fired down here. (**DAMIAN** *stands motionless.*) Aren't you going to open the holster? No, no; it's not easy to use that gun, because Lola will hear the shot and never forgive you, no matter what lie you tell her about what happened. Maybe you'll say I attacked you and you fired in self-defense. (*Pause.*) I know you want her. You're either infatuated or in love, I don't know which. But you want her, and you believe she loves me. (*Silence.*) And I love life. (*Another silence.*)

Look, how about a little test. I'll turn my back . . . Just a test . . . for both of us. (*Long pause as* AARON *turns toward the little window and waits tensely.* DAMIAN'*s facial expression and hand movements show extreme vacillation regarding the use of the weapon. The seconds drag.* AARON *sighs and, without turning around, speaks, after a few moments.*) Soldiers love life, and I'm a soldier of sorts. (*Silence.* DAMIAN *continues clutching the pistol.*) But a soldier without prejudices . . . (*Pause.*) I'll be quiet. (*Silence again.* AARON *sighs and turns slowly toward* DAMIAN. *They look at each other.*) Well, let's go up. (*He walks toward the door.* DAMIAN *opens it and is about to go up the stairs.*) All is not lost. (AARON *ponders what he has just said as he prepares to follow* DAMIAN. *As the basement zone goes dark, lights come up on the* SECRETARY. *She appears to continue reading, but it is* LOLA *who now speaks as reader, but without looking at the text.*)

LOLA: I would like for those hearing me today or reading the text tomorrow to imagine me writing this on the verge of . . . tears. Yes, I cry easily. Imagine that you are in a theater and that I'm an actress, in case the reading has moved you sufficiently. But I'm a real person. The other two will be up soon after saying to each other whatever it is they need to say without my hearing them, but I'm afraid I understand all too well what's going on . . . because the more aggressive of the two has a gun, and Aaron is definitely in his way. (*Crying.*) What solution can there be? Probably no good one; none. As I just said, whatever happened between these two may be just something I imagined; that's what one of them confided to me later. Was it really like that? I'll never know. All I know is I don't want that shot fired. . . . And I want the burning bush . . . to inspire us without flames and without words . . . (*Her voice has been fading away and is barely audible as she retreats, murmuring unintelligibly. The light on her likewise fades to darkness. The* SECRETARY *holds up the final page as lights come up on the* ADJUNCT, *seated in his place on the left with an annoyed expression on his face. Pause.*)

SECRETARY: That's the end of the story, ladies and gentlemen, for my relative's narrative is interrupted here. I didn't destroy its final pages. The author eliminated them, I suppose. Or perhaps the story's ending was so awful she couldn't bring herself to write it. (*Sitting down.*)

PRESIDENT: (*Reappearing at her side as she spoke.*) I suppose we'll never know what really happened, but with the passage of time, it's less difficult to come up with answers to the issues she and Aaron posed. I insist, therefore, that the discussion can be very revealing. I invite you, therefore, to bring your responses to our next session. The complex nature of the problems posed obliges us to schedule discussion for a future meeting. (*Smiling.*) Or maybe it will start when we leave the building. That's always an option, of course.

ADJUNCT: May I have the floor?

PRESIDENT: You may.

ADJUNCT: Aside from the fact that what you have heard may be an attempt at creative writing . . . (*The* **SECRETARY** *starts to protest but is silenced by a gesture from the* **PRESIDENT**.), the many years that separate us from that war confirm my opinion that the issue is irrelevant. The protagonists of those events, if they ever existed at all, are gone. Does anyone know anything about them other than what this interrupted story tells us? (*Short pause.*) No. Maybe Damian was a victim of the winners' repressive zeal; that painter, Aaron, left no trace of himself. Not even our secretary knows whether he was married to her famous relative. I reiterate my vote for more timely topics, even though they were proposed by other people.

PRESIDENT: (*Coldly.*) By majority vote, the board approved the relevance of today's subject.

ADJUNCT: A very strange story. We don't even know what happened to the characters! If it were a play, that ending would hardly be acceptable; as we understand theater, I mean. (*Despite the* **PRESIDENT**'s *decision, he continues.*) Before I sit down, just a question or two. Where is that famous El Greco Annunciation now?

PRESIDENT: I suppose the winners in that conflict blamed the losers . . . and the losers blamed the winners.

ADJUNCT: Blamed them about what?

PRESIDENT: The disappearance of that canvas; it's again considered lost.

ADJUNCT: So if it ever existed, it didn't leave the palace, as your relative seems to suggest, and certainly not on that ridiculous motorcycle. Are we to believe that later it fell into the hands of art speculators? There must have been some of those on both sides. I assume there has been no news of the painting since then. Am I right?

SECRETARY: All I know is what I just read.

ADJUNCT: Really! Then we're supposed to believe the part about that incredible motorcycle? (*To the audience.*) Please forgive me. That's all I have to say. (*Sitting down.*)

PRESIDENT: (*To the audience.*) Members and guests: I invite you to imagine what happened to the three people on the mission just described. I firmly believe in the validity of the narration. Like so many human beings, those three left this world without telling us what their motivations were, what they accomplished, and what their failures were. That's the way our lives are, too; that's the destiny of some and perhaps the greatness, too, of others. Just a few final words. The stubborn opposition shown our secretary by our adjunct committee member leads me to suspect, and forgive me for saying this, that the embers of our civil war burn hotter than we suspected. . . . But maybe that's just the inevitable reaction of people like me who remember that war's consequences . . . and hope that perhaps all is not lost . . . Thank you very much. (*He and the* SECRETARY *rise and bow as the curtains close on this area. When the curtains part again, the* ADJUNCT *has risen, and others—the director, actors, and perhaps even an insecure author—join him center stage to bow, all clearly illuminated.*)

CURTAIN

Select Bibliography

STUDIES IN ENGLISH RELATED TO
THE FOUR PLAYS IN THIS VOLUME

Agawu-Kakraba, Yaw B. "The Locus of Meditation of the Same and the Other: Antonio Buero Vallejo's *El tragaluz.*" *Letras Peninsulares* 10:2–3 (1997–98): 305–18.

Aggor, Francis Komla. "Derealizing the Present: Evasion and Madness in *El tragaluz.*" *Revista Canadiense de Estudios Hispánicos* 18 (1994): 141–50.

Anderson, Farris. "From Protest to Resignation: The Recent Evolution of Spain's Theatre of Social Concern." *Estreno* 2.2 (1976): 29–33.

————. "The Ironic Structure of *Historia de una escalera.*" *Kentucky Romance Quarterly* 18:2 (1971): 223–36.

Bethune, Jane Harrington. "A Comparative Study of Antonio Buero Vallejo and Alfonso Sastre." Ph.D. diss., University of Michigan, Ann Arbor, 1994.

Bleznick, Donald W., and Martha T. Halsey. "Introduction." In *Madrugada*, ix–xxiv. Waltham, Mass.: Blaisdale Publications, 1969.

Brown, Kenneth. "The Significance of Insanity in Four Plays by Antonio Buero Vallejo." *Revista de Estudios Hispánicos* 8 (1974): 247–60.

Casa, Frank P. "The Darkening Vision: The Latter Plays of Buero Vallejo." *Estreno* 5:1 (1979): 30–33.

————. "The Problem of National Reconciliation in Buero Vallejo's *El tragaluz.*" *Revista Hispánica Moderna* 35 (1969): 155–94.

————. "The Theatre after Franco: The First Reaction." *Hispanófila* 66 (1979): 109–22.

Dixon, Victor. "The 'Imersion Effect' in the Plays of Antonio Buero Vallejo." In *Drama and Mimesis*, ed. James Redmond, 113–37. Cambridge: Cambridge University Press, 1980.

————. "Music in the Later Dramatic Works of Antonio Buero Vallejo." *Bulletin of Spanish Studies* 82:3–4 (2005): 567–88.

————. "Pintar de otra manera: Art in the Life and Work of Antonio Buero Vallejo." *Estreno* 27:1 (2001): 13–21.

Donahue, Francis. "Spain's Tragic Voice: Antonio Buero Vallejo. *Revista / Review Interamericana* 9 (1979): 209–17.

Dowling, John. "Buero Vallejo's Interpretation of Goya's 'Black Paintings.'" *Hispania* 56 (1973): 449–57.

Dugo, Carmen Caro. *The Importance of the Don Quixote Myth in the Works of Antonio Buero Vallejo*. Lewiston, NY: Mellen University Press, 1995.

Edwards, Gwynne. *Dramatists in Perspective: Spanish Theatre in the Twentieth Century*. Cardiff: University of Wales Press, 1985.

————. "Spain." In *European Theater, 1960–1990: Cross-cultural Perspectives*, ed. Ralph Yarrow, 161–80. London: Routledge, 1992.

Fedorchek, Robert M. *"The Weaver of Dreams: Marvels & Tales." Journal of Fairytale Studies* 18:1 (2004): 95–101.

Foster, David William. *"Historia de una escalera*: A Tragedy of Aboulia." *Renaissance* 17 (1964): 3–10.

Fraile, Medardo. "Twenty Years of Theater in Spain." In *The Texas Quarterly: The Image of Spain*, 97–101. Austin: University of Texas, 1961.

Gillespie, Edward V. "Intellectual Blindness in Six Works by Antonio Buero Vallejo." Ph.D. diss., University of Michigan Microfilms, Ann Arbor, 1991.

Giuliano, William. "The Role of Men and Women in Buero Vallejo's Plays." *Hispanófila* 39 (1970): 21–28.

Halsey, Martha T. *Antonio Buero Vallejo*. New York: Twayne, 1973.

————. "Buero Vallejo and the Significance of Hope." *Hispania* 51:1 (1968): 57–66.

————. *"El tragaluz*: A Tragedy of Contemporary Spain." *Romanic Review* 63 (1972): 284–92.

————. *From Dictatorship to Democracy: The Recent Plays of Buero Vallejo*. Ottawa, Canada: Dovehouse Editions, 1994.

————. "More on 'Light' in the Tragedies of Buero Vallejo." *Romance Notes* 11 (1969): 17–20.

————. "The Politics of History: Images of Spain on the Stage of the 1970s." In *The Contemporary Spanish Theater: A Collection of Critical Essays*, ed. Martha T. Halsey and Phyllis Zatlin, 93–108. New York: University Press of America, 1988.

————. "Theatre in Franco Spain." In *The Cambridge History of Spanish Literature*, ed. David T. Geis, 659–76. Cambridge: Cambridge University Press, 2004.

————. "Women as Author Surrogates in Four Tragedies of Antonio Buero Vallejo." In *Spanish Theatre: Studies in Honor of Victor Dixon*, ed. Kenneth Adam, Ciaran Cosgrove, and James Whitson, 41–55. Woodbridge, Suffolk, UK: Tamesis, 2001.

————, and Phyllis Zatlin. "Is There Life after Lorca?" In *The Contemporary Spanish Theater: A Collection of Critical Essays*, ed. Martha T. Halsey and Phyllis Zatlin, 1–24. New York: University Press of America, 1988.

Holt, Marion Peter. "Artaudian Affinities in the Theater of Antonio Buero-Vallejo." In *Antonin Artaud and the Modern Theater*, ed. Gene A. Plunka, 252–262. London: Fairleigh Dickinson University Press, 1994.

————. *The Contemporary Spanish Theater (1949–1972)*. New York: Twayne, 1970.

————. "Remembering Antonio. The Mysteries of Chance." *Estreno* 27:1 (2001): 29–36.

Kirsner, Robert. *"Historia de una escalera*: A Play in Search of Characters.*" In *Homenaje a Rodríguez-Moñino: Estudios de erudición que le ofrecen sus amigos o discípulos hispanistas norteamericanos*, 279–82. Madrid: Castalia, 1966.

Kronik, John W. "Antonio Buero Vallejo: A Bibliography (1949–1970)." *Hispania* 54 (1971): 856–68.

————. "Buero Vallejo's *El tragaluz* and Man's Existence in History." *Hispanic Review* 41 (1973): 371–95.

Londré, Felicia Hardison. "Introduction." In *Plays of the New Democratic Spain (1975–1990)*, ed. Patricia W. O'Connor, v–xiv. New York: University Press of America, 1992.

Lott, Robert E. "Functional Flexibility and Ambiguity in Buero Vallejo's Plays." *Symposium* 20:2 (1966): 150–56.

Lyon, John. "History and Opposition in Franco's Spain." In *Spanish Theatre: Studies in Honor of Victor Dixon*, ed. Kenneth Adam, Ciaran Cosgrove, and James Whitson, 91–109. Woodbridge, Suffolk, UK: Tamesis, 2001.

McSorley, Bonnie Shannon. "Buero Vallejo's *Mito* and *El tragaluz*: The Twilight Zone of Hope." *Science-Fiction Studies* 10:29 (1983): 81–86.

————. *"Historia de una escalera* and *El tragaluz*: Twenty Years and One Reality." *Modern Language Studies* 10 (1979–80): 69–74.

————. "Poco Loco: The Paradox of Madness in the Theatre of Antonio Buero Vallejo." *Cuadernos de Aldeeu* 17:1 (2001): 91–96.

Molina, Ida. "The Dialectical Structure of Buero Vallejo's Multi-faceted Definition of Tragedy." *Kentucky Romance Quarterly* 22 (1975): 293–311.

————. "Dialectics of the Search for Truth in *El otro* and in *El tragaluz*." *Romanistisches Jahrbuch* 24 (1973): 23–29.

————. "Vita activa and vita contemplativa: Buero Vallejo's *El tragaluz* and Hermann Hesse's *Magister Ludi*. *Hispanófila* 53 (1975): 41–48.

Moore, John. "Buero Vallejo: Good Mistresses and Bad Wives." *Romance Notes* 21 (1980): 10–15.

Moreno, Antonio. "The Theater of Antonio Buero Vallejo: A Cry in the Dark." *A Journal of the Liberal Arts* 29 (1975): 21–31.

Newman, Jean Cross. "Mission as Constant in Antonio Buero Vallejo." *Estreno* 27:1 (2001): 38–42.

Nicholas, Robert L. "Antonio Buero-Vallejo: Stages, Illusions and Hallucinations." In *The Contemporary Spanish Theater: A Collection of Critical Essays,* ed. Martha T. Halsey and Phyllis Zatlin, 25–48. New York: University Press of America, 1988.

——. "History as Image and Sound: Three Plays of Buero Vallejo." *Estreno* 14:1 (1988): 13–17.

——. *The Tragic Stages of Antonio Buero Vallejo*. Chapel Hill, NC: Estudios de Hispanófila, 1972.

Noble, Beth. "Sound in the Plays of Buero Vallejo." *Hispania* 51:1 (1958): 56–59.

O'Connor, Patricia W. "Buero Vallejo Deals Directly with the Spanish Civil War in His New Play: *Misión al pueblo desierto*." *Hispania* 83:2 (2000): 327.

——. "Censorship in the Contemporary Spanish Theater and Antonio Buero Vallejo." *Hispania* 52 (1978): 282–88.

——. "Introduction." In *Plays of Protest from the Franco Era,* ed. Patricia W. O'Connor, 7–13. Madrid: SGEL, 1981.

——, ed. *Plays of the New Democratic Spain (1975–1990)*. New York: University Press of America, 1992.

——. "Post-Franco Theater: From Limitation to Liberty to License." *Hispanic Journal* 5:2 (1984): 55–73.

——." A Theater in Transition: From Paternalism to Pornography." In *The Contemporary Spanish Theater: A Collection of Critical Essays,* ed. Martha T. Halsey and Phyllis Zatlin, 201–213. New York: University Press of America, 1988.

——. "Torquemada in the Theater." *Theater Survey* 14:2 (1973): 33–45.

O'Leary, Catherine. *The Theatre of Antonio Buero Vallejo: Ideology, Politics and Censorship*. Woodbridge, Suffolk, UK: Tamesis, 2005.

Pasquariello, Anthony M., and Patricia W. O'Connor. "Introduction: Confrontation and Survival." In *El tragaluz: Experimento en dos partes*, 1–15. New York: Charles Scribner's Sons, 1977.

Pennington, Eric Wayne. "Biblical Motifs in the Theater of Antonio Buero Vallejo." Ph.D. diss., University of Michigan Microfilms, Ann Arbor, 1987.

——. "The Forgotten *Muñeco* in *El tragaluz*." *ULULA Graduate Studies in Romance Languages* 2 (1986): 117–24.

——. "Life, Death and Love in *El tragaluz*." *ULULA Graduate Studies in Romance Languages* 2 (1986): 29–40.

Ruple, Joelyn. *Antonio Buero Vallejo: The First Fifteen Years*. New York: Eliseo Torres and Sons, 1971.

Sánchez, José. "Introduction." In *Historia de una Escalera*, ix–xxvii. New York: Charles Scribner's Sons, 1955.

Schweizer, Dawn Jeanette. "Ibsen and Buero Vallejo: A Comparison of Their Tragic Presentation of Life." Ph.D. diss., University of Michigan Microfilms, Ann Arbor, 1996.

Sheehan, Robert Louis. "Buero Vallejo as 'el médico de su obra.'" *Estreno* 1:2 (1975): 18–22.

———. "Censorship and Buero Vallejo's Social Consciousness." *Aquila* 5:1 (1968): 121–37.

Shelnutt, William L. "Symbolism in Buero's *Historia de una Escalera*." *Hispania* 42 (1959): 61–65.

Sikka, Linda Solish. "Buero's Women: Structural Agents and Moral Guides." *Estreno* 16:1 (1990): 18–22.

———. "Mario, Cain and Me: Interrelatedness in *El tragaluz*." *Estreno* 16:2 (1990): 29–32.

Weiss, Gerard R. "Buero Vallejo's Theory of Tragedy in *El tragaluz*." *Revista de Estudios Hispánicos* 5 (1971): 147–60.

Wellwarth, George E. *The Theatre of Protest and Paradox*. New York: New York University Press, 1971.

Zatlin, Phyllis. "Plays of Conscience and Consciousness: Psychological Drama in Contemporary Spain." In *The Contemporary Spanish Theater: A Collection of Critical Essays*, ed. Martha T. Halsey and Phyllis Zatlin, 63–78. New York: University Press of America, 1988.

———. "Theatre in Madrid: The Difficult Transition to Democracy." *Theatre Journal* 32:4 (1980): 459–74.

———. "Twentieth-Century Spanish Theatre on the American Stage." *Theatre Survey* 42 (2001): 69–84.

FEATURE FILMS OF PLAYS IN THIS VOLUME

"Historia de una escalera" ("Story of a Stairway"), 1950. Director: Ignacio F. Inguino.
"Madrugada" ("Before Dawn"), 1958. Director: Antonio Román.

PUBLISHED ENGLISH TRANSLATIONS OF BUERO-VALLEJO'S PLAYS

The Weaver of Dreams (*La tejedora de sueños*). Trans. William I. Oliver. In *The Genius of the Spanish Theater*, ed. Robert O'Brien. New York: Mentor, 1964.

The Dream Weaver (*La tejedora de sueños*). Trans. William I. Oliver. In *Masterpieces of the Modern Spanish Theater*, ed. Robert W. Corrigan. New York: McMillan-Collier Books, 1967.

The Concert at St. Ovid (*El concierto de San Ovidio*). Trans. Farris Anderson. In *The Modern Spanish Stage: Four Plays*, ed. Marion Peter Holt. New York: Hill and Wang, 1970.

The Double Case Story of Dr. Valmy (*La doble historia del doctor Valmy*). Trans. Farris Anderson. *Hispanic Arts* 1:2 (Fall 1977).

The Basement Window (*El tragaluz*). Trans. Patricia W. O'Connor. In *Plays of Protest from the Franco Era*, ed. Patricia W. O'Connor. Madrid: SGEL, 1981.

In the Burning Darkness (En la ardiente oscuridad). Trans. Marion Peter Holt. In *Antonio Buero-Vallejo: Three Plays*, ed. Marion Peter Holt. New York: Trinity University Press, 1985.

The Foundation (La Fundación). Trans. and ed. Marion Peter Holt. In *DramaContemporary: Spain.* New York: Performing Arts Journal Publications, 1985.

The Foundation (La Fundación). Trans. Marion Peter Holt. In *Antonio Buero-Vallejo: Three Plays*, ed. Marion Peter Holt. New York: Trinity University Press, 1985.

The Sleep of Reason (El sueño de la razón). Trans. Marion Peter Holt. In *Antonio Buero-Vallejo: Three Plays*, ed. Marion Peter Holt. New York: Trinity University Press, 1985.

Las Meninas (Las Meninas). Trans. and ed. Marion Peter Holt. In *Antonio Buero-Vallejo: Las Meninas, a Fantasia in Two Parts.* New York: Trinity University Press, 1987.

Today's a Holiday (Hoy es fiesta). Trans. James A. Dunlop, C. Lucía Garavito, León Narváez, and Frank L. Odd. New York: University Press of America, 1987.

Judges in the Night (Jueces en la noche). Trans. John Koppenhauer. *Modern Internacional Drama* 23:1 (Fall 1989): 5–72.

The Shot (La detonación). Trans. David Johnson. Warminster, England: Aris and Phillips, 1989.

Lazarus in the Labyrinth (Lázaro en el laberinto). Trans. Hazel Cazorla. In *Plays of the New Democratic Spain (1975–1990)*, ed. Patricia W. O'Connor, 381–479. New York: University Press of America, 1992.

The Skylight (El tragaluz). Trans. John Koppenhauer and Susana Nelson. *Modern International Drama* (Fall 1992): 37–88.

A Dreamer for the People (Un soñador para un pueblo). Trans. Michael Thompson. London: Aris and Phillips, 1994.

The Music Window (Música cercana). Trans. Marion Peter Holt. University Park, PA: Estreno, 1994.

Two Sides to Dr. Valmy's Story (La doble historia del doctor Valmy). Trans. and ed. Gwynne Edwards. In *Burning the Curtain: Four Revolutionary Spanish Plays.* London: Marion Boyars, 1995.

The Sleep of Reason (El sueño de la razón). Trans. Marion Peter Holt. University Park, PA: Estreno, 1998.

The Story of a Stairway (Historia de una escalera). Trans. Donald Gibbs. Rock Hill, SC: Spanish Publications, 2003.

The Weaver of Dreams (La tejedora de sueños). Trans. Robert M. Fedorchek. *Marvels & Tales: Journal of Fairy-Tale Studies* 18:1 (2004).

BUERO-VALLEJO'S THEATRICAL HONORS

In 1971, Buero received the highest honor accorded any Spanish writer: he was inducted into the Royal Spanish Academy. His major honors for theater include, in addition to the Lope de Vega Prize in 1949, two Medals of Merit (1957 and 1958); the Fine Arts Medal (1993); National Theater Prizes for the best plays of 1956, 1957, 1958, and 1980; and the National Theater Award for Lifetime Achievement (1980). Moreover, Buero is the only dramatist ever to receive either of Spain's two most prestigious literary awards: the Cervantes Prize (1986) and the National Award for Literature (1996).

In addition to productions in many other Spanish-speaking countries, Buero's plays have come to life on the stages—and in the languages of—France, Italy, Germany, England, the United States, Russia, Japan, China, Korea, Poland, Sweden, Denmark, Hungary, Finland, Iceland, Estonia, and Bulgaria. In Germany, no fewer than twenty Buero plays have been professionally produced.